Sweet William
or
The Butcher?

Sweet William
or
The Butcher?

The Duke of Cumberland and the '45

Jonathan Oates

Pen & Sword
MILITARY

First published in Great Britain in 2008 by
Pen & Sword Military
An imprint of
Pen & Sword Books Ltd
47 Church Street
Barnsley
South Yorkshire
S70 2AS

ISBN 978 1 84415 754 9

A CIP catalogue record for this book is available from the British Library

Typeset in Ehrhardt by Phoenix Typesetting, Auldgirth Dumfriesshire

Printed and bound in England by Biddles Ltd., King's Lynn

Pen & Sword Books Ltd incorporates the Imprints of Pen & Sword Aviation,
Pen & Sword Maritime, Pen & Sword Military, Wharncliffe Local History,
Pen & Sword Select, Pen & Sword Military Classics, Leo Cooper, Remember
When, Seaforth Publishing and Frontline Publishing

For a complete list of Pen & Sword titles please contact
PEN & SWORD BOOKS LIMITED
47 Church Street, Barnsley, South Yorkshire, S70 2AS, England
E-mail: enquiries@pen-and-sword.co.uk
Website: www.pen-and-sword.co.uk

Contents

List of Plates

Battlefield of Killiecrankie (1689). (Author's collection.)

Scene of the massacre of Glencoe (1692). (Author's collection.)

Statue to Charles Edward Stuart at Glenfinnan. (Author's collection.)

Edinburgh Castle (Author's collection.)

Monument at Prestonpans, 2007. (Author's collection.)

Gravestone at Clifton, 2005. (Author's father (Mr David Oates).)

Blair Castle, c.1910. (Author's collection.)

Charles Edward Stuart, 1720–88. (Richard Sharp's collection.)

Miss Flora MacDonald. (Richard Sharp's collection.)

William Augustus, Duke of Cumberland (1721–65). (E. Charteris, *William Augustus, Duke of Comberland*, 1913.)

Thomas Pelham-Holles, Duke of Newcastle (1693–1768). (Author's collection.)

Regular soldier, 1745. (Author's collection.)

Jacobite re-enactors at Culloden, 2007.

Culloden Moor, looking west towards the Jacobite lines, 2007. (Author.)

The Well of the Dead, Culloden Moor, c.1900. (Author's collection.)

Cairn and graves of the clans, Culloden Moor, c.1910. (Author's collection.)

Culloden Cottage, Culloden Moor, c.1910. (Author's collection.)

House in Inverness where wounded regular soldiers were taken after Culloden, 2007. (Author.)

Church in Inverness where Jacobite prisoners were taken, 2007. (Author.)

Ruin of Glengarry castle, Loch Oich, c.1900. (Author's collection.)

Troops searching the area.

Isles of Rhum and Eigg, c.1910. (Author's collection.)

Isle of Skye, c.1910. (Author's collection.)

Fort George, 2007. (Author.)

Acknowledgements

First of all my thanks go to her gracious majesty, Queen Elizabeth II, for permission to cite from the Royal Archives. To all those archivists and librarians in England and Scotland for having brought out copious amounts of archives and books, thank you. The eminent historians Professor Speck, Professor Taylor and Stuart Reid were all kind enough to read through my first draft and made comments accordingly. Any mistakes of fact, are of course, mine, and the opinions expressed herein are not necessarily theirs. I would also like to thank Richard Sharp for allowing me to use a number of images which appear here. My long-suffering and ever patient wife has not only endured my absences in research and writing, but has also accompanied me in several research visits.

I dedicate this book to Professor Stephen Taylor, for all his help and encouragement in my eighteenth-century studies since my undergraduate days.

Introduction

'The actions of the great are viewed through so false a medium, that
they seldom receive their just proportion either of applause or censure,
till a long accession of events has removed the influence of prejudice.
A heavy train of fawning flatterers, or envious rivals, like the different
extremes of a telescope, always exhibits them either dwarfs or giants . . .
In what light posterity will view the actions of the late duke of
Cumberland, requires no depth of penetration to ascertain; his services
are too strongly felt by Englishmen, for the remembrance of them
to die away in their minds'.[1]

Most of those who have heard of the Duke of Cumberland automatically think of him as 'The Butcher', even though they will often not be able to say much more than this. This appellation is on account of cruelties allegedly committed to wounded and fleeing Jacobites immediately after the battle of Culloden and the repression in the Highlands of Scotland which followed.

Cumberland's epithet does not dispose anyone to adopt a kindly attitude towards him. Anything but. Yet other well-known eighteenth-century figures, Frederick II of Prussia (1712–1786) and Catherine II of Russia (1730–1796), better known as Frederick the Great and Catherine the Great, immediately shine through their epithets, though both pursued militarily aggressive policies abroad and essentially illiberal and repressive ones at home. Cumberland's epithet is therefore unfortunate and perhaps unfair.

My immediate interest in writing specifically about him stems from a rereading, in 2002, of the novel by Josephine Tey, *Daughter of Time*, in which the twentieth-century hero investigates the alleged crimes of one of history's greatest villains; Richard III, in order to ensure he receives a fairer judgement. One character in this book makes the following observation:

It's an odd thing but when you tell someone the true facts of a mythical tale they are indignant not with the teller, but with you. They don't want to have their ideas upset. It rouses some vague uneasiness in them, I think, and they resent it. So they reject it and refuse to think about it. If they were merely indifferent it would be

ix

natural and understandable. But it is much stronger than that, much more positive. They are very annoyed.[2]

Thus inspired, I began to write an article on the subject, but failed to complete it. Then the idea was revived four years later, and this book is the result.

The phrase 'History is written by the victors' is one which is trotted out at regular intervals. It could not be less true as regards the Forty Five. 'Bonnie Prince Charlie' and his Highland supporters are certainly associated in the common mind as heroic and romantic, whereas Cumberland and the victorious regular troops are identified as the enemy. The losers seem to have won the battle for a favourable posthumous judgement. Certainly anyone visiting the battlefield of Culloden would come away with that impression and the annual commemoration there, with flowers and flags put next to the 'clan' graves add to that impression.

That said, there are a number of works which do not present such a view. These include the near-contemporary histories, which present a favourable image of the defenders of the status quo and denigrate the Jacobites. More recently, historians such as Professor Speck, the late General Whitworth and Stuart Reid have presented the Duke and his forces in a more sympathetic light. Of course, from the nineteenth century onwards, books have been published to give another viewpoint, such as those written by Frank McLynn, Jeremy Black and John Prebble in the second half of the twentieth century, to name but three. As far as fiction, TV and film goes, the Jacobites win hands down. Even passing references to Cumberland saddle him with the epithet 'Butcher'; one example being Evelyn Waugh's *Vile Bodies*, where Mr Isaacs, proprietor of a film studio, refers to 'Part of Butcher Cumberland's army'. At the Jacobite Studies Trust conference in July 2007, a casual reference was made by one speaker, without any need for further comment, to Cumberland's genocide in Scotland.

Such comments were not new In 1751, Horace Walpole wrote of Cumberland, re Culloden:

> that victory made him in the end more unpopular than all his defeats;
> for the Scotch, the Jacobites, and his brother's jealousy never rested
> till they had propagated such stories of his tyranny and severity, as
> entirely lost him the hearts of the nation.[3]

The purpose of this book is to focus squarely on the Duke and his role in the suppression of the Forty Five. Unlike Whitworth's book, this is not a biography of the Duke from birth to death. Unlike those of Speck and Reid it is not a history of the campaign of the Forty Five, although one chapter of the book will survey the campaign prior to Culloden. The Jacobites are thus very much in the shade. The question to be asked is whether Cumberland can be anachronistically termed a 'war criminal'. Is his soubriquet 'The Butcher' justified?

In order to answer the question, it is first necessary to explore the debate which has raged from 1746 to date. What have historians said about the Duke and why? What themes have emerged? Then, in order to properly judge him, the perceived rules of war and the actual standards of warfare of the eighteen century must be examined. The Duke, as with any other historical figure, cannot be judged by the standards of later times. He can only be judged in the light of the society in which he lived. We may not approve of these values, any more than twenty-fourth-century pundits may approve or disapprove of our twenty-first-century standards and values.

In order to understand the Duke, we also need to survey his life and military career prior to the Forty Five. Cumberland was youthful, but was also a seasoned soldier, having taken part in two continental campaigns, with mixed success. His reputation and actions in these will be examined. Was he habitually cruel to his enemies in this period? How was he viewed by contemporaries? It is important to understand the man as much as we can before examining his later exploits. Then we will move to the campaign of the Forty Five. I will also note contemporary attitudes both to the Duke and to the Jacobites themselves. The views of Cumberland's fellow soldiers, politicians and others will be examined. I will note the actions of the Jacobite army themselves. Were the Duke's opponents the romantic heroes of popular myth?

Then we will come to Culloden; to the preliminaries before the battle, the encounter itself and the immediate aftermath. Particular attention will be paid to the aftermath of the battle. Were atrocities committed? If so, who was responsible? Or were these 'merely' commonplace after battles in this period and this impression heightened by Jacobite propaganda?

Next are two chapters covering the Duke's campaign in the Highlands after Culloden. The first month was spent in the vicinity of Inverness and the second in the west of the Highlands. Although the Jacobite army was decisively defeated at Culloden, Charles Stuart had escaped and many Jacobites wished to fight on. Cumberland had to try and root out the Jacobites in order to prevent a further rebellion. Yet his methods have been called into question, at the very least. But what were these methods and to what extent were they justified?

What were the responses of contemporaries to the Duke and towards the

Jacobites? Was the Duke a popular man among Britons in 1746? At last we come to the verdict. Was Cumberland the Butcher of common legend? Or was this unfair? Contemporary values, motivation and ultimate results need to be borne in mind.

The book uses many primary sources to investigate the matter. First there are the manuscript sources of the State Papers for Scotland, State Papers Domestic, the Cumberland Papers and the Newcastle and Hardwicke Papers, located at the National Archives, the Royal Archives and the British Library Manuscripts. These contain Cumberland's official and personal correspondence, and that of his military secretary, Sir Everard Fawkener, with their political master, the Duke of Newcastle. Then there is the published correspondence and diaries of others in senior political and religious circles, such as Lord Hardwicke, Thomas Herring, Archbishop of York, Horace Walpole, the Duke of Richmond and the Earl of Chesterfield, but also of more humble folk. Other sources include material from the National Archives of Scotland and the National Library of Scotland, contemporary newspapers, but the Jacobite sources will not be ignored either. These include the memoirs of Jacobite soldiers and the *Lyon in Mourning*, a Jacobite collection of material. This book will quote extensively from these sources.

Having examined all these sources, the author will deliver his verdict. The reader may or may not agree; but at least they will have been given matter for thought.

A word on the terms used in this book – often a matter of great controversy and a method of identifying authorial prejudice straight away. The attempt here is to use terms, except those in quotations, which are as neutral as possible.

Charles will be used instead of Prince Charles or the Young Pretender/son of the Pretender. His followers will be known throughout as Jacobites, not the perjorative rebels. The Duke of Cumberland will be referred to as the Duke or Cumberland, not as the 'Butcher'. His soldiers will be referred to as the regulars, not as British, English, Hanoverian or government troops.

All dates are in Old Style, which was used in Britain until the calendar reform of 1752.

Chapter 1

The Duke and the Historians

Who now remembers the victor of Culloden
except as 'butcher Cumberland'?[1]

This chapter will examine how historians and others have dealt with Cumberland and his part in the Forty Five. But first we need to bear in mind a few points about the nature of history and the pitfalls that await the unwary.

Our perception of any historical event or character is usually formed for us by those who write about them, whether in books, films or other performances. This image is not a static one. History is as much an art as a science and is neither impartial nor objective. This is for several reasons. First, every historian is human, with his or her own likes and dislikes. Figures whose values and actions are favoured by the writer will tend to be viewed and written about in a better light than a figure whose behaviour is found by them to be unsavoury. The historian is also a product of his environment and his times. He may be as much influenced by contemporary values as by those of the time he is investigating, though any good historian will guard against this. Secondly, historians have to be selective if they are writing about anyone about whom there is a mass of documentation, such as a ruler, an author or an important military figure. It would be impossible to write everything about that individual. The question then is how to select information for inclusion and what to reject. Again, the historian's judgement is required – objectivity again. Here, deliberate bias can occur, as favourable information can be included and even exaggerated and derogatory material be left out or minimized, or vice versa.

Thirdly, there is a question about the material used in the first place. Primary sources, such as correspondence, diaries, memoirs and newspapers, are usually subjective and the latter two doubly so, for they aim to give one particular view to a wide audience. But even the former will be shaped by the writer's own views of people and events, and also their own knowledge of them, which is usually only partial and may be second hand. If one source is the only account of a particular event, how truthful and accurate is it? With varying accounts giving differing views and even 'facts', a historian needs to choose one version, but how is he to choose which one? Surviving evidence often comes from a small and not necessarily representative circle of individuals. In the case of the Duke of Cumberland, most of what was written about him comes from men of a fairly senior rank in the army and government, or from his virulent political enemies. We only have a few accounts written by the men in the ranks of the army he commanded, nor is there anything written by Jacobites below the rank of the officers. In any case, the surviving evidence is often incomplete and open to interpretation. Assumptions can be made which may not necessarily be accurate.

Finally history can easily be written as propaganda. This does not mean that the writer is writing lies. Every fact included can be utterly genuine, but the work is still a propaganda piece. A history of the Soviet Union could be written (and has) without any account of the gulags and other methods of extermination and repression by the state. Such an account would be a grotesque distortion of reality, but every word of it could be entirely supported by fact.

History is not, therefore, a monolith of facts which are unchallengeable. It would be a very tedious subject if it were so. An eminent military historian has recently written, 'Nobody can pretend to offer the last word on the '45. History is constantly reinventing itself' and 'Nobody is so divorced from origins and instincts as to be able to avoid "taking sides", once exposed to this subject matter'.[2] Yet there is such a thing as historical orthodoxy, in which certain characters are usually cast as heroic and others as villains, and this is how the mass of the public perceive them, though many historians would not accept such black and white delineations. Those deemed heroic include Elizabeth I, Winston Churchill and Lord Nelson. Villains would include Sir Oswald Mosley, King John and the Duke of Cumberland. Of course, it is possible to make a case against the first three and for the second three.

I shall now survey how historians have written about Cumberland since 1746, in roughly chronological order. A number of histories of the Forty Five appeared just after the campaign was over. These include those by John Marchant, James Ray and Andrew Henderson and were all published in Britain. Naturally enough, all of them were favourable towards the Hanoverian status quo and virulently opposed to the Jacobites.

These authors did not think they were writing propaganda. Andrew Henderson wrote that his book was 'By an Impartial Hand, who was an Eye Witness to most of the Facts'.[3] Likewise, James Ray wrote in his preface:

> I took all opportunities of writing a Journal; which contains the most material Things that happen'd during that period; and those

Circumstances that did not fall directly under my Observation, I have taken Care to collect from the most Authentic accounts I could procure . . . I have taken care through the whole of my History, to relate Facts with the greatest Perspicuity and Exactness.[4]

Yet perhaps what Ray meant was that the facts he included would be accurate, but that he would also be highly selective in deciding which he would use. Unlike later historians, Ray nails the purpose of his history to his mast at the first possible moment. He wrote:

I hope that great Example of theirs will spread its Influence, through the Dwellings of the Disaffected and convince them (and such are of unsettled Opinions and Prejudices) that it would be wise Part of them to discountenance all Popish Imposters, and to defend to the last Drop of their Blood that illustrious and heroick Family, which kind Providence has made us a free and happy People.[5]

It is interesting to note that Henderson, writing as he was, just a few years after Culloden, does not omit that the regulars killed wounded Jacobites after the battle of Culloden, though he excuses such behaviour. Ray, on the other hand, does not allude to such activity.[6] Cumberland is portrayed favourably in these works, Ray writing about the soldiers' behaviour at Culloden, 'Who could do otherwise when animated by the Presence of so brave a Commander? That ordered all the Dispositions, perhaps, as just as the mind of Man could conceive'.[7] Henderson went on to write the first biography of the Duke, which was published in 1766, a year after the latter's death. It shows Cumberland in an impossibly good light during every phase of his life.[8] Marchant's book does not hint at any wrongdoing by the Duke or his army, either.[9]

Yet Douglas's *History*, published in 1755, does reveal wrongdoing by the soldiery after Culloden. He retails the suffering in the Highlands and how some innocent people had their property stolen from them. Cumberland is not explicitly blamed for any of this, however. It is interesting to note that both Henderson and Douglas were Scottish.[10]

At the onset of the nineteenth century, two histories of the Forty Five were published, the last to be by those who were alive at the time of events. One was by John Home and the other by Giulo Caesare di Antonio Cordara, an Italian nobleman, who knew the exiled Stuarts at Rome. The latter was written in 1751, but not published for decades. It was the first account to show what many other writers have; namely that Cumberland and his forces dealt savagely with their beaten foes. One extract reads:

The King's troops, pressing round them in ever-growing numbers and becoming more savage as the victory became more complete, killed every one in their way. Edward [Charles] succeeded in escaping from the horrible butchery with the utmost difficulty. Every one had already fled from the field, hurrying wherever terror and the hope of safety carried them . . . Many were caught and killed. In vain did the wretches beg for mercy on their knees, in vain did they implore help from Heaven and from man. Neither prayers nor piteous appeals moved the cruel butchers to spare them. [11]

Cordara's writing is based on accounts of fugitive Jacobites in Rome. However, like Ray, Home (another Scot) does not mention any savagery after Culloden; perhaps it was too soon after events to do so.

It is a truth, almost universally acknowledged, that history is written by the victors. Although, as we have just seen, this was true in the immediate aftermath of the Forty Five, perspectives changed in the nineteenth and twentieth century. Professor Speck notes: 'Though it is often complained that historians record successes and have little time for failures, the reverse is true of the Forty Five. Hardly a year goes by without the appearance of a new life of Bonnie prince Charlie, or a Jacobite saga.'[12]

In the nineteenth century, a number of memoirs written by former Jacobite officers were published and these have been used by historians as key sources. However, they do, somewhat naturally, give a Jacobite bias, and though the Jacobites indulged in quarrelling and infighting, they could all agree on their common enemy. The sources for the Forty Five as written by Cumberland and other key figures in the British state have mostly not been published and lie in manuscript or microfilm form in the National Archives, Windsor Castle, the British Library and elsewhere and are therefore less easy to access, and so are less well-known and less used.

Unfortunately, many of the Jacobite accounts only offer vague and generalized statements about the alleged brutality after Culloden. James Maxwell of Kirkconnell (1708–62), a Jacobite officer and an otherwise excellent source for the military history of the Forty Five, writes:

There is hardly an act of violence to be found in the histories of the most barbarous nations, but may be matched in the Duke of Cumberland's expedition to the Highlands . . . The reader will be satisfied with the manner of treating this subject in general, when he reflects, that it saves him abundance of shocking scenes he must have seen had I been particular.[13]

Had Maxwell been less concerned about his readers' sensibilities, we would be better able to judge the veracity of his comments. But the impression he makes is very unfavourable to Cumberland.

Similar remarks come from the pen of James Johnstone (1719–*c*.1800), another Jacobite officer, who wrote:

> The Duke of Cumberland never failed to say to the commanders of these detachments at the moment of their departure, 'Make no prisoners, you understand me'. They had particular instructions to stab the Prince if he fell into their hands . . . the sanguinary Duke, whose officers and their detachments – his executioners – inflicted more cruelties on the brave but unfortunate Highlanders than would have been committed by the most ferocious savages of Canada.[14]

Again, it is a pity that the second half of this quotation is so vague, and the fact that the veracity of the first half is questionable at best does not bode well for that of the second. Furthermore, it seems unlikely that either Maxwell or Johnstone was an eye witness to the events referred to.

Another good source of apparently primary material about the atrocities is the *Lyon in Mourning*. This was a collection of letters, poems and accounts written by Jacobites after the rebellion which detail their sufferings at the hands of their enemies. It was gathered together by the Revd Robert Forbes (1708–75), the Scottish Episcopal bishop of Ross and Caithness, who was a staunch Jacobite. Some of its contents may, however, be suspect, and there is no doubting its bias. Although this was not fully published until 1895, some of it did appear as early as 1834 and Forbes wrote,

> The humanity displayed, and the regular and honourable payments made on all occasions by the Chevalier, in contrast with the licence and barbarity, now for the first time fully brought home to the royal army, will hardly fail to disturb some of the prepossessions of the English race.[15]

It is hard to find any military campaign in which atrocity stories are absent. However, as one historian cautions, 'We are usually dependent for details on enemy accounts produced largely for propaganda purposes, so there can be considerable difficulty in establishing the exact circumstances of each incident, and sometimes indeed whether the actually happened at all.'[16]

It was in the nineteenth century that the portraits of Charles and Cumberland that we know today were established. Scotland, long seen in

England as remote, backward and barbarous, began to be shown as a centre of historical romance and contemporary patriotism. Royal approval was granted when George IV visited Scotland in 1822 (the first reigning monarch to do so since the seventeenth century) and this was reinforced by the visits of Victoria and Albert in subsequent decades. Walter Scott's Jacobite novels, such as *Rob Roy* and *Waverley*, featured incidents from the Jacobite rebellions, depicting the Highland warrior as a heroic and an honourable man, albeit as a noble savage. Now none of this was explicitly anti-Cumberland, but it did show his opponents, Charles Edward Stuart and his supporters, in a favourable light. The damage had been done.

Alexander Ewald, in his *The Life and Times of Prince Charles Stuart*, published in 1883, stated what was by the late nineteenth century the orthodox view on Cumberland:

> We are so accustomed to connect the character of William, Duke of Cumberland, solely with the awful barbarities that followed Culloden, that we are liable to overlook everything else in his conduct, and every other event in his history. One most foul blot overshadows his escutcheon that we do not care to inquire into its quarterings. History having recorded him as a merciless enemy, an inhuman victor, and a glutton for all that was brutal, we pass him by with loathing.[17]

Ewald proceeds to list Cumberland's virtues: liberality, honour, bravery and respect for authority. But he then goes on to enumerate his failings, which are in part because Cumberland's morals were not those of the conventional Victorian (whose were in the eighteenth century?) and in part are questionable, and overlook much in Cumberland's actions. The point to be made, though, is that Cumberland's reputation was already at a low ebb by the Victorian era. He had already been condemned.

Historians in the first half of the twentieth century tended to be sympathetic towards Charles in the same romantic vein, and so hostile towards Cumberland. Foremost among these were Alistair and Henrietta Tayler and Sir Charles Petrie.

Petrie has no good word for Cumberland, and first attacks him by allusion, writing 'his real nature was not fully disclosed until after Culloden, but enough was already known of it to give him no better reputation than the rest of his family', though as to what this is, or why, the reader is initially given no clue.[18] Petrie spends but two pages on a generalized account of the situation in Scotland after Culloden, but it is enough to damn Cumberland:

Cumberland fully determined that Culloden should be the end of Jacobitism in Scotland, and his ferocity once again proved, not only the peculiar sadism of his nature, but the fright which he and his family had received . . . the most repellent barbarities were perpetrated by Cumberland's orders. All Highlanders who had been out with the Prince were treated like vermin.[19]

Petrie also relates how Cumberland ordered Major Wolfe to shoot a dying Highlander and how girls were stripped naked to take part in horse races for the delight of the troops.[20]

In the popular mind, it is Charles Edward Stuart who takes their imagination. He was young and good-looking, attractive to both women and men (much of the same can be said about Cumberland, too, though he was portly). It is his face that can be seen on countless packets of 'Highland' biscuits, toffee and shortbread tins. The only film about him, starring the English actor David Niven, *Bonnie Prince Charlie* (1950) is entirely favourable. There is even a statue of him in Derby (erected in 1995, to mark the 250th anniversary of the Forty Five). Jacobite societies currently exist in both England and Scotland. It is true that serious studies, even those sympathetic towards him, do refer to his alcoholism in later life, and other negative aspects of his personality, but the overall impression is a favourable one. It is important to realize this, because by explicitly showing Charles as a romantic hero, it implicitly casts Cumberland as the principal villain. Although there was a statue of the Duke in Cavendish Square, London, it was taken down in the nineteenth century and the Cumberland obelisk in Windsor Great Park is known only to a few. Although Cumberland was the victor at Culloden, it is hard, perhaps impossible, to find postcards or other imagery of him – unlike those for Charles.

Diana Preston made the comparison between the two men in her book in 1995:

So the story of the '45 is truly the stuff of theatre and legends. It comes complete with heroes and villains. Bonnie Prince Charlie converts into the perfect hero, brave, handsome and chivalrous. 'Butcher Cumberland' makes an appropriately villainous foil, corpulent as Charles is slender, harsh as Charles is merciful, a libertine in contrast with Charles' virginal aloofness. Both transcend the centuries, larger than life, like one dimensional characters from a melodrama.[21]

Preston makes no attempt to question this stereotype of Cumberland.

It has always been the case that the British public, sentimental, perhaps, have favoured lost causes – whether the Jacobites or Charles I or the Confederacy of the nineteenth. It is always easy to romanticize a lost cause because it can be imbued with hopes that can never be realized and it is impossible to criticize its actions as these never occurred. Reality, on the other hand, is full of compromise and disillusionment. But it is worth noting that before these causes were lost, they were highly controversial and often the subject of much suspicion, fear and hate by contemporaries. The Jacobite Highlanders and their leader were unpopular in England and much of Scotland when they posed a threat, as they did in 1745–6. Charles I was duplicitous and the Confederate States supported the institution of slavery.

Perhaps the most influential single work about Culloden and its aftermath is John Prebble's *Culloden*, first published in 1961 and, unlike any other book about the subject, has never been out of print since. This book also spawned a low-budget, almost documentary, film. Prebble has no time for romantic nineteenth-century myths and has a low opinion of Charles. He is no Jacobite supporter, as many historians to date had been. However, this does not lead to a revised treatment of Cumberland and the forces under his command. If anything, Prebble is more systematically opposed to them than anyone else had been before, detailing the ill treatment of Jacobites and others in the Highlands from Culloden onwards. His sympathies, which soon become those of the reader, are with the common people of Scotland, who are portrayed as the victims of both Hanover and Stuart. It is a powerful work and makes a strong impact on the emotions of the reader. Yet much of the book is the product of the writer's imagination as well as the relatively few primary sources referred to. Prebble was a journalist, after all.

He writes:

> This is not another story of the Forty Five . . . It is an attempt to tell the story of the many ordinary men and women who were involved in the last Jacobite Rising, often against their will. For too long, I believe, the truth of this unhappy affair has been obscured by the over romanticised figure of the Prince.[22]

This is a book written about the sorry lot of the Common Man in the Highlands in 1746, but unfortunately it is now somewhat outdated and inaccurate in places.

Diana Preston, writing for the 250th anniversary of the rebellion has little to say about Cumberland, and all of it serves to blacken his character. Here are some samples of her comments:

> Culloden was the beginning of a new and greater nightmare. Cumberland's men were already showing that they were more than victors on the field – they were a merciless army of occupation . . . Cumberland may have disliked Scotland in general, but he left no doubt that he loathed and despised the Highlands and its people in particular. He ordered the extermination of the wounded at Culloden and this was the beginning of a campaign of suppression . . . Martial law was imposed, fugitives were hunted down and indiscriminately hanged and shot.[23]

Then there is Dr John Roberts. He discusses atrocities after Culloden, but also states that those same 'victims' would have killed their undefended opponents should the night march before Culloden have succeeded. He notes other atrocity stories but produces evidence to cast doubt on some of them. Yet he then goes into detail about the campaign in the Highlands in 1746 in the usual manner.[24]

Raab Houston, writing in *BBC's History Magazine* for January 2006, named Cumberland as the most evil Briton of the eighteenth century. His article not only repeats what most of his predecessors had accused the Duke of, but dresses them up in contemporary language. He writes 'he used the full power of the British state to commit genocide on mainland Britain' and 'He even suggested transporting whole clans . . . to the colonies – a sort of ethnic cleansing'. He received 'blood money earned by war crimes' and 'contributed to the racist views responsible for their [the Highlanders] later misfortunes'. By twenty-first-century standards there was not a crime he had not committed.[25] In fact, others have used Nazi terms for the Duke and his followers – comparing them to the Waffen SS and gauleiters. Similar remarks have been made by another historian, who comes up with a figure of 3,000 dead in the 'genocide' which followed Culloden, though there is no explanation of how the figure mentioned was arrived at.[26] A short defence of the Duke appeared shortly afterwards by Max Hastings in the *Daily Mail*.

But it is not only those writing for a popular market who have censured Cumberland. Many academic historians of great fame have done so. Character assassination was a technique employed by Bruce Lenman, introducing Cumberland to the reader as George II's 'unpleasant but competent younger son' and 'ever ready to use the noose and the lash on his own troops', an image which is indelible, though inaccurate.[27]

Jeremy Black comments, after writing of a contemporary and favourable judgement on Cumberland, that:

> Most judgements are less charitable. As a man he was popular with few, as a politician he was distrusted by many and as a general his only major success had been at the expense of an outnumbered and outgunned force of hungry men, obliged to fight on disadvantageous terrain as a result of poor generalmanship. There were brave men on both sides at Culloden, but it is difficult not to feel sympathy with the Jacobites.[28]

Black writes about harsh repression, plunder and violence, claiming that forged orders gave an excuse for such behaviour at Culloden and afterwards, adding 'Militarily there was no need for such activity'.[29]

Frank McLynn's magisterial biography of Charles Stuart has a number of points to make about Cumberland, and none of them are favourable. True, McLynn lumps most, if not all, of the government's soldiers together: 'The Hanoverian officers in general betrayed a frightening, sickening callousness in pursuit of their aims. They did not believe in sparing civilians, pardoning deserters, conniving at insolent townsfolk or treating enemy wounded'.[30] McLynn often refers to Cumberland as the Butcher and contrasts him with his subject in an unfavourable fashion.

The most thorough survey of the Forty Five – one is tempted to call it the definitive history – was written by Christopher Duffy and published in 2003. Here can be found numerous statements which support the 'butcher' thesis. After Culloden Duffy writes that 'The process of destruction was completed by the murder squads which Cumberland sent out into the fields, parks and scattered buildings in search of the Jacobite wounded' and relates how, in one incident, nineteen men were taken from a barn and shot.[31] Duffy states that Cumberland wanted to return to 'proper soldiering' on the Continent and that he therefore wanted quick results. No leniency such as that which had allegedly followed the end of the 1715 rebellion was to recur. A number of his subordinates, including Captain Scott and Major Lockhart, were enthusiastic advocates of such a policy. Duffy writes:

> Were such proceedings unduly harsh by international standards? They were consonant with British practice as carried through by Lieutenant Governor Lawrence when he devastated Acadia (Novia Scotia) and deported its French inhabitants in 1755. Their descendants in Louisiana are still aggrieved . . . By way of contrast the

French general D'Asfield adopted a successful policy of conciliation when he pacified the island of Minorca in 1716.[32]

Passing references to Culloden and Cumberland in textbooks, even the best of them, tend to reinforce the view of him as 'the Butcher'. Michael Barthorp writes in his summary 'Cumberland stamps out all vestiges of rebellion in the Highlands with great severity'.[33] Williams writes, 'Cumberland proceeded to earn his nickname "The Butcher", by terrorising the Highlands'.[34] According to Plumb, 'The Highlands were remorselessly, and finally, conquered'.[35] A slightly modified picture was given by Langford, writing of 'the often exaggerated but none the less harrowing tale of Cumberland's campaign of terror in the Highlands'.[36] It is, perhaps, hard to censure such views, because they are, after all, aiming at far wider canvasses, and so summary treatment of issues is unavoidable. The problem is that in doing so there is a tendency towards simplifying often complex and controversial issues.

Children's books also give this impression. The well-known series of Ladybird books includes one titled *Bonnie Prince Charlie*, which shows Charles in a very favourable light and his nemesis in a malevolent one:

> It was after the Battle of Culloden that the Duke of Cumberland earned, and deserved, the name of the 'butcher'. He ordered hundreds of prisoners to be shot, and his soldiers were permitted, and may well have been ordered, to cut down all fugitives with savage cruelty. This terrible policy of brutal murder was continued for many months in the Scottish glens. Farmsteads were burnt, and cattle and sheep killed or stolen.[37]

The vast majority of historians depict Cumberland and his troops as being responsible for killing wounded Jacobites and slaughtering fleeing ones on Culloden Moor. They then describe, in varying detail, the repression which occurred in the Highlands in the months following the battle. The impression given is that such behaviour was unnecessary and unique. For them, Cumberland's reputation as 'The Butcher' is well deserved.

It is not only writers sympathetic to Jacobitism that have damned the Duke. Notably, Speck, who is usually termed 'pro-government' in his sympathies, and has little time for Jacobitism, is critical of Cumberland. His views, untainted by pro-Jacobitism, are thus worth noting and are to be found in *The Butcher: The Duke of Cumberland and the Suppression of the Forty Five*. Speck informs the reader at the outset, 'During the ensuing campaign, however,

Cumberland's nickname was to change from "the martial boy" to "the Butcher"'.[38] Yet he also writes:

> Until allegations of atrocities committed at and after the battle of Culloden began to call his honour into question he was regarded as in every way a worthy opponent of the Young Pretender. Any account of the rebellion which sees it as a duel between a Prince Charming and a Monster uses hindsight literally with a vengeance. [39]

Much of Speck's account is a narrative history of the rebellion and its after-math from the point of view of the government and its supporters, which was then a novel interpretation of events. Speck sees the first sign of Cumberland's attitude when he wrote to the Duke of Newcastle in December 1745, hinting that the country people be given licence to murder Jacobite stragglers. Speck writes: 'Those brutal words ominously portend his reputation as a butcher. It is significant that he apparently felt no qualms about communicating them to the secretary of state.'[40]

When remarking on events after Culloden, Speck is careful to 'avoid being unduly influenced by the biased testimony of hostile witnesses' and bases his account on contemporaries who were not Jacobites. He find that 'Such evidence nevertheless demonstrates that there is no necessity to turn to suspect sources in order to document acts committed by the British army, which were outrages even by the standards of contemporaries, who were not remarkable for being squeamish'.[41] Speck proceeds to recount brutality towards the Jacobites after the battle.

He also discusses the controversial order that was apparently found on a dead Jacobite after Culloden, stating that the Jacobite orders were to give no quarter to their enemies. This is usually written off as a crude forgery by a government sympathizer in order to license butchery on the army's part. Speck considers the possibility that it was indeed written by a Jacobite, but relates to orders given on a day prior to 16 April. It does not seem to have been written by Cumberland or his staff and so Speck concludes that its provenance is not proven.[42]

Yet his final verdict is impressively fair-minded:

> This was unfair. He had, undeniably, authorised butchery in the campaign in Scotland. But then he had been the mouthpiece of the whole political establishment. He was a young commander, much influenced by older men whom he respected, both in the high command and in the cabinet. They gave him no reason to expect that

his behaviour would meet with disapproval, but on the contrary he received every encouragement from them. When some withdrew in horror he became the scapegoat.[43]

If even a historian who is examining the campaign and the Duke from the point of view of the loyalists is certain that he was indeed the butcher of legend, albeit with reservations, is there any hope for his reputation?

The answer has to be yes. But there are only a few historians who have cared to defend him. The first important one was the Hon. Evan Charteris, a Scottish lawyer. He wrote a two-volume biography of Cumberland at the beginning of the twentieth century which covered his career up to 1757. Charteris notes the current thinking about Cumberland:

> his memory has been associated with a dull obloquy and odium. To the great majority of those among whom his name is familiar, he is merely known as that 'Butcher of Culloden' who extinguished the last hope of a romantic cause by a series of acts of savage brutality. This is a reputation from which, hitherto, no very serious effort has been made to reclaim him. It has been customary to approach the rebellion of 1745 from the Jacobite side, and to view it with eyes dazzled by the glamour that has been gathered around the personality of 'Prince Charlie'.[44]

According to Charteris, the major defence of Cumberland is centred around contemporary standards, 'In fact the charges which have been brought against the Duke, in so far as they are not tainted by exaggeration, are charges applicable to England of his time.'[45]

General Rex Whitworth, soldier and historian, wrote in his biography of Cumberland:

> history has never done him the service of a full assessment. By posterity he is remembered chiefly as 'the Butcher of Culloden', his name thus linked to the image of a capricious sadist. Nothing is further from the truth . . . And yet the reality has been outweighed by the myth.[46]

Whitworth lays the blame on Cumberland's political enemies of his own time, and on the historians writing subsequently, who were mostly sympathetic towards the Jacobite cause and therefore more critical of those who were anti-Jacobite. Whitworth writes:

Most of the lies can be traced to the Jacobites . . . But the Jacobites, whether imprisoned, in hiding or in exile, now had time on their hands: time to weave elaborate lies, embroidered with half truths and delusions. 'Bonnie Prince Charlie' was never so much the hero as when he was on the run from the Duke of Cumberland's troops, but the glamour of the Young Pretender's sojourn in the Highlands belongs to the realm of fantasy. Nevertheless, a pretty story is worth retelling; when the Jacobite threat to the Hanoverian throne had faded, even the English began to repeat the tales.[47]

However, Whitworth spends relatively little time on the campaign in Scotland – arguably because in a biography he must allot space to other episodes in the Duke's life. His account of Culloden does not mention anything after the Jacobite army has been routed. There is no account of any savagery, except for a few suggestions such as the following account of the work of some of Cumberland's subordinates:

Campbell's zeal was to prove excessive, matched only by that of Captain John Ferguson of HMS *Furnace*; together they and their men would wreak havoc among the island clans – killing, pillaging, raping and forcibly disarming even anti-Jacobites . . . It was some weeks before Cumberland heard of their antics and, although he strongly disapproved, by then the damage was done.[48]

Generally speaking, Whitworth asserts that Cumberland kept his troops in fairly good order and punished any who overstepped the line. Jacobites who handed in arms were pardoned, and the whole campaign was fairly orderly. The account, as said, lacks much detail, and one could have wished for a more substantive one.

Another military historian, Fortescue, writes:

The campaign ended, as a victorious campaign against mountaineers must always end, in the hunting of fugitives, the burning of villages and the destruction of crops . . . But enough has been written of the inhumanity which earned for Cumberland the name of butcher; his services were far too valuable to be overlooked, and himself of far too remarkable a character to be tossed aside with the brand of a single hateful epithet.[49]

Although Fortecue does not deny the destruction, 'at a time of extreme national peril, the Duke lifted the army in a few weeks, from the lowest depth which it has ever touched of demoralisation and disgrace, to its old height of confidence and self respect'.[50]

The most recent historian to reappraise the Forty Five is Stuart Reid, in various books which concentrate on Culloden. Reid is a military historian, unlike many writers on the Forty Five, and has made detailed studies on the moorland battle, using both archaeological evidence and primary sources to illuminate the accounts.

Like Ray, Reid aims at neutrality, writing in one of his books:

> My aim in writing this book has been to provide a factual and above all impartial study of the military aspects of the campaign. This draws not only on the familiar Jacobite sources, but also on the British army's own records and the letters written at the time by its officers and soldiers . . . but it is by no means a history of the rebellion as seen from the British army's point of view.[51]

Reid does his best to minimize the impact of the alleged atrocities carried out by that army, writing that, after Culloden,

> Although the vigorous and undoubtedly bloody pursuit was after-wards represented in some quarters as tantamount to a war crime, it was in reality nothing out of the ordinary, and indeed the Highlanders had proved themselves equally ruthless when the position was reversed.[52]

He argues that a few wounded Jacobites were killed out of hand by the 'Vestry Men', the criminal or unemployed poor drafted into the army by magistrates, but that 'these were on the whole isolated incidents carried out by unsupervised parties'.[53] As to the later harrying of the Highlands of which so much is made of by others, Reid writes,

> Aimed at destroying the clans' ability to sustain a partisan war which they had already abandoned, the campaign was necessarily cruel, but, though in time popular historians would weave it onto a legacy of bitterness, it would prove no hindrance to the recruitment of Highland regiments for the British Army.[54]

Reid's accounts have not gone without criticism. On the Amazon website are a number of book reviews. One is virulently hostile towards his views;

almost accusing him of whitewashing the British Army's actions after Culloden (Reid once served as a soldier) and of anti-Scottish racism (perhaps the strongest term of opprobrium in the early twenty-first century), which is odd as Reid is an avowed Scots Nationalist!

A more neutral opinion comes from Sadler in his recent book, who states, 'The Duke was neither butcher nor fiend, but the "police action" which followed on from this [Culloden], his only triumph in the field, would damn his memory forever.'[55]

There are a number of charges which most historians have made about Cumberland. These can be summarized into three main headings.

> 1: His conduct of the campaign prior to Culloden. In December 1745, he urged the country people to murder any Jacobite stragglers they could; he gave the garrison of Carlisle no terms and wished they would receive no mercy (alternatively he granted terms and then did nothing to prevent these being broken) and finally in February 1746, property in Aberdeenshire was destroyed.
>
> 2: His actions immediately after the battle of Culloden, either explicitly or implicitly, allowing his troops kill wounded Jacobites, whilst taking no prisoners and having his pursuing cavalry show no mercy to fleeing Jacobites.
>
> 3: Finally, his campaigns of terror in the Highlands in May and June 1746, allowing his troops to destroy Jacobite property with 'fire and sword', to steal their livestock and other possessions, and to kill anyone deemed to be in opposition to him. Even property belonging to loyalists was not safe.

These are grave charges indeed.

We now turn to the defence, to those few historians who do not deem Cumberland to have been the butcher of popular repute.

> 1: They have argued that the tales of terror spread about are the work of Jacobites, their sympathizers and Cumberland's political enemies, both in England and Scotland, and are exaggerations at best, fabrications at worst.
>
> 2: The conditions of the time need to be taken into account. The eighteenth century was a time of harsh punishments to those who tried to rock the social and political order – about twice as many men were hanged after the Monmouth rebellion of 1685

than after that sixty years later, and fugitives fleeing defeat on the battlefield were often slaughtered by the victorious cavalry. And were the actions of the Jacobites morally any better?

3: Necessity is another argument. There had been a number of Jacobite rebellions since 1689 and senior Whig politicians were anxious that there would be no more. They had great influence over the young Duke. Indeed, Cumberland's father's throne was at risk and to him the campaign was personal.

4: Hatred and fear of the Jacobites and especially the Highlanders ran through English and some of Lowland society. They celebrated Cumberland's victory over their old enemies.

It is not the place to give a verdict until the end of the book, and even then readers are well within their rights to disagree. But it is worth recalling the points made above when reading through the remainder of this book. Evidence will be taken from those loyal to the Hanoverian dynasty and the Jacobites. The accused man will also be allowed to speak in his defence – will his words condemn him or exonerate him? The issue is a far from simple one and the evidence will have to be weighed carefully as a man's posthumous reputation lies in the balance.

Chapter 2

The Theory and Practice of the Times

The past is a foreign country: they do things differently there.[1]

This chapter will examine justice in eighteenth-century Britain, contemporary views of violence and contemporary military ethics. It will also explore how contemporary English society viewed the Highland Scots. This will be followed by a survey of the often brutal nature of eighteenth-century warfare. Finally, I will examine how the early modern state dealt with internal rebellions which failed, both in Britain and elsewhere.

There is little doubt that eighteenth-century British society was a violent one. Professor Plumb wrote:

Perhaps the most obvious but least recognised feature of English life in the eighteenth and early nineteenth century was its love of aggression. Rarely has the world known a more aggressive society, or one in which passion was more openly or violently expressed . . . No nation rioted more easily or more savagely – from 1714 to 1830 angry mobs, burning and looting, were as prevalent as disease, and as frequent in the countryside as in the great towns. Time and time again the gentry were forced to assemble and put down the rioting workmen by force.[2]

It was not only those who took part in demonstrations who were violent, but equally – and more so – those who had to suppress them. Britain's two bloodiest riots – at Hexham in 1761 and in London in 1780 – both occurred in the eighteenth century and almost all the fatalities in each encounter were from among the rioters. In an age before a universal police force, the only recourse was to the militia or, more often, the regular army, both of which were well trained and well armed, against those who were neither. Yet it is worth noting that most riots did not cause loss of life, though property might be damaged and participants injured. In the great many riots in 1714–15, only one man lost his life (and even this is not certain).

The state certainly believed in meeting illegitimate violence with legitimate violence. Thus, the legal system was robust, to say the least, partly to compensate for the difficulties in the deterrence or detection of crime. Flogging, hanging and transportation were the three more common punishments for a variety of offences. Gaol sentences were all but unknown, except for debtors. Prison conditions for those awaiting trial or final punishment were also grim, as the Archbishop of York, Thomas Herring (1693–1757), noted when seeing the Jacobite prisoners in York Castle in 1746, 'The filth and sickness and close confinement of these wretches may breed a contagion' and 'when the wind sets fair, I can almost fancy I can smell them, as they do hogs at a distillery'.[3]

The criminal code was a bloody one. Jeremy Black has written, 'The repression of crime was often brutal, especially in England and Wales'.[4] Indeed, penalties for crime had risen in this century. By 1718, theft of property valued at one shilling or over was termed grand larceny and potentially could be punished by death. More offences were deemed as carrying the capital penalty. Fifty were added in 1723, with the introduction of the Waltham Black Act, which made deer stealing a capital offence. In Scotland, criminals could be branded or have their ears nailed to the pillory.[5]

We shall now survey a variety of crimes and punishments, taken from *The Gentleman's Magazine* of 1745:

> [18 January] Ended the Sessions in the Old Bailey, when only Mary Stacey, for robbing a chairman of a guinea in the Strand, received sentence of death.

> [27 April] At the Sessions at the Old Bailey, receiv'd sentence of death, Mary Cut and come again (who would own no other name) for a street robbery, Hester Fowler, for felony, Stephen Parsons, the footman to Sir Simeon Stuart, for stealing his silver chocolate pot, Edw. Ryan, for stealing a silver tankard, Edw. Gilbert, a weaver, for the murder of Tho. Salter, his apprentice, Samuel Keep, for stealing a box of wearing apparel from the Bell Inn, Woodstreet, and Lettice Lynn, for felony.

> [11 July] The sessions ended at the Old Bailey, when Wm. Kelly, Tho. St. Leger, and Patr. Cave, for robbing Tho. Piggott, Esq., of a watch and 40 guineas in the Strand, and John Rigleton, a labourer at Stanmore, for the murder of his wife, by cutting her throat, and ripping up her belly, receiv'd sentence of death.

All were executed on 26 July except Cave, who was transported.[6]

It was not only the criminal law which was violent. Violence of sorts was a fact of life for all. Nicholas Blundell (1669–1737), a Catholic squire of Lancashire, was a most peaceful and amiable gentleman. Yet his diary records him not only attending cock fights but bringing a cock along himself to participate. He also casually refers to having whipped a disobedient servant. Such behaviour, by modern eyes, would seem not only disgraceful but illegal. But in the eighteenth century it was a social norm.[7]

Unsurprisingly, then, military discipline, as laid out by the Articles of War, was also stern. Soldiers who deserted, mutinied, pillaged, disobeyed their officers, fled from the enemy and committed many other misdemeanours were dealt with in a like manner. Floggings were not uncommon, but men could also be branded or made to run the gauntlet. In the worst cases, they could be shot. Many, though, including fellow soldiers, doubtless agreed that such punishments were necessary in order to deter potential criminals both within and without the armed forces. For example, Private Wheeler, a British soldier in the Napoleonic Wars, supported the use of corporal punishment, even though it was 'painful' to watch men punished for fairly minor offences. This was because the army was 'composed as it was of men of all grades of character', including 'men who had committed thefts'.[8]

We shall now examine English attitudes towards the Scots, and towards the Highlanders in particular. The Jacobite Rebellion of 1745 was not a war between Scotland and England – most Scots of fighting age either remained neutral or sided with the government. But the majority of the Jacobite army was Scottish, with a few Englishmen and a few French units making up its composition. Although England and Scotland had shared a joint sovereign since 1603 and a joint Parliament since 1707, differences and old animosities lingered, to say the least. The Jacobite invasion into England in 1745 stirred up all these feelings.

It is therefore worth bearing in mind the opinion of the Scots and Scotland held by many in England. The Jacobite army consisted of Lowlanders and Highlanders, but it is the image of the Highlanders that is indelibly stamped on their army and that the Jacobites tried hard to foster. The Highlanders were generally viewed as barbarians, warlike savages who were very different from Englishmen or even Lowland Scots. They were not seen as fellow Britons; just as in nineteenth-century America, the colonists and the Indians certainly did not see each other as fellow 'Americans'. Those English diarists writing in 1745–6 invariably refer to the Jacobites as 'Rebels' and Charles as 'the Pretender'. William Jessup (1682–1751), a Dissenting apothecary of Holmfirth, Yorkshire, reported rumours, such as 'the Rebels in Carlisle took the women and children and bound them hand and foot and chained them together and set them in the forefront of the castle so that they could not shoot at them but they would kill their wives and children first and so took the castle' and 'We hear this morning the Rebels have burnt Sawforth'.[9] Gertrude Saville (1697–1758), a well-to-do spinster of London, wrote that in Scotland, 'the Rebells committed great outrages and crueltys; plunder'd and destroy'd all round'.[10] That these tales were untrue is not the point; they were believed and were circulated.

Many had been greatly frightened by the Jacobites on their advance southwards. According to Jessup, in late November, 'The Clothiers are gone to fetch their Cloth from Leeds and Halifax' and on the following day, 'They say that they are recovered from their fright at Leeds and hear the Rebels are gone to Lancashire.' A few days later he wrote 'They are in a terrible Consternation in Huddersfield, Holmfirth, Wooldale, Scholes and all places hereabouts.'[11] Dr Richard Kay (1716–51), a Dissenting physician of Bury, Lancashire, wrote, 'All Things are in a Hurry. Business is confused. We have conceal'd our Valuables mostly, the Press has been so strong for Horses for that fear lest Ours should be seized we have sent them away. Lord send us better Times.'[12] James Clegg (1679–1755), a Presbyterian minister and doctor of Derbyshire, wrote 'We hear the Rebels are advancing fast towards Manchester and the people are removing and concealing their best effects.'[13] John Graves of York referred to the Jacobites as 'rascally banditti'.[14]

On the retreat, there were similar fears. Jessup wrote, 'They say that the Rebels are vastly more cruel and inhuman since they left Preston and Manchester.'[15] Horses and goods from homes in Penistone where Jacobites lodged were allegedly stolen. It was said that other houses were also plundered.[16] Miss Saville wrote 'They now plunder wherever they come and more cruel'.[17] With the return of the Jacobites to Scotland, Clegg wrote 'Blessed be God the silk mill is safe'.[18]

John Tucker, an MP for Dorset, remarked in a letter to his brother on 23 November:

> They commit all manner of violent disorders wherever they go. This kind of behaviour must exasperate the country prodigiously against them & when they come to be dispersed as I hope they will do, they must expect to be massacred wherever they are found.[19]

Although these stories of looting and pillage were highly exaggerated, there was a kernel of truth in them. Although the Jacobite army behaved in an exemplary fashion on their march southwards, their retreat northwards was less so. John Daniel, an Englishman in the Jacobite army, wrote, 'And now few there were, who would go on foot, if they could ride; and mighty taking, stealing and pressing of horses there was amongst us.'[20]

There was other prejudice against the Jacobites. Jessup wrote:

> It hath been often affirmed that the Rebels leave abundance of Lice behind them where they come, and that Manchester is very full of Lice, and that a great many of the Rebel army are such Lousy tatter'd Creatures as never was seen.

He later wrote: 'They say the Rebels are such a Shabby lousy crew as was never seen, they stink abominably that nobody can come near them'.[21] Richard Webb, an army officer, wrote that captured Jacobite Highlanders in 1746 were 'full of the Itch & dirt'.[22]

James Ray, a Whitehaven gypsy and contemporary historian of the Forty Five, outlines a number of prejudices held against the Highlanders, passing these off as facts, which he may well have believed himself. They were 'indolent', 'not free of the Itch' and played 'dumb Musick'. Yet it was their violent nature which was most dangerous, 'The Highlanders in all Reigns, have been remarkable for disturbing the established Government of Scotland, by taking up Arms on every Invasion for the Invaders . . . They are desperate in Fight, fierce in Conversation, apt to quarrel, mischievous and even Murders.'[23] Finally, 'Mr McKay tells us, that the Highlanders differ as much from the Lowlanders, in their Dress, manner, and Language, as the Indians in Mexico do from the Spaniards; that the old Scots Language is here spoken in its native Purity.'[24]

Such views were widespread and especially propagated during 1745–6. Anti-Scottish remarks were also heard from the pulpits. Clergymen spoke out against the French and the Catholics, but the Scots were also singled out. James Bate, Vicar of Deptford, wrote of 'his [Charles's] hungry and naked fiends of the north' in a sermon in 1745.[25] John Hill, chaplain to the Archbishop of York, referred to the Jacobites as 'an uncivilized and barbarous multitude . . . a band of mountaineers headed by a Papist'.[26] And there were many more such sermons throughout England, which reinforced anti-Scots attitudes.

Another means of mass circulation was the press, where these diatribes also appeared as a regular staple. In 1745, there were references to 'Popish Highlanders', 'Highland robbers', 'Highland Banditti' and a 'a ragged hungry rabble of Yahoos of Scotch Highlanders'. In the following year there was published a letter, allegedly by a gentleman of Derby, which displayed great animosity towards the Highlanders. A number of Jacobites were billeted on the householder who viewed them as 'so many fiends turn'd out of hell, to ravage the kingdom, and cut throats; and under their plaids nothing but a various sort of butchering weapons were to be seen'. They proceed to eat and drink the contents of his larder. Their language was curious, 'Their dialect seemed to me as if an herd of Hottentots, wild monkies in a desart, or vagrant gypsies, had been jabbering, screaming and howling together; and really this jargon of speech was very properly suited to such a sett of banditti.' Finally, on their departure, they left 'a regiment of lice, several loads of their filthy excrements, and other ejections of different colours, scatter'd before my door, in the garden, and elsewhere about my house'.[27]

Others, who were seen as authorities on the matter, shared, and perhaps stimulated these feelings. Captain Burt, in his book about Scotland, wrote 'But that the Highlanders, for the most part are cruel, is beyond dispute'.[28] Daniel Defoe (1660–1727), writer and journalist, wrote of Breadalbane in the Western Highlands as being inhabited by 'some of the worst, most barbarous, and ill governed of all the Highlands of Scotland; they are desperate in fight, cruel in victory, fierce even in conversation, apt to quarrel, mischievous, and even murderous in their passion'.[29] A volunteer in the Duke's army in 1746 noted: 'A people they are of firm compact Bodies, of great strength, swift of Foot, high minded, inured to Exercise of war, or rather Robbery, and desperately bent upon Revenge'.[30] Dr Samuel Johnson (1704–84), a Tory and also notoriously anti-Scottish, wrote in 1773 that the Highlanders were 'so addicted to quarrels', 'ignorantly proud and habitually violent'.[31]

Such views were long-standing. Dudley Ryder (1691–1757), a lawyer, in 1715 claimed the Scots were 'very fit for business, intriguing, cunning, tricking sort of men that have not much honour or conscience'. In the following year, he observed that one Mr Bowes said 'he hated the name and sight of a Scotchman, for it was the genius and nature of that nation to be tricking, cheating rogues'. Ryder thought this was an exaggeration, but 'I think they have more generally a disposition to play the knave than the English'.[32]

Anti-Scottish feelings derived from fear. This was not only the fear of invasion from Scotland which occurred in 1715 and 1745, but also because increasing numbers of Scots came to play prominent parts in British political, military and commercial life and were thus competing with Englishmen for positions of power that the latter had regarded as theirs of right. The fact that the Highlanders were different in manners, habits, speech, religion and costume was also held against them and shown as proof of their backward and barbaric nature. And given the fact that the Jacobites were allied to the

Catholic powers of France and Spain, the Scots were seen as acting with England's old enemies.

Crucially, these views were also held by those in the political and military elite who formed Cumberland's circle. Charles Lennox (1701–50), second Duke of Richmond and a lieutenant general, had written in 1746 to Thomas Holles-Pelham (1693–1768), Duke of Newcastle and principal Secretary of State to George II, that 'I allways did & always shall despise them as the scum of Scotland which is certainly the sinke of the Earth'. Newcastle later wrote back, remarking 'As to Scotland, I am as little Partial to it, as any man alive. I believe they are not better pleased with me, than wth other people but however, we must consider that they are within our Island.'[33]

Opinions of the Scots on the part of other leading members of the government and their supporters were low. They were always referred to as 'rebels'. Horace Walpole (1717–97), man of letters and son of the late chief minister, Sir Robert Walpole, referred to them as 'banditti'. In a poem in 1743, he wrote of 'Mixed rascal Highlanders, a lawless brood'.[34] Herring had much to say about the Scots throughout the period of the rebellion. According to him they were 'savage', 'rascals', 'wolves', 'vermin', 'Highwaymen' and 'ruffians'. Likewise, another correspondent, Philip Yorke (1690–1764), first Earl of Hardwicke and Lord Chancellor, referred to them as 'rabble'.[35] Sir John Ligonier (1680–1770), a lieutenant general, wrote of the pursuit of the Jacobites in 1746 as 'the disagreeable Hunting of these Wild Beasts'.[36] Henry Pelham (1694–1754), chief minister from 1743 to 1754, referred to the Jacobite Highlanders as 'the rabble' and 'those savages', thinking them not entirely civilized.[37]

Herring repeated stories he had heard about the conduct of the Jacobites. On one occasion, he wrote: 'The brave English were butchered in cold blood, a plain proof of the savageness of the rebel Highlanders, and that their leader is a man of blood'.[38] During the Jacobite occupation of Edinburgh, Hardwicke wrote 'It is writ that the rebels have begun to commit devastations and cruelties.'[39]

Nor was the behaviour of the loyalist Scots seen as impressive. Herring wrote:

> What shall we think of the behaviour of the Scotch nobility on this occasion? Strong marks of treachery, my Lord, when they fled their country, which they might have saved by only standing up in Edinburgh in their own defence, and lending Cope their advice and countenance. Lord Loudon is an exception of this.

Later he wrote, 'I never had an opinion of Scotch faith, and now I am sure I never shall.'[40]

It is almost certain that these attitudes were shared by Cumberland and the officers and men under his command. A soldier who was also a correspondent of Richmond's, and who was in Edinburgh after the end of the campaign, wrote that 'I hope, I am not naturally ill natured' but felt that he 'could with infinite pleasure' have played his flute 'whilst that damn'd nest of Jacobites and Rogues [Edinburgh] was in flames'.[41] These attitudes towards the Scots in general and the Highlanders in particular help explain the level of animosity felt towards the Jacobites by Cumberland and his troops.

We now move onto the practice of warfare and counter-rebellion in the early modern era. Warfare is never a pretty business in practice, yet conventional warfare of this era has often been termed 'the Lace Wars' and 'Warfare in the Age of Reason'. Certainly the full dress uniforms could be splendid and, compared to the horrors of the Second World War in the Far East or on the Eastern Front, warfare was, perhaps, less systematically brutal. Yet it is also worth noting what happened in the aftermath of a battle in which one side was the clear victor, or was able to pursue its enemies from the field. It was common for the cavalry of the victorious army to pursue its enemy. For instance, during the battle of Dunblane on 13 November 1715, the right wing of the regular army broke that of the Jacobites. Colonel Harrison wrote:

> They [the Jacobites] . . . were pursued above two Miles by five squadrons of Dragoons . . . we concluded it an entire Rout, and resolved to pursue as long as we had Day-light.[42]

Although we do not know how many Jacobites were killed in the rout, a modern historian estimates total Jacobite casualties at the battle at between 750 and 1,500, and the majority probably occurred during the rout (elsewhere on the field of battle, the Jacobite right wing had successfully routed the left wing of regular army).[43] The Earl of Argyll (1680–1743), commander of the regular troops on this occasion, is never regarded as a 'war criminal' nor a 'butcher'. When one side clearly vanquished an opponent, losses for the latter were heavy, especially if the victor had troops who could move quicker than those of the defeated army – usually this meant having a strong cavalry arm, but it could also mean that lighter clad troops could outrun more heavily equipped troops. As we shall see, the latter occurred at the Jacobite victory of Prestonpans in 1745 as well as at Culloden in the following year.

During the Civil Wars, similar treatment was meted out to the losers as they tried to flee the stricken field. At Kilysth, after Montrose's troops beat their

Covenanting enemies, his Highlanders hacked down their escaping enemies, whom they had grudges against. In the same year, after the battle of Naesby, Cromwell's troopers slashed and hacked at fleeing Royalists.[44]

Such was not uncommon after battles on the Continent either, as these examples from Marlborough's campaigns will show. On 2 July 1704, Marlborough's allied army attacked entrenched Franco-Bavarian positions on the Schellenberg. After a bloody battle, the allies routed their enemy. Marlborough ordered his dragoons to remount and pursue them. Many of the pursued were denied quarter and were killed. Mrs Christian Davies (a woman who had enlisted in the army) wrote: 'The Bavarians were now soon routed, and a cruel slaughter made of them.'[45] Historian James Falkner noted: 'Such a merciless pursuit was the ruthless custom after a bloody assault . . . the allied horsemen were off the leash and would continue their bloody work while the light lasted.' As to the enemy wounded: 'Little is said of the care offered to the fallen French and Bavarian defenders, and it may be assumed that their fate was generally an unhappy one. It was a rough age.'[46]

Nor were civilians immune from the bloody business of war. Attacks on civilian property were not unknown in this era. In the 1704 campaign, just after the battle just mentioned, Marlborough's forces pillaged the Bavarian countryside. Apparently, 3,000 cavalrymen were sent to burn and destroy. If crops could not be seized for the army's use, they were burnt, as were the barns in which they were stored, and often the adjacent property, too. Mrs Davis wrote: 'We spared nothing, killing, burning or otherwise destroying.' Adam Cardonnel, Marlborough's military secretary, noted 'We have made no progress since our success at Schellenberg, except that it be burning and destroying the Elector's country wherein we have not been sparing', yet he added 'I wish to God it were all over'. Hans Bellingh, a Hanoverian officer, was more forthright in his criticism, 'The villages were prosperous and thickly populated and it distressed every officer to see over 40 or 50 more villages go up in smoke in an hour.' Another wrote 'With fire and sword the country round was wasted far and wide, and many a childing mother then and suckling baby died, but things like that, you know, must be, at every famous victory.' Interestingly enough, the personal property of the Elector was ordered not to be touched. The military rationale for such a policy was to force the Bavarians to disperse their forces and so be unable to aid their allies with a substantial force.[47]

Another eighteenth-century campaign in which civilians and their property were destroyed by soldiers occurred in Canada during the Seven Years War (1756–63). In 1755, much of the French population of Nova Scotia was deported. During the siege of Quebec, the city was bombarded. There were also a number of destructive raids on villages along the Saint Lawrence River in 1759, where property was burnt. Major General James Wolfe (1727–59) wrote: 'I propose to set the Town on fire with Shells, to destroy the Harvest, Houses, & Cattle both above and below, to send off as many Canadians as possible to Europe, & to leave famine and desolation behind me.' Such action was allegedly an attempt to force Montcalm's French army within Quebec to leave the city to fight, but the real reason may have been the frustration Wolfe and his colleagues felt during the prolonged siege.[48]

After a battle or siege, it was common for soldiers to commit acts against person and property which would ordinarily be termed criminal. This was usual for the victors in the English Civil War. Likewise, during the eighteenth century Peter Clarke was writing after the Jacobite defeat at Preston in 1715:

> they [the regulars] with force and armes broke open doers and locks of chambers and closets, and the moneys, plate, goods, and chatles of most of the inhabitants of that towne (who were and still are good subjects to his MAJESTIE'S king Georges government) contrary to the will of the owners of the said goods, felonyously did steal, take, and carry away contrary to his said Majestie's peace, crowne and dignity, and also contrary to the laws of the nation.[49]

That said, the Jacobite troops also damaged property belonging to local loyalists.

The military experience while on active campaign could be brutal by the standards of more peaceful times. In the year after Waterloo, Private Wheeler wrote: 'If you knew but the hundredth part of the atrocities committed by men calling themselves British soldiers it would chill your blood . . . I know many have plundered when there has been no excuse.'[50] After the storming of Badajoz in 1812, Rifleman Costello wrote: 'The scenes of wickedness that soldiers are guilty of on capturing a town are often truly diabolical, and I shudder at the memory.'[51]

However, it was more common that 'atrocities' occurred either on the fringes of Europe, or on other continents, or in conflicts between regular forces and 'irregular' opponents. As Jeremy Black writes, 'In general, warfare was more savage both in eastern Europe, where religious and ethnic differences appear to have increased human cruelty, and when regulars fought irregulars.' Soldiers often reacted violently towards irregulars, destroying property as well as taking the lives of civilians. Revolts against the Habsburgs and the French monarchy, as well as against the Hanoverian monarchy in 1745, were all put down ruthlessly. So was the Irish rebellion in 1798.[52]

The eighteenth-century state dealt firmly with domestic rebellion. It is worth noting that these rebellions took place when the country was at war, as those in revolt could hope to succeed when their enemy's strength was diluted and they themselves could expect direct aid from their enemy's enemy. Therefore the government would be all the more likely to want a quick end to the rebellion and would want no more recurrence of it. Therefore, methods employed would usually be quick and brutal.

Armstrong Starkey's study of warfare in the Age of the Enlightenment provides insights into the mindset of the eighteenth century. With reference to the attitude and actions of those in authority against internal rebellions in general, he writes:

> These were not the 'cabinet wars' devised by eighteenth century monarchs and their ministers for limited national gains – but wars of peoples in which the line between civilian and combatant was blurred. When this occurred, war could be 'total' for those involved.[53]

With specific reference to our interest, he writes:

> Charles Edward's Highland followers were unfortunate in that they were not considered regular soldiers protected by military custom, but rebels and 'savages'. They were thus beyond the protection of 'civilised' warfare praised by contemporaries. Emmanuel von Vattell never included 'savage' peoples in his rules of war, and there is no reason to assume that Cumberland should have. This view was shared by almost all the governing class and Cumberland was its willing agent.[54]

It is worth reflecting further on the Swiss von Vattell, the 'most important eighteenth century expert on international law'. His theories were based on Christian teachings and humanist writers, such as Thomas of Aquinas, St Augustine and Hugo Grotius. These writers said that war should only be fought for 'legitimate' reasons, usually self-defence, and that it should be limited. 'Never let us forget that our enemies are men', Vattell wrote.

Yet he was not always an advocate of mercy and forbearance. He said that necessity could override humanity and that all subjects of an enemy state were enemies if they contributed in any way to that state's war effort. Although he said that women and children should be dealt with mercifully, they could also be legitimate targets if they contributed or resisted. Vattell was suitably vague here. He also wrote, 'When we are at war with a savage nation, who observe no rules, we may punish them in the person of any of their people whom we take.' It is interesting that Vattell praised Cumberland's humanity after the battle of Dettingen.[55]

The penalty for unsuccessful rebellion on the Continent was severe. During the War of Spanish Succession (1702–13), rebellion broke out in France, Spain and the Austrian Empire. The Freys, in their study of these rebellions, conclude: 'In early modern Europe authorities customarily reacted with repression, the violence of which dehumanised and traumatised the population.' During the rebellion of the Camisards in France in 1703–4, troops sent to put down the rebels made little distinction between the innocent and guilty and referred to their enemy as 'vermin'. Loyal militia terrorized the local populations of the rebellious districts. 466 villages were razed to the ground and their inhabitants removed to walled areas and strategic hamlets. Many died of starvation. Other village populations were massacred. One order was 'Let their dwellings be decimated and let there be none to dwell in their huts.' Forty churches were burnt or pillaged and between 200–300 were abandoned. Later an amnesty was offered to some rebels. The rebellion was not over until 1710.[56]

Likewise, when Barcelona fell in 1714, the leaders of the garrison, though guaranteed their lives, were executed. In the aftermath of the Corsican revolt in 1769, villages and churches were burnt. After Pugachev's failed rebellion in Russia in 1774, his followers were severely dealt with by the forces of that exponent of the Enlightenment, Catherine the Great. According to Starkey, 'These events seldom elicited much sympathy from Enlightened thinkers. Highland Scots, and Cossacks were not portrayed as freedom fighters, but as barbarians who threatened Enlightened civilisation.'[57]

The three major rebellions to threaten to overturn the British state in the years between the Restoration of 1660 and the 1745 rebellion were those of the Duke of Monmouth (1649–85), a bastard son of Charles II, in 1685 and the Jacobite rebellions of 1689 and 1715. As with the Forty Five, all of these were serious attempts to replace the existing sovereign with another, whom some believed to be the rightful king. In all cases, the existing ruler was in a precarious position, having only been king for a year or less.

Monmouth arrived in England on 11 June 1685 and his venture came to a bloody end less than a month later on 6 July at Sedgemoor. About 200 men were killed in the fire fight with the regulars, but perhaps 1,000 more were killed in the rout, when the regular cavalry pursued the fugitives. The survivors were hunted in later weeks by the local gentry, militia and constables as well as the regulars. Cash incentives were given to soldiers for each rebel they captured and villagers were threatened into revealing the whereabouts of the escapees.[58]

Those Englishmen who had supported Monmouth and were captured did not have an easy time. It is impossible to know how many were captured, nor precisely how many suffered each fate. One contemporary estimate was that 854 men were transported and 334 were hanged. Bearing in mind that Monmouth's army consisted of about 3,000 men, this is a very high proportion indeed. Armed rebellion was no light undertaking. In Scotland, there had been an abortive rebellion under the Earl of Argyll, with the same objective, and though this was defeated without even a battle, the consequences for Argyll's supporters were severe. About 100 were hanged and 1,700 transported. Trials were often short and men condemned on minimal evidence.[59]

There had been two major Jacobite rebellions prior to 1745. Both had been defeated in the field, though neither after a militarily decisive battle, as in 1746. The Jacobite rebellion of 1689 lingered until 1691, despite two defeats (at Dunkeld in 1689 and at Cromdale in 1690). The rebellion ended by the Jacobite chiefs being asked to take an oath that they would not take up arms against the government of William III (1650–1702) and Mary (1664–94). Most did so and were pardoned. The famous atrocity which resulted was the massacre of Glencoe of 1692 when the MacDonalds of Glencoe did not meet the deadline for making their peace with the authorities on 31 December 1691 and an order was sent to 'fall upon the rebels, the MacDonalds of Glencoe, and to put all to the sword under seventy'. Thirty-eight people, men, women and children, were killed in cold blood.[60]

Suffering was worse in Ireland, where the conflict was as much a civil war as a conventional war between regular armies. There were claims that the victorious regular troops had plundered the property of both sides. Catholics lived in fear and slept in fields lest they be attacked in their beds. Even so, a Catholic chronicler wrote of 'the vast Number of poor harmless natives, who were daily Kill'd up and down the Fields, as they were following their Labour, or taken out of their Beds and Hanged, or shot immediately'. As well as human casualties, there was further misery, for cattle were seized and property plundered.[61]

The other major effort by the Jacobites took place in 1715. The battle of Dunblane had not destroyed the Jacobite army, but a detachment of it, with its English allies, had been forced to surrender at Preston. The Jacobite clans retreated in early 1716 and the regular army moved through the Highlands. There was virtually no resistance. Clans surrendered their weapons. Little action was taken against them. It was the prisoners taken after the battle of

Preston who suffered death, or more commonly, transportation, though many were released by 1717.[62] In neither case was there any serious attempt to subdue the Highlands. In each case, the Jacobites rose again, like a phoenix.

A later, and last, major rebellion against the eighteenth-century British state occurred in Ireland in 1797–8, during the French Revolutionary War. The regular army and loyalist Irish forces eventually put the rebellion down. When Enniscorthy was taken in 1798 by the regulars, it was observed, 'it was not easy to restrain the troops in many instances. Excesses, doubtless, were committed, which it is painful to reflect, in some degree accompany every war, but which abound in a civil war more than in any other'.[63]

Whilst war in the eighteenth century was usually for limited goals, such as the capture or recapture of a piece of territory, such as Silesia, seized by Frederick II of Prussia in the War of Austrian Succession from Austria and fought over again in the Seven Years War, rebellion (not to be confused with riot) was another matter. In this case, the conflict was not for any limited objective or imperial playing piece. It was for control of a kingdom and there could only be one winner and total victory – as in the World Wars – was therefore the aim of both participants. There was, then, an element of total war here.

While prisoners of war were often dealt with in a chivalrous manner, and exchanged for other prisoners of war (cartels were often arranged, in order to exchange prisoners), for men captured in rebellion, different standards were applied by governments. A prisoner of war was a man who was loyal to another ruler. A man who rebelled was meant to have been loyal to his ruler. Therefore the offence of the former was only to obey his master and the offence of the latter was to disobey his master. The hierarchical nature of society depended on these bonds of loyalty holding or, if they were broken, on the offender being given exemplary punishment 'pour encourager les autres', as Voltaire remarked about Admiral John Byng (1704–57) on the latter's execution for failing to press home an attack in 1756. The Jacobite rebellions were often referred to as being 'unnatural' by the supporters of the government, and this is why. Furthermore, governments insist on their own legality and instinctively condemn those who seek to challenge their authority. Those whose task it is to uphold that authority and are identified with it, find themselves at the sharp end of any threat to the status quo. They are unlikely to be sympathetic to it.

Eighteenth-century British society was held together in part by violence or at least its threat. Criminals were well aware of this, as was everyone else. But governments and societies throughout Europe also recognized this. Battles could be bloody if one side routed and, if the fighting took place between regular and irregular forces, they could be even bloodier as each side harboured a hatred born out of this difference for each other. Those involved on the losing side of such a conflict were in grave danger from the victors. Violence was a salient feature of life in the eighteenth century – both by the enemies of the state and by the state itself.

Chapter 3

Cumberland's Early Life, 1721–1745

by his brave behaviour upon the Day of the Battle, by his love of the
service, by his generosity & compassion to prisoners, & by all the good
qualitys that ever a young Prince [Cumberland] was endow'd with: he
has justly got the love and esteem of everybody.[1]

William Augustus was the third son of George II (1683–1760) and Queen
Caroline (1683–1737) and was born on 15 April 1721. He was the first
Hanoverian prince who was also British – born here and who spoke English
as his first language. He was the favourite son. His parents despised his
elder brother, Frederick (1707–51), Prince of Wales, though it seems the two
brothers got on well together (at the theatre in 1738, Cumberland bowed to
his brother, but his sister did not). When George came to England in 1714,
he had left Frederick behind in Hanover, and when the latter arrived in
England in the following decade, his bitterness towards his father led him to
consort with politicians who opposed his father's ministers. The Hanoverians
were good haters.[2]

It would appear from the following quotation from the diary of John, the
first Earl of Egmont, on 31 January 1730, that Cumberland had the making
of a child prodigy:

I was told to-day that the King, jesting with the Duke his son, and
asking him which he had rather be, a king or a queen, he replied: 'Sir
I never yet tried; let me be one of them a month, and I'll tell you.'
And yesterday, the Queen, chiding him for asking eagerly for his
dinner, it being the thirtieth of January, on which he ought to fast, it
being the anniversary day of cutting off King Charles's head, she
asked him whether he thought it was right in the people to have done
it, to which he replied he could not tell what was his crime till he read
his history. These are very early marks of quickness and parts in a
child not nine years old.[3]

33

His first biographer claimed his military interests were first evident when he was a 5 year old and he 'raised a company of young boys, much about his own age, whom he marshalled and trained up according to the method which at that time appeared to him most convenient'. He rode on horseback before he was 8.[4]

He was heaped with honours at an early age. He was made a Companion of the Bath in 1725, was created Duke of Cumberland in 1726 and Knight of the Garter in 1730. In 1731, he was given his own suite of rooms in all royal residences, and an allowance of £6,000 per annum (trebled in 1739).[5] In return for such honours, much was expected of him. On her deathbed in 1737, his mother urged her son to be loyal to her husband, his father. Accord to John, Lord Hervey (1696–1743), a courtier:

> 'As for you, William,' continued she to the Duke, 'you know I have always loved you tenderly, and placed my chief hope in you; show your gratitude to me in your behaviour to the King; be a support to your father, and double your attention to make up for the disappointment and vexation he must receive from your prolifigate and worthless brother. It is in you only I hope for keeping up the credit of our family'.[6]

Cumberland's reaction to such a plea was not recorded by Hervey, but it would seem that he took it to heart and so any enemy of his father's became one of his.

He was educated by a distinguished array of tutors, one of whom, Sir Jacob Acworth (1668–1749), interested him in a naval career. As well as learning about mathematics, history, geography and law, he was also taught military subjects – the art of gunnery and fortification. In 1740, his father gave him his first military commission, as colonel of the Coldstream Guards. This was a relatively late age for a young man to receive his first commission; James Wolfe was 14 when he gained his. Cumberland spent some of this summer at the military camp at Hounslow.[7]

Yet, perhaps because of the influence of Acworth, it appeared that he might have pursued a naval career. In 1739 he had visited Portsmouth to inspect the ships and fortress there and paid another visit the following year. He enlisted as a volunteer on board the flagship of Sir John Norris (1671–1749), *The Victory*, in 1740, in order to see some action in the war against Spain. This was a naval conflict and had broken out in 1739. Yet it was not to be. Cumberland's seafaring career was over before it began because his ship was damaged by another.[8] Back on land again, Cumberland was appointed as a major general in 1742.

It is important to remember Cumberland the man as much as Cumberland the soldier. The genesis of two of Cumberland's other loves first developed in these years. First, he was given the use of a hunting lodge in Windsor Lodge, sowing the seeds of his lifelong enthusiasm for hunting and horse racing. During a royal hunt in 1737, a hound had jumped into the river after the stag and George II wanted the dog rescued 'whereupon the Duke immediately plunged in on horseback'. On another occasion, he was injured and much bruised by a fall whilst hunting.[9]

He was also interested in the fairer sex. The Earl of Egmont noted in his diary on 13 January 1739: 'Miss Williams, the player, was complimented in the green room by her fellow comedians for the honour done her by the Duke of Cumberland in taking her for a mistress; but 'tis to be hoped this is scandal.'[10] But it would appear that this was not a rumour, as Egmont later records that Lord Clinton (1720–94) offered her money to be his mistress, not the Duke's. When the Duke found the two of them together, understandably, he became very angry and challenged him to a duel.[11] His amorous activities might have been curtailed if the proposal in 1742 that he marry a foreign princess had gone ahead. Yet, with Lord Orford's help, he avoided matrimony, by asking for too large an allowance from his parsimonious father. All this was perfectly natural in a young man (or prince). Horace Walpole wrote in 1745 that 'he will be as popular with the lower class of men, as he has been *for 3 or 4 years* [my emphasis] with the low women'.[12]

Cumberland could be passionate about more than just women. He was involved in politics, and on 1 January 1742, Egmont wrote 'the Duke of Cumberland was in a great passion that my son and Mr Edwin were elected [to Parliament] without any opposition'.[13]

His martial ambition was not to be frustrated for long. The British Army was on campaign on the Continent in the spring of 1743, with its Hanoverian and Dutch allies in the War of Austrian Succession (1740–8) in which Britain came to the aid of Maria Theresea, Empress of Austria, whose throne was being disputed by Prussia, France and Spain.

On 16 June 1743, the allied army and that of France clashed at Dettingen. It was a great triumph for the allied army, led by George II, the last reigning monarch to lead a British army into battle. Marshal Noilles, leading the French army, planned to trap his enemies between the River Main and the forested hills. The allies had to deploy under fire in order to be in position to assault the French lines. But the French attacked first. Showing great resolution, George II led his forces on foot and the infantry and artillery beat off the attack, and with the French falling back, the cavalry was ordered ahead to complete the victory. The casualties of the vanquished were treble that of the victors.[14]

During the battle, Cumberland, who acted as an ADC to General Clayton, issuing orders and ensuring their compliance, was wounded, and the injury which at first appeared slight, became more serious. Horace Walpole initially reported, 'The Duke is wounded in the calf of the leg, but slightly', although later he wrote 'The poor Duke is in a much worse way than he was at first apprehended: his wound proves a bad one, he is gross; and has had a shivering fit which is often the forerunner of mortification'. Eventually he recovered, but always had difficulty walking thereafter.[15]

The Duke's reputation soared. Sir Horace Mann (1706–86), the British Minister in Florence, noted: 'His behaviour on the battle and after it has gained him great honour, which nobody endeavours to rob him of.' Lieutenant-Colonel Charles Russell wrote thus to his wife: 'The Duke also charged with General Clayton in the first line in the warmest part of the action, riding about, animating the men with great bravery and resolution.'[16] Cumberland was humane as well as brave. The Duke of Richmond told the Duke of Newcastle,

> by his brave behaviour upon the Day of the Battle, by his love of the service, by his generosity & compassion to prisoners, & by all the good qualitys that ever a young Prince was endow'd with: he has justly got the love and esteem of everybody.[17]

According to Voltaire, there is a story that when the wounded Duke was being seen to by a surgeon, he saw the wounded Count Fenlon, a French soldier, nearby and told the surgeon, 'Begin with the French officer: he is more wounded than I am, and I shall be certain of assistance, which he is not.'[18]

Wolfe wrote admiringly of Cumberland:

> the Duke behaved as bravely as a man could do. He had a musquet-shot through the calf of his leg. I had several times the honour of speaking with him just as the battle began, and was often afraid of his being dash'd to pieces by the cannon-balls. He gave orders with a great deal of calmness, and seemed quite unconcerned. The soldiers were in high delight with him so near them.[19]

In the following year, Cumberland remained in England. His only military command was to be put in charge of the troops defending London in early 1744, when a French invasion force was to set sail to restore the Stuarts to the throne. Since storms at sea prevented a landing, his military talents went unused on this occasion.

Cumberland was back in action in April 1745, taking sole command of the allied army in Flanders, having been appointed Captain General, a title that had been abeyance since it had been held by the Duke of Marlborough. That army was made up of British, Hanoverian, Dutch and Austrian troops. This was his first independent command and it was a grave responsibility. It also demonstrated the trust and esteem in which his father held him.

The principal action in this campaign was the battle of Fontenoy, four miles from Tournai, on 11 May 1745. The French army under Marshal de Saxe, one of the foremost military captains of the age, was besieging Tournai, held by Dutch/Swiss troops. Cumberland's army sought to relieve the stronghold.

After some initial skirmishing on the flanks, the main body of the allied army advanced, led by Cumberland. Despite being unsupported by some of the Dutch, they were able to beat off attacks by the French infantry and cavalry. However, French reinforcements arrived. Cumberland was then concerned that his smaller army might be outflanked as well as outnumbered, so gave the order to withdraw, albeit in good order and the French did not pursue. Losses were severe on both sides.[20] Although it was a defeat, it was an honourable one, and no one seems to have thought less of Cumberland because of it.

Again, as at Dettingen, Cumberland's conduct drew praise. Lieutenant-Colonel Joseph Yorke (1724–92), one of Cumberland's aides, wrote on the following day:

> I never heard of such behaviour as the Duke's: he rode everywhere, he encouraged the wavering, he complimented the bold, he threatened the cowards. In the midst of the greatest dangers, in the heat of the action, whilst death stared him on every side in the face, he delivered his orders with a steadiness and coolness worthy of himself: had the nation seen him they would have adored him.[21]

As well as displaying great bravery, Cumberland revealed another side to his character. The Hon. Charles Yorke (1722–70), a lawyer, reported that during the retreat,

> His R. Highness turned his eyes on the field of battle and burst into tears: having acted the part of a general, he acted that of a man. Nothing can be stronger than his expressions of tenderness and humanity in the private letter he wrote to the Princesses.[22]

In his early years, therefore, Cumberland distinguished himself as a brave, compassionate and conscientious soldier, winning plaudits even in defeat. He was also a loyal subject and son to his father, the King. Perhaps we can see in these years that Cumberland was destined to be an implacable foe of the Jacobites as they sought to overthrow his father's throne and he sought to defend it in the best and most permanent manner that he could.

Chapter 4

Cumberland and the Campaign of the Forty Five, July 1745–April 1746

*don't imagine that threatening military execution and many other such
things are pleasing to do to me but nothing else will go down without
in this part of the world.[1]*

Before Cumberland's role in the Forty Five is examined, a brief survey of the
campaign prior to his direct involvement in it will be made. The Jacobite
rebellion of 1745 was but one of a series of internal uprisings, which had
occurred since 1689. Although he was not initially involved, once he was, he
became the key figure in the defeat of the Jacobites.

The Background to the Forty Five, 1688–1744

The Jacobite Rebellion of 1745 was one of a succession of armed attempts
made by the exiled Stuart dynasty to regain the throne of Great Britain which
James II had lost to William and Mary in 1688. Their supporters were known
as Jacobites from the Latin *Jacobus* for James and there were Jacobites
throughout the British Isles and at all ranks of society. Catholics and Scottish
Episcopalians were particularly sympathetic towards Jacobitism, as were a
number of the Highland clans, though by no means all. They also had occa-
sional supporters on the Continent, chiefly Spain and France. There had been
civil war in Scotland and Ireland in 1689–91, assassination plots against
William and invasion attempts in the 1690s. Notable incidents among these
had included the battle of Killiecrankie in 1689, the battle of the Boyne in the
following year and the massacre of Glencoe in 1692. None of the Jacobite
attempts, though, had been successful. In 1701 the Act of Succession stated
that, on the death of the childless Queen Anne (1664–1714), who succeeded
William III in 1702, the crown would pass to Sophia, dowager electress of
Hanover, a small Protestant German duchy. She died in 1714 and so the
crown passed to her eldest son, George Lewis (1660–1727), the Elector. In

1701, James II died and his son, James Francis Stuart (1688–1766), was recognized by the Jacobites and the French as James III. There was a French-backed invasion attempt in 1708, but storms and the Royal Navy forced the ships back to France.

George I was crowned in 1714, but the first years of his reign were troubled by a spate of rioting throughout England. Worse still, there were major attempts in both England and Scotland in 1715 to put James on the throne. Both were defeated by the following year. Other plots occurred throughout the reign, but again came to nothing. Although, on George I's death, his son, George II, was peacefully crowned in 1727, Jacobitism remained a danger. By this time, a new hope for the Jacobites had emerged; James's first son, Charles Edward Stuart (1720–88), known to history as Bonnie Prince Charlie or the Young Pretender (his father being known as the Old Pretender). This young man was passionate to restore his father to the throne which he saw as rightly his.

It is hard to ascertain how dangerous the Jacobite threat was to the Hanoverian throne after 1716. Active and vocal sympathy in England was at a low ebb from the early 1720s, though drinking clubs existed throughout the country. These were meetings of men who were sympathetic towards a Jacobite restoration and their existence showed that there was some hostility to the Hanoverian dynasty. Yet it is one matter to drink with like-minded fellows and quite another to rise in arms. In Scotland it was another matter. The clan system ensured that the chieftains had the option of raising their tenants for battle, though clan warfare by 1745 was almost unknown. England, on the other hand, was virtually unmilitarized, except for the regular forces. If Britain was at war, the French and Spanish were always potential allies to the Jacobites. Sir Robert Walpole (1676–1745), chief minister from 1721 to 1742, was convinced of the danger that Jacobitism posed and did all he could to monitor and quell it and to keep it diplomatically isolated. In peacetime, Jacobitism was easily containable, but in wartime, it was more dangerous.

In early 1744, with Britain and France at war in the War of Austrian Succession, as we have seen, Charles had intended to set sail with a French army in order to invade Britain, having been invited over by a group of Tory noblemen and gentry, mostly based in Essex. This bold move was thwarted by poor weather in the Channel.[2]

The Forty Five in Scotland, Part 1, July–October 1745

Charles was undeterred. Lacking much concrete French support, he gathered arms and money. In July 1745, he set sail with his two ships, the *Du Teillay* and the *Elizabeth*, and seven companions. The *Elizabeth*, carrying the money and arms, was forced to return after an encounter with the *Lion*, a Royal Navy vessel. But by the end of the month, Charles had arrived in Scotland and his bid for the throne had begun in earnest.

Initially it did not appear that the Jacobite attempt would be successful. The Hon. Philip Yorke (1720–90), eldest son of Lord Hardwicke, wrote 'I shall think the Young Pretender very ill advised'.[3] The Highland response was at first lukewarm. Horace Walpole wrote 'if the Boy has apparently no enemies in Scotland, at least he has openly very few friends. Nobody of note has joined him, but a brother of the Duke of Atholl, and another of Lord Dunmore.' When Charles first asked for support, 'the Majority were of Opinion, it was risking too much, and therefore declined'. Lacking French troops, money and arms, he was told to go home.[4] Once again, Charles was adamant that he had come home and that he would see his father crowned.

Eventually, though, the Camerons, Stewarts of Appin and the MacDonalds flocked to Charles's standard, which was officially unveiled at Glenfinnan on 19 August. Lord George Murray (1694–1760), sixth son of the Duke of Atholl, and James Drummond (1713–46), self-styled Duke of Perth, were appointed as lieutenant-generals. One of their first triumphs was to ambush and capture a detachment of soldiers marching to Fort William. Their little army was not well armed and only numbered about 2,000 men. Lieutenant-General Sir John Cope (1690–1760) was in command of the regular forces in Scotland, though his troops were similar in number and inexperienced (the bulk of the veteran regiments were with Cumberland on the Continent). He issued orders on 13 August that all his troops should gather at Stirling.[5]

From there his forces, which were made up of infantry and artillery, marched northwards on 21 August. His two dragoon regiments remained in the Lowlands, to the west of Edinburgh, because the terrain would be too difficult for horses and their food supply would be limited. Despite hopes of loyalist Highland support, not a man joined his army. Furthermore, he was unable to bring the Jacobites to battle in favourable circumstances and so marched north to Inverness, there to take ship to Edinburgh.[6]

Despite this ultimately ineffectually marching in Scotland, few of the government's supporters were apt to see the rebellion as anything to worry about. Walpole recorded that 'Lord Granville and his faction persist in persuading the King that it is an affair of no consequence'. He also noted that there was apparently no sign of any support for the Jacobites from England or France and so 'never was so desperate an enterprise'. Furthermore, the Channel was well guarded by Admiral Vernon's ships and noblemen in England were raising the militia and regiments of volunteers to support George II.[7]

Yet some were concerned. The Duke of Newcastle, foremost Secretary of State, was one. His brother, Henry Pelham, was another. Newcastle wrote that the rebellion might be aided by a French invasion and noted 'all true friends of the government are extremely alarmed'. He requested that troops abroad be recalled from the Continent.[8] At this point, Cumberland, with the bulk of the regulars, was on the Continent, facing the French. Yet he agreed, 'if England wants them, I am intirely of [sic] opinion that this country and even the whole alliance ought not to be considered comparatively with our own country'. Yet he thought Newcastle was exaggerating the danger, writing 'I don't see the danger at home as so imminent' and later 'that this cloud of the Pretender will blow over'. Once ten battalions of regular infantry and eight battalions of Dutch/Swiss troops had been dispatched, Cumberland was convinced that they should be more than enough, and spoke of his contempt for the Jacobites, 'I hope Great Britain is not to be conquered by 3000 rabble gather'd together in the mountains'.[9]

Whilst Cope marched northwards, the Jacobites advanced on Perth and proclaimed James Francis Stuart as James III of England and VIII of Scotland. They then moved towards Edinburgh. The two regiments of dragoons there felt that they were too weak to oppose them and retreated eastwards and so there were no regular troops between the Jacobites and Edinburgh. There was debate in the Scottish capital over whether to defend the city with the volunteers and militia. During the negotiations with the Jacobites the coach carrying the city's representatives returned and the gates opened. When they did so, an advance party of Camerons slipped inside and took the city without a fight. Many in the city enthusiastically welcomed Charles.[10]

When Cope's forces arrived by sea on 17 September, they found themselves a defensive position just east of the city, at Prestonpans. The Jacobite forces were able to march around this and attacked on the morning of 21 September. Cope's gunners fled and though the officers lit the cannons' fuses, little damage was inflicted. The cavalry refused to charge and left the field. The infantry, being attacked on the flanks, were unable to make much effectual resistance. Many fled. Andrew Henderson, a Scottish schoolmaster and contemporary historian, wrote thus of their fate:

> The Infantry in the first line were miserably massacred by the Rebels. Such as threw down their Arms, and begged for Quarters upon their knees, were inhumanely mangled; and such as fed into the Inclosures were pursued and kill'd. But the great Carnage was at the Grange Park Dyke, which when the poor Men were climbing, they were

massacred in the most barbarous manner: twenty were killed by the sword, for one who fell by a Bullet.[11]

The Jacobite David Wemys, Lord Elcho (1721–87), ADC to Charles and commander of a troop of cavalry, wrote similarly:

> The foot Soldiers run to Gett through the Breackes in the walls that were behind them . . . but they were either cutt down or taken by the Highlanders, who in pursuit are very nimble, and had it not been for the breaches in the walls their would not have a Soul Escaped.

Yet, after this bloody episode, the wounded survivors were well treated. Almost all of Cope's men, except the cavalry, who, along with Cope, retreated to Berwick, were killed or taken prisoner. The Jacobites suffered very few casualties.[12]

The Jacobites were now masters of Scotland, save for a few scattered garrisons in forts and castles, who were in no position to do them much harm at the present. They were also all properly armed for the first time with the weapons taken from Cope's army. Some suggested that they should march immediately towards London, but there were insufficient men to do so; many having temporarily gone home. A ship from France brought money and arms, and a representative from the French court, the Marquis D'Eguilles. He promised that French troops would be sent to Britain to assist the cause.[13]

There was despondency in London. Walpole wrote 'we are sadly convinced that they are not so such raw ragamuffins as they were represented . . . This defeat has frightened everybody.'[14] Newcastle wrote to Philip Dormer Stanhope (1694–1773), the Earl of Chesterfield and Lord Lieutenant of Ireland, 'You will also see that we have for the present lost one kingdom.'[15] Now there could be no doubt that the Jacobite danger was no mere flash in the pan, but a serious threat, especially if allied to a French invasion.

But the military situation, for the government, was improving. Dutch and Swiss troops arrived in Britain, as did the ten battalions of regular infantry, under Sir John Ligonier's command. They came just as news of the defeat of Prestonpans broke, thus averting any major panic. More units were then recalled. Field-Marshal George Wade (1673–1748), a veteran soldier, was ordered to command the first army which was to assemble at Newcastle, whereas the remainder was to be led by Ligonier. The Duke of Newcastle observed on 9 October, 'we shall now soon have troops enough at home to quash our intestine rebellion, and to discourage our foreign neighbours from making any attempt upon us'.[16] Civilian responses were largely loyalist too:

with militia and volunteer forces being raised in the shires, clergymen preaching loyalist sermons and a new song being heard in Drury Lane – 'God save the King'.[17]

Attitudes towards the Scots were largely negative. The Hon. Philip Yorke wrote on 19 September:

> I am greatly shocked at the ungrateful behaviour of Lord George Murray. Besides his being pardoned for the last Rebellion, the King had just given his son a commission in the new Highland regiment. The chiefs of the clans too, had all experienced the clemency of his late Majesty. I am utterly against Western assizes [the 'Bloody Assizes' which followed Monmouth's unsuccessful rebellion of 1685], but I hope some useful examples will be made.[18]

Catholic Ireland was a country which gave much concern to Cumberland. It had been the scene of fighting during 1689–91 to restore James II and might assist the Stuarts again. Yet all there was quiet. Chesterfield told Newcastle on 5 October, 'All my good subjects here are unanimously zealous; but unanimously frighten'd too, which I confess I am not.' Chesterfield was convinced that the Jacobites thought that the contest would be resolved one way or another in England and that Ireland would follow that decision. Even so, he took all the necessary security precautions, without offending the Catholic majority.[19]

Charles and his supporters remained in Scotland until early November. The decision to be taken at the end of October was whether to invade England or not. Many Scots did not wish to enter England, but were persuaded by promises of French and English support. Then they had to decide if they should march towards Newcastle and fight Wade's army or via the traditional south-western route, in order to rally supporters in northern England prior to any battle. Lord George Murray plumped for the second option and the majority followed his lead.[20]

The Jacobite army numbered about 5,500 men. This was divided into Highland and Lowland battalions, armed primarily with muskets, but many also had swords. In many ways, they resembled a regular army, not a feudal host. There were several troops of cavalry and thirteen cannon, though few trained gunners. The army could move fairly quickly, in part because money and supplies were taken from the towns they passed through. This was not plunder. Instead, they took the money from local tax collectors in the name of James III. The Jacobites, after all, saw themselves as representatives of a legitimate government and so claimed they had the right to tax revenue. This also meant that the local population were not likely to be hostile on these grounds. On their advance south the army was certainly well behaved, paying for anything they took.[21]

The Forty Five in England: Advance and Retreat, November–December 1745

By the time the Jacobites were marching through the north-western counties of England, Ligonier's forces were gathering in the Midlands. It was uncertain, though, where the Jacobites were aiming for; whether London, Wales or Bristol. But after they left Edinburgh, Wade sent two battalions of infantry and two regiments of dragoons to Edinburgh, which they occupied bloodlessly shortly afterwards. Elsewhere in Scotland, loyalist noblemen, aided by Duncan Forbes (1685–1747), Lord President of the Court of Sessions and a leading supporter of George II in Scotland, and towns and cities formed companies of militia. The Jacobite cause could only exist where substantial numbers of Jacobite troops held their ground. Yet not all was lost; for the Jacobites were raising a second army. Lord Lewis Gordon raised battalions for the Jacobite cause in Aberdeenshire and Banff. Lords Lovat (1668–1747) and Ogilvy (1725–1803) also raised men for their Prince and levied nearly £13,000 for the cause.[22]

The Jacobites arrived outside Carlisle on 10 November after marching through the Lowlands. There had been as many as 1,000 desertions, such was the reluctance of the Scots troops to march into England. Thomas Pattinson, the deputy mayor, was asked to surrender the town or face the consequences of an assault. He refused to surrender and answered the request with cannon fire. On learning that Wade's army was apparently marching against them, the Jacobites marched towards Brampton, leaving the town with the impression they had beaten off the attack. When the Jacobites discovered that Wade was not marching against them, they returned to Carlisle and began to besiege the town. On 14 November, it appeared that an attack was imminent and the civic dignitaries and militia officers met to discuss what they should do. The outnumbered county militia and volunteers, some of whom had already deserted, had no prospect of relief from Wade's army and so a majority voted to surrender.[23]

On 15 November, therefore, the town and castle of Carlisle fell to the Jacobites in an almost bloodless victory. In fact, Wade's army had begun to march towards Carlisle on the day after the surrender, but only got as far as Hexham in spite of bad weather. When news of the surrender reached them, they turned back to Newcastle. The Jacobites recommenced their march through Cumberland, Westmorland and Lancashire. The Duke of Newcastle was dismayed, writing on 20 November of 'the miserable state of our domestic affairs' and that 'The rebellion is far from being over or to be despised . . . Every day shews this rebellion is by no means a trifle.'[24] This march southwards, however, was only possible because there were no regular troops in their path to prevent them.

Although the outnumbered militia of Lancashire dispersed before they arrived and the rather better Liverpool Blues sought sanctuary in Chester, the omens for the Jacobite cause were not wholly good. Walpole wrote on 29 November, 'The country is far from rising for them, that the towns are left desolate on their approach, and the people hide and bury their effects even to their pewter.' Ten days later he wrote, in the same vein,

> though they [the Jacobites] have thus marched into the heart of the kingdom, there has not been the least symptom of a rising, not even in the great towns of which they possessed themselves. They have got no recruits since their first entry into England, except one gentleman in Lancashire, one hundred and fifty common men, and two parsons, at Manchester, and a physician from York.[25]

Walpole was exaggerating – there were perhaps between 200 and 300 Englishmen who joined the Jacobites and others were heard giving the Jacobite army verbal support. But on the whole he was correct.

Military preparations against the Jacobites were also becoming more effectual. Cumberland was appointed to command the army in the Midlands against the Jacobites. The Duke, hitherto an onlooker, was now centre-stage, a position he would retain until the conclusion of the campaign. Walpole wrote:

> It is certain that the army adore the Duke, and are gone in the greatest spirits; and on the parade, as they began their march, the guards vowed that they would neither give nor take quarter. For bravery, his Royal Highness is certainly no Stuart, but literally loves to be in the act of fighting.[26]

Henderson wrote:

> He no sooner appeared among them, than the Hills and the Vallies repeated their Huzzas, his Heroick and unaffected Mein, his easy Greatness, and martial Countenance revived then, and raised in them a Confidence of certain Victory. [27]

Chesterfield was confident in military success, arguing on 25 November 'our regular troops I am convinc'd are fully equal to three times their own number of undisciplined rabble . . . I see an end, and a speedy one of the rebellion'. He also had a high opinion of Cumberland, writing 'I depend upon my Marcellus, the Duke, for exterminating those rascals' and despised Wade's lack of success.[28]

Despite this, the Jacobite army was able to outmanoeuvre Cumberland, who marched towards Stone, in Staffordshire, whereas they reached Derby on 4 December. This was due to a feint made by Murray. The road to London had been cleared of Cumberland's army and Wade's forces, which had left Newcastle for a second time, and were moving southwards, were still as far north as Yorkshire. London was, perhaps, ten days march away. Once London was taken, the Jacobites would have gained control of the country's financial, commercial and administrative capital and victory would then appear to be close.

There has been a great deal of discussion as to what the Jacobites should have done next. What actually happened was that Lord George Murray convinced his colleagues, quite against Charles's wishes, that the army should retreat, which is what they proceeded to do on 6 December. From then on, Murray and Charles were usually at loggerheads – they never fully trusted one another again. It should be noted that there had been similar conferences already; one at Carlisle and one at Manchester, in which the same strategic question had been posed: advance or retreat? On the first two occasions, Charles had convinced his fellows that the former option was correct, reminding them about the offers of support he had been given from allies in England and France.

Those who argue that Charles was right make the following observations. First, the faster moving Jacobite army would have won the race to London and would have swept aside the forces which were readying themselves in Finchley to oppose them. Second, once the Jacobite army moved southward, they would accrue large numbers of English supporters. Third, London was in a state of panic and opponents of the Jacobites would flee before them. Finally, there was a French invasion fleet ready to set sail which would provide the regular forces necessary to reduce any hostile strongholds. In retrospect, Newcastle noted, 'I think there can be no doubt but, if the rebels had continued in England advancing towards London, and our army been at a distance from the capital, the Duke of Richelieu would have attempted to make us a visit before now.'[29]

But there was another side to the coin. The assumptions made above are optimistic. The combined numbers of the regular troops at the disposal of

George II far outnumbered those of the Jacobites. Since Jacobite support had been so meagre in England to date, there is no evidence that there would have been any significant increase on the eve of a battle, and even if there had been, unarmed and untrained men would not have stood a chance against regulars. Furthermore, although there was some panic in London there was also evidence of anti-Jacobitsim, too. Walpole wrote 'here in London the aversion to them is amazing', with weavers and lawyers forming themselves into military units.[30] Finally, any French invasion fleet would have had to contend with the ships of the Royal Navy which were in the Channel.

Yet the Jacobites did pose a dangerous threat. The advance further south would have been a gamble, it is true, but then the whole venture had been one from the start. Although the government was not in a state of panic, they were aware that the situation was critical. The Jacobites did pose a serious military threat, albeit briefly, and even though their chances were probably slender, they were not entirely negligible. As an incentive to retreat, the Jacobites learnt that French troops and more Scots had formed themselves into another army in Scotland under Lord John Drummond. A successful retreat would make them far stronger in numerical terms. Yet the psychological advantage had been lost forever.[31]

Once they retreated, the military initiative, until then in Jacobite hands, passed over to the government. On 8 December, Cumberland marched his fastest moving troops – his five regiments of cavalry and 1,000 mounted infantrymen – in pursuit of the Jacobites. Meanwhile, Wade was ordered to move westwards across Yorkshire and cut off the Jacobites in Lancashire.[32]

The Jacobites, though, had a head start of two days over Cumberland. They reached Manchester before Wade's forces had even arrived at Halifax. Meanwhile, Cumberland's troops had to be halted at Macclesfield because of news of a French invasion on the south coast, which turned out to be a false alarm. Another setback was the withdrawal of the Dutch troops which made up such a strong component of Wade's infantry. Their commanders were instructed that they could not be employed against the Jacobites, who were now allied to the French. These Dutch troops, due to the terms of their surrender to the French earlier that year, could not be employed against the French. Hessian troops were requested to make up the loss of the Dutch.

It was noticed that, on the retreat, the Jacobites found themselves attacked by small parties of countrymen. Perth's advance guard were fired upon at Kendal and deterred from entering Penrith. At Manchester, the Jacobite quartermasters were assaulted. Stragglers were arrested and thrown into gaol; occasionally they were killed. Such attacks were encouraged by Cumberland, who wrote, 'I did not care to put them [Jacobites] to death, but I have encouraged the Country people to do it, as they fall into their Hands.'[33] Was this an early sign that he was vindictive and cruel towards his enemies, or was it a case of his suggesting that the country people harry the retreating enemy, killing them where possible? If the former, it is also proof that he was frank in his correspondence. Yet these small parties of men did not attack the main Jacobite army, as it would have been suicidal to do so. In return, the Jacobite army took to plunder, which it had not hitherto indulged in.[34]

Although Cumberland had been delayed, he was still eager to give battle to the Jacobites before they reached Scotland. His advance guard encountered the Jacobite rear guard at Clifton Moor on 18 December. Lord George Murray was in charge of the four regiments which held the village. He had requested reinforcements, but none were sent. Cumberland sent 500 dismounted dragoons forward at sunset. There was a fire fight between the opposing sides, before the Jacobites charged. There was no time for another volley, and so hand-to-hand combat occurred. The dragoons were pushed back and the Jacobite rear guard was allowed to retreat, whilst Cumberland forbade a night battle.[35]

It has been alleged by Andrew Henderson that after the Jacobites 'had wounded some Officers, they inhumanly cut them when down, crying "No Quarter! Murder them"'.[36] This is reinforced by Colonel Joseph Yorke, who was present, and reported the same story in a letter to Hardwicke. Such stories, together with tales of the massacre after Prestonpans, would hardly have made the troops more sympathetic towards their enemies; they had one more wrong to avenge. Yet Cumberland was personally merciful. Captain David Hamilton, a Jacobite officer, was about to try and kill Cumberland, but stopped on recognizing him, warned the Duke that another Jacobite officer was eager to slay him. Hamilton was captured and 'Afterwards being brought to the Duke, he [the Duke] told him he was sorry to see him engaged in such bad company, "but I will endeavour to save your life"' (though Hamilton was executed at York in the following year).[37]

Although the fighting had been indecisive, it had allowed the Jacobite forces to regroup at Carlisle on the following day. They had to decide what to do next – whether to leave a garrison there or for all of the army to retreat back to Scotland. Charles and his quartermaster and adjutant-general, Colonel John O'Sullivan (*c*.1700– *c*.1751), advocated leaving a garrison there.[38] Lord Elcho later wrote 'This was done against the Opinion of almost Everybody'.[39] About 400 men, mostly Scots, but including most of the English recruits who had not already deserted, remained.

The final encounter on English soil occurred at Carlisle, therefore. Cumberland arrived on 21 December and declared the stronghold was 'An old hen-coop, which he would speedily bring down about their ears, when he should have got artillery'.[40] Rather than risk a bloody assault, the town and castle were encircled and heavy guns from Whitehaven were brought to bear. Once the guns began to fire, on 28 December, a breach was made. Although some of the garrison wanted to fight on, morale was low and most wished to surrender and this occurred on 30 December. Cumberland greeted the news with mixed feelings, 'I wish I could have blooded the soldiers with these villains, but it would have cost us many brave men and it came to the same end as they have no sort of claim to the King's mercy and I sincerely hope will meet with none.'.[41] Cumberland wanted a victory in order to boost his troops' morale, but had been denied a fight; though it had saved the lives of his men. The prisoners were mostly sent to York and London for trial.

Some accused Cumberland of a degree of villainy on this occasion. Thomas Sydall (1709–46), an English Jacobite officer who was taken prisoner at Carlisle and later was executed for treason, said, in his last speech:

> I also forgive the pretended Duke of Cumberland for his dis-honourable and unsoldiery proceeding in putting us to death in violation of the laws of nations after a written capitulation to the contrary, and after the garrison, upon the faith of that capitulation, had surrendered the place and faithfully performed all the conditions required of them.[42]

Cumberland had in fact given no such undertaking. In the surrender negoti-ations, he remarked: 'All the terms his royal highness will or can grant to the rebel garrison at Carlisle, are that they shall not be put to the sword but be reserved for the King's pleasure.' A Scottish officer in the Liverpool volun-teer corps later wrote 'The city had surrendered to the Duke upon no other Terms than leaving themselves at the King's mercy.'[43] His actions did not constitute a 'war crime'.

After the Jacobites had surrendered, Cumberland returned to London to counter a supposed French invasion. This turned out to be another scare, but Newcastle was convinced that the French would invade at some point. Chesterfield thought that the threat was a mere feint designed to keep the regulars at home whilst the French campaign on the Continent continued to prosper. Cumberland was a popular figure at this time. Newcastle wrote 'Our young hero returned yesterday morning, highly pleased and satisfied . . . All the world is in love with him and he deserves it.'[44] The pursuit of the Jacobites was maintained by Lieutenant-General Henry Hawley (1685–1759) who took over the command of what had been Wade's army (Wade had been allowed to resign his post), which had reached Edinburgh.

The Forty Five in Scotland, December 1745–April 1746

The Jacobites crossed the Esk and then split into three bodies; one going to Dumfries and taking £2,000 and 1,000 pairs of shoes, as well as any arms and gunpowder they could find from there for the army. They all arrived at Glasgow on 25–26 December. This city was known to be loyal to the government. The city was forced to pay £10,000 to the occupying forces and to provide them with clothes and shoes. The army then marched to Stirling.[45]

Senior members of the government were concerned about the policy that should be adopted once the rebellion was crushed. None were advocates of mercy and all called for harsh measures against the enemy which had so recently almost been at the gates. Walpole wrote on 3 January 1746:

> I still think it probable that he [Cumberland] will go to Scotland. That country is very clamorous for it. If the King does send him, it should not be with that sword of mercy, with which the present family have governed those people. All the world agrees to the fitness of severity to highwaymen, for the sake of the innocent who suffer – then can rigour be ill-placed against banditti, who have so terrified, pillaged and injured the poor people in Cumberland, Lancashire, Derbyshire and the counties, through which this rebellion has stalked! There is a military magistrate of some fierceness sent into Scotland [Hawley] . . . He will not sow the seeds of future disloyalty, by too easily pardoning the present.[46]

Chesterfield had similar views. As noted, he had talked of the Jacobites as rabble to be exterminated. On 6 December 1745, he had written, 'There must be alertness and vigour in crushing of this, and unrelenting severity in punishing it afterwards.'[47] He did not trust any Scots, even those who appeared to be loyal to George II. As with Walpole, he saw the Jacobite rebels as criminals, for whom rewards should be offered. He wrote, 'They are not enemies but criminals; we cannot be at war with 'em'.[48] He did see the French troops serving with the Jacobites differently, however, 'who should be treated like fair enemies'.[49] He thought that there should be a cessation of the trade in food from Ireland to Scotland. All loyal Scots units should be marched into garrisons in England and only English and Hessian troops be employed against the Jacobites. 'I would also forbid provisions of any kinds being sent upon any pretence whatever (unless directly to the Duke's army) into Scotland, and I would starve the loyal with the disloyal if the former chose to stay with the latter'.[50] He refused to supply Scotland from Ireland, 'I have taken effectuall care that the loyallest Highlander shall not have an oatcake from hence'.[51] Chesterfield continued to pronounce such hardline views in a further letter on 20 March, 'Recall your Scotch heroes, starve the whole country indiscriminately by your ships, put a price upon the heads of the chiefs, and let the Duke put all to fire and sword.'[52]

Newcastle responded to such views on 6 April, writing:

> Your notions in general are certainly right, and I hope will be followed as far as you seriously would think they should. They are much tasted in the Closet, where I am sure you are thought at least a good minister for Scotland. Your young Marcellus writes in the same strain, and, to be serious, I have it in my heart to do something right in this respect than in almost any part of our administration, as thinking it more material for the peace and interest of this country.[53]

He held the Jacobites in contempt and was convinced that Hawley would crush them, 'you see it is only marching up to those scoundrels to put 'em to flight . . . you will see the troubles in Scotland ended in two months time at the furtherest'.[54]

The government saw the Jacobites as enemies to be crushed and that Cumberland was their instrument for enforcing such a policy. They held hardline views. Some believed that all the Scots were equally responsible for the rebellion. Cumberland's actions, therefore, need to be seen in this context.

However, the government's supporters, with their expectations of a quick victory, were to receive a rude shock. The Jacobite army was now at the peak of its numerical strength, which included two units of infantry sent from France and other Jacobite forces raised in Scotland since November 1745. They had begun to besiege Stirling Castle, held for the government by General William Blakeney (1672–1761). Hawley marched his army, which consisted of twelve battalions (5,850 men) and three regiments of dragoons (800 men), along with the Glasgow militia and Captain Thornton's Yorkshire volunteers (making a total of 8,100 men) towards them. The infantry were veteran battalions, who had fought on the Continent, unlike Cope's raw soldiery.[55]

The two armies clashed at Falkirk on 17 January 1746. Hawley ordered his cavalry, whom he had great faith in, having seen in 1715 the damage they could do to infantry, against the right wing of the Jacobite army. However, the Jacobites stood fast and discharged a murderous volley at very short range. Although some of the dragoons made contact with their enemy, most scattered and fled, disordering the regular infantry to their rear. As Hawley later wrote, 'some of the dragoons took a most shameful flight, and was followed by a great part of the infantry'.[56] The Jacobite front line charged and most of the regular troops fled before them.

The defeat was not a disaster. Three battalions of infantry, who had been posted on the right of the line, repelled those Jacobites advancing on them, before retiring in good order. They eventually retreated to Edinburgh. Yet it was undoubtedly a setback. Hawley wrote on the evening of the battle, 'My Heart is broke . . . such a scandalous cowardice I never saw before'.[57] Although the casualties suffered by the regulars were fewer than at Prestonpans, Sir Robert Munro (1684–1746) of Foulis 'was murdered in cold blood' according to James Ray, and two unarmed men who came to his aid were killed by the Jacobites and there were other reports of fleeing soldiers being killed.[58]

Two main consequences sprang from the battle. First, the Jacobites decided not to pursue their retreating foes, because their forces were too dispersed after the fighting, and returned to the siege of Stirling, which was conducted unsuccessfully. Secondly, Cumberland went to Scotland. Again, as with his being put in command in the previous year, this was a popular move. Walpole wrote on 28 January, 'The great dependence is upon the Duke; the soldiers adore him; and with reason: he has a lion's courage, vast vigilance and activity; and, I am told, great military genius.'[59]

Hawley then began a round of court martials on a number of officers and men for cowardice. On 29 January, Hawley told Newcastle that he planned to have 32 men shot for cowardice, 47 deserters to hang and 31 dragoons to be tried for cowardice.[60] On the following day, following Cumberland's arrival, they were all reprieved, as Cumberland informed Newcastle, 'I thought it better to pardon all the private men, to give a sort of mark of favour to the corps'.[61] He also declared that he relied 'upon their future courage and good conduct', that he had 'a pride in commanding' them and was 'convinced [they] will support the King to his honour and which they have so often and justly acquired'.[62] Hardly a general who was merciless towards his own troops.

A battle between the Jacobites and the regulars was anticipated in early February as Cumberland advanced and the Jacobites remained near Stirling. Joseph Yorke wrote: 'I thought this night to have wrote your Lordship an account of a victory'.[63] No such event occurred. The Jacobites retreated after spiking their artillery and blowing up their powder magazine, crossing the

Map of the campaign in Scotland, January–April 1746.

Forth and arriving in Perth. Desertion from their ranks was probably a principal cause of the retreat. Despite the recent defeat, there was a new confidence among the loyalists in the army. Yorke wrote 'I never saw the troops promise more than their appearance did this day and I am thoroughly convinced they will do as well as I wish 'em, but all the glory is reserved for our Stator Reipublicae; may Heaven preserve his life!'[64]

Cumberland hoped that the Jacobite retreat would lead to their dispersal, allowing him to return to London and then continue with the campaign on the Continent. This was not to be. He was also angry that the Jacobite retreat had denied him his battle. He proposed a ruthless solution to Newcastle, 'When once they are got into their holes and hiding places, it will be impossible to follow them in a body' and so recommended that 'small parties of men to burn and destroy that nest of robbers and orders should be given to kill all that have arms in their houses, as that will now be the only trace of treason left'.[65] He clearly assumed that the Jacobite retreat was a mere prelude to their dispersal.

Jacobite property certainly came under attack in the following weeks. On 5 February, whilst at Crieff, the troops had marched through country formerly in Jacobite control and so, 'I thought fit to let the soldiers a little loose with proper precautions that they might have some sweets with all their fatigues'.[66] In March, Jacobite property was demolished in Lochaber and cattle were seized, resulting in further desertions from the Jacobite army. This was in order to show the Jacobites that he meant business and to deprive them of aid, as well as to encourage his soldiers.[67]

On 22 February, Cumberland wrote to Alexander Campbell, the officer in command at Fort William, 'Send out Parties to Burn & Destroy all the country belonging to the Rebells in your Neighbourhood, as far as you dare go with safety to your Garrison.'[68] Captain Caroline Scott (*c*.1710–54) later replied that eighteen houses belonging to the Camerons had been burnt, these being of those who were 'mostly rebels'.[69] Some Scots who were entirely innocent, therefore, also suffered. Later Cumberland noted the effect this had had: 'a very good effect, & all the Rebels have deserted to go home to their own habitations'.[70] Cumberland also noted that 'I place great confidence in his [Scott's] courage, zeal and skill'.[71]

In fact, Campbell had almost anticipated such orders. He reported, on 17 February, that two of his officers had been shot dead in ambush and was outraged. He wrote:

> This barbarous murder induced me with the advice of the officers of my garrison to immediately send out a party with orders if possible to apprehend the Eilian [killer?] and to burn the village of Inverlochy, which place was the common receptacle of the rebels . . . there was not one inhabitant belonging to it but was in the rebellion.

Cattle were also confiscated. Campbell concluded: 'I flatter myself that we shall be so happy as to have your approbation for these proceedings . . . for the good of His Majesty's service and the safety of the garrison.'[72]

Other punitive action was taken by both the garrison and sloops of the Royal Navy which were operating off the coast of the Western Highlands. The

Terror destroyed boats off the Movern coast in February. In charge was Commander Robert Duff (1721–87), who reported in the following month that

> I arrived at St. Lindsay with a detachment . . . with orders to burn ye houses and destroy the effects of all such as are out in ye Rebellion. They began at Drummean's town and by six of ye clock at night had destroyed the Movern coast as far as Ardtornish except a town belonging to ye McDougals and ye houses of those who appeared and declared they had never been out, which were very few.[73]

Captain John Ferguson (*c.*1710–67) was in charge of the sloop *Furnace* and was on a similar expedition. In early April, having found arms and money on the isle of Barra and on South Uist, he demanded their surrender. He explained that compliance meant 'there shall not be the value of a chicken be hurt on either island'. However, refusal would have dire consequences, 'if my request is not complied with I shall take them to be all Rebels, disaffected, and am resolved to burn and destroy both islands'.[74]

Meanwhile, the men of General John Campbell (1705–82) had destroyed part of Maryburgh so that it could not harbour the enemy. General Campbell agreed with the action, writing, 'I approve of your having demolished the town of Maryburgh towards your own security'.[75] Since Fort William was being threatened by Jacobite troops who were to lay siege to it, such actions seemed necessary in order to assist in the defence of the fort in denying the besiegers support.

These orders ultimately came from Cumberland, as General Campbell acknowledged: 'orders for distressing the country of the Rebels were issued by His Royal Highness the Duke of Cumberland'.[76] They caused concern to some. Campbell acknowledged, 'I find your procedure has struck a most dreadful pannick upon some of His Majesty's dutiful subjects who have the misfortune to be raised in lands contiguous to those of the Rebels.' Commanders on the ground were reminded that they must distinguish between the Jacobites and those who were not, though how easy this was in practice is hard to discern.[77] Yet Campbell also stressed that:

> I can take the liberty to assure you that it is by no means His Royal Highness' intention that His Majesty's innocent subjects should suffer with the Guilty and that I have the confidence in His Majesty's officers by sea and land that they will take care to distinguish the one from the other.[78]

Efforts were made to deprive the Jacobites of support. Those tenants and vassals of the Duke of Gordon who were in the Jacobite ranks were told to withdraw, taking their arms with them and to submit to royal mercy. Any who did not 'will be proceeded against as Rebels, with the utmost severity, by burning their houses, immediate confiscation and seizure of their cattle, immoveable goods and Effects'.[79] Notices of similar orders were widely distributed. The Duke of Atholl told Thomas Bisset to make 'copyes of this order and have them dispersed all over the country'.[80] Lord Airlie was thought to have assisted the Jacobites and was told to desist 'as you value the security of your house and estate and the safety of your person'.[81] Civil magistrates were to proceed against local Jacobite sympathizers and to gaol them.[82] Magistrates who did not act against Jacobites were to be treated as 'Rebels, Traytors, & be proceeded against by military execution'.[83] An exasperated Cumberland wrote 'I have been forced to come to pretty vigorous methods to keep His Majesty's enemies in the Country in a little order.'[84]

Not all of his subordinates agreed with this policy. Cumberland wrote on 10 February, General Campbell 'absolutely refused to plunder any of the rebel houses, which is the only way to punish them'.[85] However, Campbell put the blame on the Jacobites, writing 'I am extremely concerned for the General Calamity these infatuated people [the Jacobites] have brought our poor country'.[86] There were also legalistic arguments. Andrew Fletcher (1692–1766), Lord Chief Justice for Scotland, also protested, arguing that 'Every subject retains the property of his own goods, unless that property is either forfeited for his crimes, or transferred by his consent.' He also objected to the wording of Cumberland's orders. He thought that 'The words military execution' were injudicious and also wrote 'I humbly submit to His Royal Highness's consideration, is that though in war with a foreign enemy, every man may take what he can of the enemy's goods, yet in a rebellion or civil war, that either appears in a different light.'[87]

At the end of March, there was even talk of two legal actions taking place as a result of Hawley's activities. The first of these was over the hanging of a spy at Stirling. Fletcher wrote:

> I never heard of any prosecution threatened against General Hawley for hanging the spy, nor do I believe it and if there were, the great law of necessity, would probably justify what was done, because without such severitys, it would be difficult to carry on any war, foreign or civil.

But as to the second, on Hawley's stealing goods from Callander House, his thoughts were different. 'I really wish it had not happened; for it occasions a great clamour, & I doubt it can be well justified in law.' Redress would have to be sought. Hawley and his ADC, Wolfe, had been staying at the house of Mrs Gordon, whose husband was an officer in the Jacobite army and they saw her property as fair game, though Cumberland disapproved, with Fawkener writing, 'The things might as well have been left, and I am sure the Duke would have been better pleased if they had.'[88]

Sir Everard Fawkener (1694–1758), Cumberland's military secretary, replied to Fletcher's remarks. He wrote that, in the case of the destruction of Jacobite property, 'his prudence or humanity may be called into question, but I don't see the case is actionable'. He differentiated between the case of a man suspected of high treason who was brought for trial, and those found in open rebellion, where the legal niceties did not have to be observed. He also argued that to threaten to destroy Jacobite property was a safeguard to loyalist property which might otherwise be destroyed by the Jacobites.[89]

Cumberland used threats against the Duchess of Perth, ordering her to ask her son to release all prisoners or 'the King's soldiers shall be let at full liberty to plunder and destroy the Drummond Estate'. An officer and seven soldiers were temporarily billeted on her, Cumberland writing 'I hope His Majesty will approve this proceeding of mine'. She did as she was told. Yet it is worth noting the temper of the soldiers who, 'it is said, have already given a specimen of what they will do, in Revenge for the Fatigues and Hardships they have been made to suffer, if they are at once let loose without controul'. A winter campaign was almost unheard of in conventional warfare, and so the additional hardships it imposed would not incline the men towards mercy for their opponents, who they saw as being the cause of their extra woes.[90]

Yet, for all this, clear boundaries were set as Cumberland not approve of unauthorized looting and pressed for heavy penalties for those who did – officers as well as men. Some soldiers were out of control. Fletcher noted 'the ill behaviour of our Regular Troops', but was confident that Cumberland's presence would put this right.[91] As a report stated:

> Some soldiers having plundered the House of Mr Gordon of Towbairdie, who is in the Rebellion, his Royal Highness the Duke not only (on information of this abuse) ordered the least Trifle to be restored, but presented his lady with a purse of 100 guineas, and gave her his own signed protection – Another apprehending herself in Danger, and having had some things carried off, tipp'd an officer wth a few Guineas to have them restor'd: but his Royal Highness detesting such infamous Methods, directly broke him, and discharg'd him from the service forever.[92]

The officer in question was Ensign Daniel Hart of Munro's, a Scot, who had extorted six guineas from Mrs Francis Ross, a merchant's wife of Aberdeen. Another ensign was suspended for six months for a malpractice, too. Two soldiers from Fleming's regiment had plundered several houses near Aberdeen, and were hanged for these offences. A letter from Aberdeen read 'his Royal Highness maintains strict discipline, without severity; his Example teaches us all our Duty, and his Care of us in all respects attracts our Affections'.[93] Another source noted 'His Royal Highness the Duke has been so careful of the property and Effects even of such as are actually in Rebellion, on the shire of Aberdeen, that he makes it Death to deprive them of the meanest of Trifles.'[94] When cornet Pitt was to escort the Jacobite Lady Perth to Edinburgh, he was told to do so 'using her civilly by the way'.[95] Yorke wrote on 20 February, 'Every Gentleman in the army is concerned that any violence is offer'd to the Fair Sex, and it is absolutely contrary to His Royal Highness' Orders.'[96] This was certainly appreciated, as a letter ran 'thank all these good officers . . . for their great civilitys to us and Major General John Huske [c.1692–1761] in particular for the guards he was so good as to place here we have injoyed a perfect tranquillity ever since'.[97]

Other plundering was not approved of either. Brigadier John Mordaunt (1697–1780) took hay from Williamston, even though 'he has no directions from the Duke nor any of the generals to seize anything'. Cumberland ordered the hay to be put into a magazine and it was to be properly accounted for in order that the rightful creditors be paid for it.[98] John Stewart, though eager to see the rebellion crushed, wrote 'the most absolute orders are given and will be punctually obeyed not in any shape to molest any person who is not found in arms, or acting against the interest of His Majesty'.[99] Woe betide any soldier who disobeyed – an order from Stirling noted 'any man that is found plundering will be hanged on the spot by the provost'.[100] There was certainly a need for such orders, for it was noted in the same month that 'the House of Sir Henry Stirling has been plundered by some of His Majesty's troops, a thing always irregular and directly contrary to the intentions of His Royal Highness'.[101] Indiscriminate attacks on the Scottish people and their property had not been advocated – so much for later claims of genocide.

It should not be forgotten that the Jacobites were not above both making threats and carrying them out. On 2 January, Fletcher wrote 'they have been very outrageous against all those who appeared zealous and active in the new levys, by plundering and Burning their houses, destroying their goods and furniture'.[102] The Duke of Atholl's order recorded that the Jacobites were 'threatening to burn and destroy the houses and carry away the moveable goods, gear and cattle of such as shall refuse to join him'. The Jacobite Lord

Drummond signed an order to the effect that, 'unless immediate compliance should be made with their demands of levy money, &c, my [Lord Findlater's] house was to be burnt'. It was pillaged.[103] Kinoull's tenants in Perthshire had 'for their Loyalty [to the Crown] have been much oppress'd and punder'd by them [the Jacobites]'.[104] John Grant wrote on 6 April: 'The Rebels upon Friday last brock open your gernall doors and carried off all the meal that was there, carried off all my threshed seed . . . and all my horses and 2 or 3 more in the neighbourhood.'[105] There was an order from Charles's headquarters on 4 March, which read thus:

> These are commanding and strictly requiring you to burn and destroy the houses and effects of all those in the aforesaid counties [Inverness and Nairn] who shall disobey our said orders [supplying horses and carriages to transport army artillery and baggage].[106]

Another Jacobite order told men to pay the levy required or be faced with 'military execution'.[107] These seem to have been standard practice; the phrase 'upon pain of fire and sword' was used in a demand signed by O'Sullivan, Jacobite quartermaster general, in March.[108]

Meanwhile, the campaign in the Highlands continued. The Jacobites made a number of localized offensives against Scots loyal to the government and against isolated garrisons of regulars. These had a large degree of success. Lord Loudon's Highlanders were pushed out of Inverness; the garrison he left there surrendered without a shot being fired. Forts Augustus and George and the barracks at Ruthven all fell to the Jacobites and Fort William was besieged, though this was rather more strongly defended.[109]

Cumberland was apprehensive. He was uncertain how far he could trust the Scots, claiming he could not procure any intelligence 'and reckons himself more in an enemy's country, then when he was warring with the French in Flanders'.[110] The Duke wrote:

> The Highlanders are almost universally a nest of knaves & they are always ready to rise in order to rob, many of them are also Papists, they have been poisoned by that connexion which has been kept up. Even those of the Episcopal Clergy who take the Oaths, retain generally their Old Principles.[111]

He was not alone in these views. Yorke agreed, writing 'the answer I made to a noble Lord who ask'd me if I found Scotland so bad a country as I imagined, shall serve my description, "Yes, my Lord, and infinitely worse"'.[112] William

Keppell (1708–54), second Earl of Albermarle, and one of Cumberland's generals, thought so, too: 'I protest, I prefer ye soil to ye inhabitants, for more malice, falsehood, cunning and self interest, was ever mett with in any country whatsoever'.[113]

Yet Cumberland did not despair of all Scots, and he relied on the civic and religious authorities in his campaign against the Jacobites. At Perth, Cumberland told the town's magistrates that

> Any person within the Town . . . who shall conceal any Rebel or arms, ammunition or anything else belonging to the Rebels, and shall not immediately bring the said Rebel or stores to the Provost James Crie, shall upon proof of Disobedience of this Order, be hang'd.[114]

He wrote to Newcastle at the end of the month, 'The only people to be trusted are the Church of Scotland . . . here in the north they own that almost all the people are Jacobites or led astray by the Episcopals, who have meeting houses all over his country' and that 'the greatest part of this kingdom are either openly or privately aiding the rebels & how it may be changed, I don't know'.[115] Cumberland also admired the Scots irregular loyalists, a source writing 'The Duke takes much Notice of them, and they are very proud of it.'[116]

It should be noted that active Jacobites in Scotland were in a minority. Charles had far fewer men under his command than had been raised for his father in 1715. Even Cumberland admitted that the Lowlands were 'as well affected as in any part of it'. Many Scots fought against the Jacobites, either in the regular army or in the independent companies raised by Loudon or the Campbells. Glasgow and Edinburgh had formed loyalist militia and the former had accompanied Hawley's army to Falkirk. Although the non–regular forces had not fought well, if at all, their presence alone shows where their political loyalties lay. Furthermore, on 30 October 1745, George II's birthday was celebrated in many Scottish towns and, if local Jacobites protested, they were chased and beaten if found. Although the Scots provided the mainstay of the Jacobite army, they represented a minority of Scots, even in the Highlands. Many Scots, of course, remained passive, and some clans were divided among themselves, whether by inclination or by political calculation.[117]

Cumberland's main force marched northwards, to Dunblane, Perth and finally to Aberdeen, arriving in early March, where they stayed for a month, gathering supplies, but also because the Spey was currently unfordable. His army was supplemented by another three battalions of infantry and at last had trained artillerymen to man his guns, which his predecessors never did.[118]

As well as the regular troops under his command, Cumberland also had a strong supplement of Hessian forces, numbering just over 5,000 men, mostly infantry, under his brother-in-law, Prince Frederick of Hesse. These had replaced the Dutch forces who had been obliged to go home because they were not allowed to fight the French. Initially Cumberland saw these troops as nothing but an encumbrance who would consume supplies but contribute little to the campaign. Yet his opinion changed when he realized that the Jacobites would not be put down as quickly as he first envisaged.[119]

The Hessian troops were deployed in Perth and Stirling in order to prevent any Jacobite thrust south, now that the bulk of the regulars were at Aberdeen. Cumberland wrote that if the Jacobites moved southwards, they were to 'march directly to attack them'. When Lord George Murray besieged the command of Sir Andrew Agnew (1687–1771) at Blair Castle in March, Cumberland urged them to attack him. They eventually did so, and after a brief skirmish, Murray withdrew on 1 April.[120]

Then a controversy erupted which is worth considering. During this skirmish, one of the Hessian officers had been captured by the Jacobites. He was returned with a letter from Murray, which suggested a cartel be arranged, in which prisoners would be exchanged. This was standard practice in conventional warfare of the Continent and both Cumberland and Prince Frederick were well aware of it. The latter deemed it to be 'reasonable and just' and wrote for Cumberland's opinion. Cumberland wrote to Newcastle thus:

> to find he should demand instructions whether he should answer or not Lord George Murray's most insolent letter. I thought myself obliged upon this occasion to write to him in a stronger manner than I before ever have done, which I hope will have the desired effect and prevent any more of these indiscretions.

Cumberland, Hardwicke and Newcastle did not view the Jacobites as honourable enemies, but rebels. The result was that the Hessians took no further active part in the campaign.[121]

Yet Cumberland did believe that the French troops in Jacobite service, and who had been captured en route to Britain, should be treated as prisoners of war. Fawkener explained in a letter:

> His Royal Highness is pleased to direct that they shall receive different Treatment. Those who are not subjects of His Majesty as well officers and men are to be treated as prisoners of war, they having been taken in the service of France; and the officers are to be allowed

the liberty of the Town, on their parole and the Men are to be confined to the citadels, with such a liberty of walking about there as may be proper. But all such of these prisoners are natural born subjects of His Majesty, are to be treated as Rebels and Traytors and to be imprisoned in the common jayl.[122]

French prisoners of war held in Hull in February 1746 certainly saw Cumberland as a man they could successfully appeal to. They were being treated badly in captivity, in not receiving the allowances and freedoms they were entitled to. As Fawkener wrote:

> he [Cumberland] totally disapproves the treatment you have met with, and orders him [their gaoler] to furnish you with subsistence, according to Louis XV's regulation of pay, to allow you the liberty of walking about the castle in the day time, and to take care that you are lodged in quarters fit for officers.[123]

As soon as the Jacobites had ceased to threaten Blair Castle, Cumberland wrote vigorous orders to Sir Andrew on 7 April:

> I desire you will send out sufficient partys, tho' none further than 6 miles to destroy and burn ye Habitations and effects of all those who were out in the present rebellion, if they should attempt to oppose this, or you should find any party of them armed, you will order ye detachment to destroy them, and for this use, you will demand the dragoons if you need them.[124]

Matters were looking increasingly bleak for the Jacobites as time went by. Attempts by the French to send troops, supplies and, crucially, money, to them were being foiled by the Royal Navy. The *Hazard* sloop, with 200 soldiers and £8,000, was taken in early April after it was driven ashore near Tongue Bay. Lord Elcho later wrote 'This was a great loss to the Prince as he was in Great Distress for want of money.'[125] A scheme to make this loss good was to plunder the territory of loyalist Scots, but this was not carried out to any significant degree. The basic problem was that while the Jacobite army moved from place to place it could be supplied easily, but once it was more or less stationary, sources of supplies dried up and men had to go further and further away to find food, whether they were authorized to do so or not. In early April, 'provisions were becoming very Scarce'.[126] Meanwhile, the siege of Fort William had to be raised and the besieging Jacobites marched away on

3 April. Shortly afterwards, Charles was told by French emissaries that there would be no support forthcoming from France. According to Elcho, Charles's distrust of many of his officers grew to an even higher pitch. Matters were not looking hopeful.[127] Cumberland was aware of this state of affairs, writing on 4 April, of the 'great Disorders and Confusions is got amongst them; which added to the want of money, has occasioned many mutinys and great Desertion among their people'.[128]

Cumberland and Newcastle corresponded with one another about what should be done in the aftermath of the rebellion. It would certainly be a difficult issue to solve, as the young general admitted:

> I really think that the éclat of it is over, but believe their will be left such seed that God knows how soon it may break out again if a care & caution unused in this Island be on this occasion kept. All this country are almost to a man Jacobite & mild measures won't do. You'll find that the whole of the laws of this ancient kingdom must be new modelled & for that purposes by the next despatch . . . don't imagine that threatening military execution and many other such things are pleasing to do to me but nothing else will go down without it in this part of the world.[129]

Cumberland was clearly of the opinion that the solution to the Jacobite issue was a mixture of threats and violence, which he saw as necessary but was also unhappy about, and changes to the Scottish legal system, which had not been altered at the time of the Union in 1707. Newcastle agreed with him about the need to reform the laws, writing: 'The great object will be to pass such laws, after the Rebellion is over, as may effectually reduce the power of the Highlanders.'[130]

Newcastle gave Cumberland only a few general outlines as to his conduct of the campaign. He told him on 2 February that his task was 'the speedy Extinction of the Rebellion and of the Re-establishment of the Peace and Tranquillity of every Part of this Kingdom'.[131] As he wrote on 23 March, 'it has been found impracticable to give any more particular Direction than is therein contained'.[132] On the one hand, he was 'not to suffer you to omit anything, that might be necessary, for putting a speedy end to it', yet he was neither to 'give any just cause of complaint to a country, so ill disposed to the King'.[133]

Cumberland was not entirely idle while his forces remained around Aberdeen. Parties of soldiers were sent out into districts thought to be sympathetic to the Jacobites, such as Angus and Mar. They searched for weapons and threatened the inhabitants not to support the Jacobites. Jacobite gentry in Banff and Aberdeenshire had their properties plundered. He approved of the fact that the garrison of Fort William would 'seize all the cattle and demolish the habitations of those in Lochaber, who were actually out in rebellion' so that 'all the rebels of that country have deserted to go home to their own habitations', which would 'discourage the men and add to their present Distraction'.[134] He also sent Major La Fausille and 300 soldiers to Glen Esk, at the end of March, 'one of the most rebellious parts, to destroy all them he finds in arms and to burn the habitations of all those who have left them and are with the Rebels'.[135]

It is worth examining the major's actions. Between 27 March and 2 April, his men marched through the Highlands from Montrose, making a round trip. On 28 March he had the nonjuring meeting house burnt at Lethnot. He had eighteen sheep and seven cows taken from a Jacobite property to feed his men. On this day and the following he received arms from the locals. On 29 March the meeting house at Brechin was torched. That of Carristown was also destroyed, and so were two others. At least forty weapons were handed in. Laird Airlie's tenants, to the number of over 100, swore their allegiance to George II before La Fausille. Jacobite property was plundered – the house of David Gibb at Brunkern, that of Alexander Mather at Craik and several others. Another house belonging to a Jacobite was set on fire, but when they found the man's wife was a loyalist the flames were extinguished. Some cattle, 'but no great quantity', were also captured and would be sold at Montrose. La Fausille thought it had been a success, 'I think the country is quiet & terify'd'. However, he was unsure if he should have spared Lord Airlie's house. 'I declare it solemnly no tenderness for him has sav'd his house, but ignorance & fear of exceeding my orders.'[136]

Loyalist Scottish opinion backed his action. Presbyterian clerymen aided him in his task. The authorities in Brechin noted:

> Major Lafausille has, so far as we can judge, acquitted himself very well. He has disarmed the Countys where the spirit off the rebellion most prevailed and has so effectually intimidated them that we hope they will not so easily be prevail'd on to make any open appearance against His Majesty's government.[137]

Cumberland wrote of 'Major LaFausille's having disarmed all the Clova and Glenesk people'.[138]

A contemporary journal noted, approvingly: 'The seizing all the cattle and demolishing the habitations of those in Lochaber, who were actually out in

Rebellion, has had a very good Effect, as all the Rebels of that Country have deserted to go to their own Houses.'[139] Yet there were limits. If complaint was made to Cumberland, he usually had the goods recovered and restored to the householders or would give compensation out of his own pocket.[140]

Apart from active Jacobites, the property of the Episcopal Church and of Non Jurors was attacked. Both these branches of Protestantism favoured Jacobitism and the latter had been founded after the overthrow of James II. Non Jurors believed that only the Stuart line directly descended from James II were lawful monarchs of Britain. Some were active Jacobites. An anonymous contemporary noted:

> His Royal Highness on coming to Aberdeen immediately stopped all the Nonjurant Ministers, and soon after ordered their Meeting Houses and the Mass Houses to be destroyed, which was accordingly executed, both in town and country as the Army marched along, and indeed none were surprised at this piece of discipline, as these houses were not only illegal, but had in fact proved such Nurseries of Rebellion.[141]

In order to increase the troops' confidence for their next encounter with the Jacobites, Cumberland taught them a new drill. Ordinarily, when the Highlanders closed in on them, soldiers would thrust their bayonets at the man in front of them. However, he could then parry it with his targe. Therefore, they were taught to strike at the unprotected flank of the man on his right. The soldier on his right would then thrust at the man who was attacking him.[142]

Cumberland had wanted to take the offensive earlier than he did, complaining to Newcastle at the end of March that poor weather and heavy rainfall meant that the Spey was too deep and so prevented a march to Inverness. Although he knew that desertions in the Jacobite army were taking place due to lack of money, he was concerned that he would not have the decisive battle he thought crucial to end the campaign. Perhaps he recalled the instance of 1715 in which there had been no climactic battle and the Jacobites had simply dispersed and gone home. He told Newcastle:

> For, should this rebellion end any way but by the sword, I apprehend that for the lenity of our government and from the ill placed compassion which be had, when our Frights are over, the authors and actors of, and in this Rebellion, will not be sufficiently punished to prevent another, I am sorry to be forced to say, that I see such seeds

of rebellion, and so much Disaffection to any government established upon an English foot, that there is little Reason to flay ourselves, but that we shall have other Scenes of this kind, wherever an opportunity presents itself, except the whole government and constitution of this part of the kingdom shall be changed.[143]

Cumberland was not advocating wholesale severity. His letter continued:

As His Majesty has been graciously pleased to entrust me with the power of promising his pardon to those who shall entitle themselves to it, I will endeavour to make the properest use of that power.[144]

Earlier in the month he had signed an order pardoning Jacobites who surrendered, although he had not wholly agreed with it, explaining

I have been advised and desired to publish some sort of an order to bring the ignorant people back who have been pressed into the Rebellion. I have had it worded as cautiously as I could, and I neither hope or desire any great benefit from it.[145]

This was published on 24 February and read as follows:

His royal highness having received information that sundry persons, who have been concerned in this wicked rebellion, are returned to their dwellings, or are lurking about the country, some of them with their arms, and others without: And likewise, that sundry arms, and other effects belonging to persons who have been engaged in the rebellion, and concealed in various parts and places of these countries of North Britain where the rebels have resorted: These are therefore, in his royal highness' name, strictly to require and command all ordinary common people who have bore arms, or otherwise have been concerned in this rebellion, bring in their arms to the magistrate or minister of the church of Scotland, where this notice shall reach them, and likewise to give in their name and place of abode: And in case they have no arms, then to declare their names and places of abode, and are all to submit themselves entirely to the king's mercy. And all manner of persons, who have in their possession, or have knowledge of arms, or effects of any kind whatsoever, belonging to persons who are, or have been in the rebellion, or aiding and assisting to such as have been in the rebellion, are in like manner commanded to declare such arms or such effects, and to deliver them up to the magistrate or minister of the church of Scotland, and the place of their abode: And all such as shall any ways fail in the most exact obedience to this order, are to take notice, that they will be pursued with the utmost severity as rebels and traitors, by due process of law, or military execution.[146]

This order was republished in April. How effective such orders were is doubtful. The Argyll militia had distributed circulars to the people of Stratherl, Glenshee and elsewhere in late February, but no arms were received. This was because the notices had given the Jacobites advance information and so were able to conceal arms.[147]

Cumberland wanted to ensure that the Jacobites would never rise in arms again. For this, he believed that he needed a decisive military victory to bring the campaign to an end, in contrast to the experience thirty years previously. The Jacobites needed to be shown, in no uncertain terms, that they had been defeated in the field, which, it was thought, would act as a great discouragement to any future campaigns. Punishment was certainly required. Yet he also realized that this was not enough in itself. Pardoning some of the Jacobites was important, too. Finally, a remodelling of the laws of Scotland was also needed. But first there had to be a battle.

Cumberland was thus impatient to advance against the Jacobites who were in and around Inverness. He constantly had scouting parties out to see when the Spey was fordable. He planned to march from Aberdeen on 6 April, but his departure had to be delayed for two days. There were skirmishes between advance parties of both sides in the region of the River Spey. On 8 April, Cumberland finally struck camp at Aberdeen and marched towards the Jacobites. Once again, a climactic battle was apparently near at hand.[148]

The Jacobite rebellion of 1745 had lasted for almost eight months; the longest military campaign on British soil for almost a century. Though that of 1715 had attracted considerable English and Scottish support, it had lasted six months and the Jacobites had never beaten the regulars in battle, nor had they marched into the heartland of Britain. Nor had the Jacobites the promise of substantial French military aid. How realistic their chances were in this is a moot point. There had been a possibility of success at Derby, though caution had overridden audacity at that turning point. From then on the Jacobites had been on the defensive, despite localized successes in January and February 1746. It had been potentially dangerous to the government, but that moment was now long gone.

From the viewpoint of the government, the Jacobite threat was real, as it had been to an extent, for several decades. There was now a chance of dealing the cause a mortal blow and Cumberland was thought to be the man to do this. He had the confidence of senior figures in the government as well as in the army. What does the military campaign reveal of his character? Although he did authorize attacks on Jacobite property in Scotland, this was hardly evidence of systematic brutality. After all, the Jacobites themselves did not disdain the use of such tactics. In fact, Cumberland was well aware that such methods alone would not be a useful long-term solution. He and Newcastle had concluded that changes in legislation would be required. These would destroy the method that the Jacobites had at their disposal to raise a fighting force in Scotland. In fact, compared to Chesterfield, Cumberland appears rather moderate. Legality, not brutality, was the solution. But first the Jacobites had to be decisively defeated in battle and their army destroyed as a fighting force. It was, after all, undefeated to date.

Chapter 5

The Battle of Culloden and its Aftermath, 8–18 April 1746

The battle was so desperate, that the soldiers bayonets were stain'd and clotted with the blood of the rebels up to the muzzles of their muskets.[1]

Prelude to the Battle, 8–15 April 1746

According to Elcho, there was a possibility that the Jacobite army could have made the first move in this stage of the campaign and attacked Cumberland at Aberdeen. This was not to be because the supply situation was so dire that the army could not move far from its supply base at Inverness. Crossing the Spey and giving battle was just not an option for them.[2] Rather, it was Cumberland who seized the initiative and moved first, striking camp at Aberdeen on 8 April. His second column, under Albermarle, moved from Strathbogie on the same day, and likewise the third, from Oldmeldrum. He was at Banff on 10 April (Albermarle's was at Keith) and all were reunited and encamped at Cullen on the following day. On the morning of 12 April the army approached the River Spey. This was the last geographical barrier between the two armies.[3]

En route, two spies were discovered, one making notches on a stick so as to estimate Cumberland's numbers. The two were summarily hanged, as the rules of war dictated. A notice was pinned to one 'All you that does pass here, Take warning by me, a Rebel spy'. The troops also acted as wreckers, at Turriff, 'a miserable small town with a Non Juring meeting house, but our soldiers took the liberty to disrobe it'.[4]

Expecting resistance at the river, Cumberland decided to spearhead the advance over it with his three regiments of cavalry and all fifteen grenadier companies, the latter to be led by Huske. Two cannons and all the Argyll highlanders made up the remainder of the vanguard.[5] Cumberland accompanied them. The men won plaudits from their commander, as Private Alexander

Taylor of the Royal Scots later wrote, 'He that had seen him reviewing the Lines on that long March, would have seen pleasure in his eyes; for we were a fine Sight; with clean Arms on as fine a Sun-Shine Day as it was.'[6] They tried to draw the Jacobites on the other side of the river away by a number of feints. Although about 2,000 Jacobites under Perth and Drummond were seen on the other side, they did not contest the crossing, but 'marched away with great precipitation leaving however a corps of Horse and what they call Hussars to skirmish with our people on the banks of the river', according to Yorke.[7]

The regulars managed to cross the river, which was at a relatively low depth. The water was only at waist height. Cumberland wrote 'they went on with great cheerfulness'. The only losses were one dragoon and four women.[8] There was some question as to whether the Jacobites should have defended the crossing. Yorke thought so, writing later that day, 'If The Rebels had defended this river, we should have found some difficulty to have past so cheap; for I never saw a stronger post in my life by nature, and a very little art would have rendered it very strong and tenable'.[9] Cumberland agreed, writing: 'It is a very lucky thing that we had to deal with such an enemy. For it would be a most difficult undertaking to pass this river, before an enemy who should know how to take advantage of the situation.'[10] Yet none of this was obvious to the Jacobites. Elcho wrote, 'it was not possible to prevent the passage of the river, as it was Fordable every where'.[11] Similarly, Maxwell said

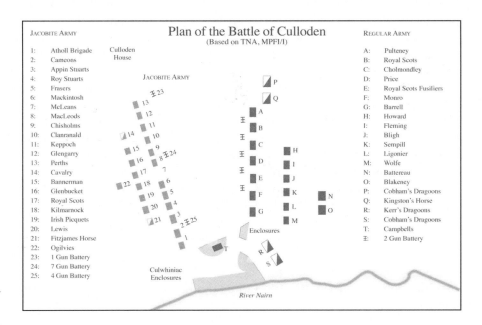

Plan of the Battle of Culloden
(Based on TNA, MPFI/I)

JACOBITE ARMY

1:	Atholl Brigade
2:	Cameons
3:	Appin Stuarts
4:	Roy Stuarts
5:	Frasers
6:	Mackintosh
7:	McLeans
8:	MacLeods
9:	Chisholms
10:	Clanranald
11:	Keppoch
12:	Glengarry
13:	Perths
14:	Cavalry
15:	Bannerman
16:	Glenbucket
17:	Royal Scots
18:	Kilmarnock
19:	Irish Picquets
20:	Lewis
21:	Fitzjames Horse
22:	Ogilvies
23:	1 Gun Battery
24:	7 Gun Battery
25:	4 Gun Battery

REGULAR ARMY

A:	Pulteney
B:	Royal Scots
C:	Cholmondley
D:	Price
E:	Royal Scots Fusiliers
F:	Monro
G:	Barrell
H:	Howard
I:	Fleming
J:	Bligh
K:	Sempill
L:	Ligonier
M:	Wolfe
N:	Battereau
O:	Blakeney
P:	Cobham's Dragoons
Q:	Kingston's Horse
R:	Kerr's Dragoons
S:	Cobham's Dragoons
T:	Campbells
⊥:	2 Gun Battery

Culloden House

Enclosures

Culwhiniac Enclosures

River Nairn

that the Jacobites had only 2,500 men to oppose 9,000, that they lacked artillery, whereas their opponents did not, the water was low and so easily fordable. The position was therefore not defensible.[12]

Those Jacobites who had faced them retreated to Elgin, reaching there at noon. A scouting party of Highlanders and fifty cavalrymen found a body of Jacobites ahead, so Major-General Humphrey Bland (1686–1763), who was also the author of a well-known treatise on military discipline, was given charge of all the cavalry in order to push them back, which he did, the Jacobites retreating in good order.[13]

By 14 April, the regulars had reached Nairn, after having been refreshed by 300 guineas worth of drink from Lord Bracco.[14] It had been fine marching weather, and forage and straw was plentiful. Perth sent troops to attack them, but finding the advance guard was composed all of cavalry, retreated in good order, and though they were followed, little damage was done.[15] Cumberland rested his men on the following day, which was also his twenty-fifth birthday. To celebrate, he gave each battalion a half anker of brandy to drink his health with.[16] After all, they had had five days of hard marches since Aberdeen and Strathbogie.

The speed of their advance had caught the Jacobites off guard. Many of the Jacobite troops were unable to gather together quickly. According to Elcho, 2,100 men were too far away to be able to reach their comrades at Inverness. These included some of the Frasers and Mackintoshes, the MacPhersons and the Mackenzies.[17] Another account describes the effect caused by the news of the regulars' approach: 'The town was in a general alarm, and even in confusion. Nothing was heard but the noise of bagpipes, the beating of drums and the clash of arms.'[18]

Cumberland used the day of rest to make preparations. According to Wolfe, now a brigade major on Hawley's staff, 'We wanted to have fought the 15th, his Royal Highness' birthday, but his charity for the men after many marches prevented it.'[19] Cumberland gave orders for marching on the morning of 16 April. He called a council of war, even though in private he was not certain that a confrontation was imminent, because so many of the Jacobites were not gathered together. 'I can't bring myself to believe that they propose to give us battle.' But he told the assembled men that there was a possibility of action on the following day and told them how he expected them to act in leading their men, and assured them if they acted as he wished, victory was theirs.[20]

A decision now confronted the Jacobite high command. O'Sullivan gave a succinct account of the dilemma and, though the Jacobites were outnumbered, the only party he had was to retire, towards Fort Augustus, but there were difficulties to be met with there to; how cou'd yu keep nine or ten thousand men together wth out meal or mony, there was none to be had in the mountains. You cou'd not get them even cows without mony, yu cou'd not keep them out on the feelds, in the season we were in . . . yu cou'd never assemble them time enough in case the enemy come upon yu . . . It was better to risqué a Battle, where it was morally sure yu wou'd abeat them if his royal Highness orders were follow'd, then give up all for lost, as yu wou'd if yu retired.[21]

Meanwhile, a couple of days before, Charles had told Perth to halt his column at Culloden in order that he might meet him there with as many of his troops as he could muster. Charles was determined to fight a battle – in all probability there was little option if the army was to keep together. Although there was meal in plenty, none of it had been baked and it had not been brought by John Hay, who was in charge of the commissariat, from Inverness. According to Elcho, 'This neglect of provisions would have made it impossible to have kept the army together in a body.'[22] The Jacobite army stood to arms on the night of 14 April and were reviewed by Charles on the following morning. On this day, there was debate as to the choice of battlefield. Murray was unhappy about the initial choice of battlefield on Culloden Moor. He wrote in his memoirs:

> Early on Tuesday morning, we all drew up in a line of battle, in an open muir, near Culloden. I did not like the ground: it was certainly not proper for Highlanders. I proposed . . . the other side of the water of Nairn . . . It was found to be hilly and boggy; so that the enemy's cannon and horse could be of no great use to them there.[23]

He proposed the other site as being more suitable. On Murray's preferred location, near Dalcross Castle, which O'Sullivan said he took 'to be the finest thing in the world', the Irishman 'found it was the worst yt cou'd be chosen for the highlanders & the most advantagiouse fore the enemy'. O'Sullivan thought that the ravine he had seen on the site would serve to separate the two forces. Therefore, musketry and cannon fire would resolve the issue and thus the regulars would fight at an advantage. The Jacobites needed to get to grips with their enemy to use their swords at close quarters. Any obstacle in their path was therefore to be avoided.[24]

Traditionally, Murray's choice has been applauded and O'Sullivan's has been dismissed; perhaps because it was on Culloden Moor that the disaster for the Jacobites occurred. Yet the open moor surely had much to recommend itself, for it gave the Highlanders fairly flat terrain over which to charge to get at their enemy (the ground at Prestonpans had been similar, and the Jacobites gained a decisive victory there). The uneven ground at Falkirk had not helped them. In this, O'Sullivan was correct, though the terrain was also ideal for their opponents' artillery and cavalry.

There was, in fact, no ideal site in which to fight. But there was no alternative – if they did not fight, the army would disintegrate due to the lack of money and supplies. The Jacobites had been on the defensive for some months – ever since Derby – and now the enemy, well led, well supplied and well equipped, and in good spirits, was advancing towards them. The Jacobites could fight, with the odds stacked against them, or they could cease to exist as a fighting force. The former provided, perhaps, a slim chance, the second none.

About 7,000 troops were drawn up in battle order on Culloden Moor. They had not eaten for at least a day as supplies were not reaching them. Keeping them together in a body for any length of time would be impossible. But Charles was determined on a battle. Sending out scouts to reconnoitre Cumberland's camp, they noted that it was stationary and likely to remain so for the rest of the day. The Jacobites had suddenly been given the initiative.[25]

Charles called together a general council of his principal officers, which he had not done since Derby. According to Elcho:

> Lord George Murray made a Speech, wherein he enlarged upon the advantages Highlanders have by Surprising their Enemy, and rather Attacking in the night time than in the day Light, for as regular troops depend intirely upon their discipline, and on the Contrary the Highlanders having none, the Night was the time to putt them upon an Equality, and he concluded that his Opinion was that they Should march at dusk of ye Evening. [26]

Matters were so desperate for the Jacobites that such an orthodox leader as Murray should insist on a night march – Monmouth's army had tried a similar tactic at Sedgemoor in 1685 and it had gone horribly wrong. Murray wrote: 'I thought we had a better chance by doing it, than by fighting in so plain a field'.[27] Certainly, attacking troops in camp meant that the regulars' advantages in numbers, training, drill and equipment would all be negated. In order that Cumberland be surprised, the plan was to march around the town of Nairn and so attack his army in the rear in a pincer movement of three columns. Everyone agreed to the plan, and the only concern was that they might not be able to march the eight miles before daylight, but Murray said he would take responsibility for that. They may have thought that, as it was Cumberland's birthday, all the soldiers would be drunk and therefore an easy victory could be forecast.[28] Yet their men were hungry. Only one biscuit per man had been issued that day.[29]

Despite their hunger, the army began to march at nine. The timing was to stop their being seen by their enemy. Likewise, all human habitations had to be given a wide berth in order for the attack to be a surprise. The men thus marched to the south of the main road from Inverness to Nairn. They only succeeded in marching five miles before daylight, perhaps in part because they lost their way en route, and men were ankle deep in mud. Johnstone elaborated on the difficulties encountered:

> This march across the country, in a dark night which did not allow us to follow any track, had the inevitable fate of all night marches. It was extremely fatiguing and accompanied with confusion and disorder. The Highlanders, who could not keep together from the difficulty of the roads, were more or less dispersed and we had many stragglers. As there were a great many bad places to cross, it would have been impossible for the best disciplined troops to have preserved anything like order.[30]

Murray, who was at the front, called a halt at Culraick, sending Cameron of Lochiel to tell Charles of the news and that it was better to withdraw, because their enemy would be prepared by the time they arrived and so the whole point of the night march had failed. They marched back using two routes, no longer caring if they were seen or not. Charles was angry and was in favour of pressing on, arguing that to fight later would leave the men even more exhausted than they were then. But, as at Derby, his enthusiasm for daring was frustrated.[31] He allegedly declared 'God Damn it! Are my Commands still disobeyed?'[32]

Was this the correct decision? Was this, as at Derby, another case of withdrawing at the moment of possible victory? John Daniel, an English Jacobite, certainly thought so, believing the regulars had seen 'the jeopardy they had been in'.[33] According to Henderson, they 'really knew nothing of the danger they were in'.[34] Home wrote 'if it had been executed as it was projected, would, in the opinion of some of the bravest officers in the Duke's army, have proved not a little dangerous'.[35] However, Yorke said that the Jacobites did not reach within five miles of the camp and Cumberland had scouts and other patrols who were observing them.[36] Johnstone thought retreat was the best policy, 'A shameful repulse would have been the inevitable consequence of such an attack'.[37]

The abortive night march had not only failed, but it had rendered the army in an even worse condition in which to fight. On their return to Culloden, Elcho wrote:

> Every body seemed to think of nothing but Sleep. The men were prodigiously tired with hunger and fatigue, and vast numbers of them went into Inverness, and the Villages about, both to Sleep and to pick up what little nourishment they Could gett.

The officers were also exhausted and tried to sleep. They had little chance.[38]

Incidentally, there was another defeat for the Jacobites on 15 April. The Earl of Cromartie with a party of 400 men moved against Lord Ray and his loyalist Highlanders. The former were ambushed at Golspie; some were killed and others taken prisoner. Some fled to Dunrobin, where Cromartie and the others also gave in; in all 164 prisoners were taken.[39]

The Battle of Culloden, 16 April

There was some further discussion about whether the Jacobites should have fought at Culloden. Some later suggested that a retreat to Inverness, where their stores were located, would have been a better option. There was enough food there for the army for two or three days and this would also have allowed the stragglers and other men to join them there. Yet this was surely only to delay the battle.[40] Elcho wrote 'No council was held; everyone knew that he wished to fight; and yet there was only one proper course to follow, viz to retreat, but there were no provisions.'[41]

Meanwhile, at the camp at Nairn, patrols and spies brought news of the abortive night march. Between four and five that morning, Cumberland's troops began to march towards Culloden. It was a gloomy, unprepossessing day, as Taylor wrote:

> It was a very cold, rainy Morning, and nothing to buy to comfort us: But we had the Ammunition-loaf, thank God; but not a dram of Brandy or Spirits, had you given a Crown for a gill, nor, nothing but the Loan and the water. We had also great Difficulty in keeping the Locks of our firelocks dry; which was absolutely necessary.[42]

They marched cautiously forward in four columns. The first three columns, from left to right, were each composed of five battalions of infantry. The fourth column, on their right, was made up of the three regiments of cavalry. The artillery and baggage went behind the first column of infantry. Ahead of this main body was an advance guard of forty men from Kingston's Horse and all the Argyll Highlanders. The key concern was to prevent the army being ambushed en route to Culloden. Colonel Whitefoord noted that the reason for such a formation was that, if the Jacobites attacked from any angle, the troops could form up quickly and easily in order to repel them. Each infantryman had had his weapon checked on 13 April and each had been allocated twenty-four musket balls. [43] According to Ashe Lee, 'he [Cumberland] settled the disposition of our march and the order of battle, in a manner most justly admired, and worthy the experience of the oldest and ablest general'. [44]

Among the general orders of the day were the following: 'Ye cavalry to pursue ye Enemy as far as they can' and 'The Surgeons to take immediate care of ye wounded'. [45] The strength of this army is uncertain. It was composed of fifteen battalions of regular infantry, who numbered about 6,410 men, according to the official returns taken before the battle. Then there were two regiments of dragoons and one of horse, numbering 787 men. There were ten 3-pounder cannon and six coehorn mortars, all of which were manned by regular soldiers of the Royal Artillery Regiment, about 100 men. Finally there were Highland militia – companies of Argyll Highlanders (360 men plus officers) and a company of Lord John Murray's Highlanders. [46] Traditionally, the army has been numbered at about 9,000 men, but perhaps the true figure is about 7,800. It was the strongest force that had been sent against the Jacobites, made up of experienced troops, well supplied (by sea), confident in their commander and whose guns were manned by professionals. Neither Cope at Prestonpans, Wade at Newcastle nor Hawley at Falkirk had such a fine force under their leadership.

This array was observed by a party of Jacobite cavalry sent to watch their motions. Only two hours after the Jacobites had returned from their failed night march, Charles and his senior officers ordered the drums to beat and the pipes to be played, 'which Alarm Caused great hurry & Confusion amongst people half dead with fatigue'. The army was also considerably numerically weaker; perhaps by about 2,000 men, according to Elcho, who had fallen asleep too far away to hear the reveille or had gone further afield in search of food. The army numbered only about 5,000 men. [47] It was a rainy, misty day and the rain and wind blew in the faces of the Jacobites. There was no time for another council of war, but the dispositions of the day before were adhered to.

At least one final attempt was made to persuade Charles against fighting on that day. The Marquis D'Eguilles, the accredited envoy of Louis XV of France, later wrote:

> The Prince who believed himself invincible because he had not yet been beaten, defied by enemies whom he thoroughly despised, seeing at their head the son of the rival of his father; proud and haughty as he was, badly advised, perhaps betrayed, forgetting at this moment every other object, could not bring himself to decline battle even for a single day.

D'Eguilles argued that the Jacobite army was below its full strength, the men were hungry and tired. He suggested that a retreat to Inverness or to the mountains would put the army in a better condition in which to do battle. It was to no avail, 'finding him immovable in the resolve he had taken to fight at any cost', the Frenchman went to Inverness and burnt all his papers.[48] Although there were proposals for a retreat, it was claimed that Thomas Sheridan and other advisers 'having lost all patience and hoping no doubt for a miracle . . . insisted upon a battle'.[49]

It was alleged that the clan chiefs were opposed to fighting on that day until goaded by Brigadier Stapleton, who commanded the Irish Picquets. He claimed 'the Scots were always good troops until things came to a crisis'. Cameron of Lochiel answered, 'he did not believe there was an Highlander in the army who would not have run up to the mouth of a cannon, in order to confuse the odious and undeserved aspersion'.[50]

After having marched eight miles from Nairn, partly on the road, before turning south-west towards Culloden, and on being informed that the Jacobites were 'making a motion towards our left', Cumberland had the army form up in lines for battle. Yet, as the Jacobites did not stir, he ordered his troops into their column of march again. These movements were accomplished quickly and easily. There was another similar manoeuvre, but once again it proved unnecessary. These manoeuvres were impressive, as Yorke wrote, 'the Duke made the army form immediately in line of battle, which they did with the ease and alacrity as surprised every spectator, and gave the greatest hope for eventual victory'.[51]

Yet for the men, it was unsettling. Taylor wrote:

> We marched but four Miles till we was alarmed by their Out-parties, and drew up in Order of Battle, and marched that Way for two Miles,

with our Arms secured and, Bayonets fixed (a very uneasy Way of marching).[52]

The weather was still unfavourable, too – Private Edward Linn of the Royal Scots Fusiliers writing 'it was a very bad day both for Wind & Rain, But Thank God it was straight upon our Backs.'[53] Yet this worked against the Jacobites. Andrew Lumisden, Charles's secretary, remarked upon the 'great storm of hail and rain that blew in our faces'.[54]

Spies gave useful information about the Jacobites' disposition. The walled grounds of Culloden Park were on the Jacobite left and these they planned to use as a method of ambushing the regulars as they approached them. On their right were the Culwhinniac enclosures.

Eventually the army formed up a mile to the east of the Jacobites. The first line was made up of six battalions of infantry, the second of six, with three in reserve. Lord Albermarle and Brigadier Hew Sempill (1688–1746) were in command of the first line, Huske the second and Mordaunt the third. The first two lines were separated by 50 yards. Two cannons were placed between the battalions of the first line, making ten in all. Six coehorn mortars were placed in front of the battalions on the right wing of the second line. Kingston's Horse (two squadrons) and one squadron of Cobham's dragoons were also placed in the third line as reserves. The remainder of the cavalry (Kerr's three squadrons of dragoons and two squadrons of Cobham's) were on the left. These cavalry were led by Hawley and Bland, and planned to fall on the Jacobites' right flank if possible. Most of the Argyll Highlanders were sent to guard the baggage in the rear, but 140 were sent with Hawley's cavalry. Both sides manoeuvred for about half an hour in order to gain the best position prior to the battle.[55]

The Jacobite army's main strength lay in its front line, which was composed of fourteen mainly clan regiments, under the command of Murray, Perth and Lord John Drummond. There were, perhaps, twelve guns scattered here, but there is much doubt over the number of batteries; one map suggests three of four guns each, another four batteries of either two or three guns each and a lone gun to the far left. The French troops guarded the flanks of the second line, whilst in its centre were the small units of Jacobite cavalry and non-clan regiments, eight units in all, under Stapleton. Finally, there was a small reserve.[56] Their numbers are unclear. One source lists 4,150 men in the front rank, 1,600 in the second and 700 in the reserve, with 176 cavalry, totalling 6,626 in all, but this is probably an overestimate, perhaps based on numbers from 15 April, not the following day. As noted, Elcho thought the true number to be about 5,000. Their position was to the south-west of the battlefield selected on the previous day.[57] Yet their disposition was such that their left wing was considerably further from the regulars than their right.

Initially a morass was before the battalions on the right of the regulars' front line. This protected their flank. But as they advanced, the morass was crossed and so no longer offered any protection. Cumberland ordered Kingston's Horse and the squadron of Cobham's dragoons from the third line to that spot.[58] He also moved Pulteney's battalion of infantry from the reserve to the right flank of the first line and Battereau's battalion from the reserve to the right of the second line, too.[59]

The Jacobite army's right wing was apparently protected by the walled enclosures of Culwhinniac, which were six feet high. O'Sullivan suggested to Lord George Murray, whose men were on the direct left of the walls, that he put men inside the walls and pierce them so that they could fire out of them and this would deter any flanking move that might otherwise be attempted. Murray refused to do so and reminded him that he held the superior rank.[60] On the following day, Murray blamed O'Sullivan for having 'committed gross blunders on every occasion of moment'. In particular, he accused O'Sullivan of allowing the enemy army the chance of occupying the walls.[61]

Relations between those in the Jacobite high command were sour. It was not only that Murray and O'Sullivan were at loggerheads. Charles was 'enraged against Lord George Murray', presumably for halting the night match without his orders.[62] Another problem was that the MacDonalds, who were on the left of the Jacobite line, complained to Charles that they should be allowed to be on the right instead, and to displace the Atholl brigade who were currently there. He told them that they should remain where they were.[63]

Cumberland's army advanced to within 500 yards of the Jacobite front line. In order to encourage his men, Cumberland rode down the lines and gave a short speech:

> My brave boys, your toil will soon be at an end; stand your ground against the broadsword and target; parry the enemy in the manner you have been directed, be assured of immediate assistance, and I promise you that I shall not fail to make a report of your behaviour to the King; and in the meantime, if any are unwilling to engage, pray let them speak freely, and with pleasure they shall have a discharge.[64]

According to Michael Hughes, a volunteer in the ranks, the speech was 'followed by a full acclamation of all the soldiers, testifying their intire satisfaction and Loyalty'.[65] Cumberland then rode to the right wing of his army, in front of Howard's battalion in the second line, 'imagining the greatest push would be there', to use his own words.[66]

Meanwhile, according to Daniel, the Jacobite troops who opposed them were also in good spirits. He wrote, 'Those, however, who staid, put the best face on the affair they could, and all of us presently appeared surprizingly courageous, who only seemed to survive and animated by the spirit of loyalty and love for our dear Prince.'[67] When they saw the regulars approaching, 'we began to huzza and bravado them in their march upon us'.[68] Finally, Charles and other Jacobite leaders 'rode from rank to rank, animating and encouraging the soldiers by well-adapted harangues'.[69] Maxwell wrote 'The Highlanders, though faint with hunger, and ready to drop with fatigue and want of sleep, seemed to forget all their hardships at the approach of the enemy.'[70]

Parts of the battlefield were wet underfoot. Horses pulling the regulars' artillery began to sink and had to be removed, being replaced by soldiers who dragged the cannon into position. Elsewhere, Wolfe's battalion were standing up to their ankles in water until they moved.[71] The weather at this stage in the conflict was variable. There was a rainstorm, followed by wind and then there was fair weather at about one.[72] The weather's effects were injurious to both sides: wind blew against the Jacobites, but some of the regulars' cartridges were wet. Yet most men kept their muskets dry with their coats and only a very few did not fire.[73]

Cumberland sent Lord Bury (1724–72), a staff officer, towards the Jacobite lines for a closer reconnaissance in order to see where the Jacobite batteries were. The time was about one o'clock. It was at this point that the Jacobite artillery opened fire and the first shots of the battle were heard. However, as Cumberland later remarked, they were 'extremely ill served and ill manned'. According to Ray, this 'did us little or no Damage'.[74] Apparently 'the Balls flew mostly over the heads of the Royalists'.[75] Home relates that a soldier of Bligh's battalion in the second line was wounded, but that was all.[76] An anonymous contemporary writing from Edinburgh wrote 'the shot when [sic] entirely over the army (except a few) and killed some person guarding the baggage, a great distance behind the army'. He blamed the ineptitude of the French gunners manning the Jacobite guns.[77] Yet, since some of the units in the second rank had a few men wounded, it is probable that the Jacobite guns were responsible for these casualties.

The guns of the Royal Artillery, placed in batteries of two between the front-line battalions, opened fire and, in Cumberland's words, 'began their confusion'. There is great controversy over how long such a barrage lasted and how effective it was. At one extreme, Home estimates that it lasted an hour and was deadly, 'The Duke's artillery did great execution making lanes through the Highland regiments.'[78] Another source claims it lasted fifteen minutes.[79] However, according to Yorke, only two or three minutes elapsed, which had given the guns time to have fired only two balls each. A recent estimate is that the cannonade lasted nine minutes and killed or wounded about 90–100 of the Jacobite front line.[80] Some of the guns' fire affected the second line of the Jacobite army and a number of accounts state that this was how Charles's servant was killed and that Charles himself was in danger.[81]

It was not long before the artillery fire provoked a response from the Jacobites. The Jacobites had either to charge forward or to flee. They could not remain where they stood. A few fled and some lay on the ground. At some point, Charles sent an aide with orders that the front line regiments charge, but the messenger was killed by a cannon ball before he could deliver his message. Another man was sent, and finally the orders were received and acted upon. Other accounts relate that even more messages were sent before the charge began and that Sir John MacDonald had to be sent to tell Perth to advance, which he did. The plan was for the units on the left, who were furthest from the regulars, to move first, then the centre ones, and finally those on the right, who were nearest the enemy. In this way, the front units would hit their enemies at about the same time.[82]

It was not to be, though most of the regiments in the front rank advanced. They advanced in three columns or wedges of attack, but did so in some confusion, having already taken some casualties from artillery fire.[83] This was not a coordinated assault and can be divided into two parts. Cumberland had expected the main attack on his right wing. The MacDonalds, who formed the left wing of the Jacobite front line, charged at the regulars, 'firing their pistols and brandishing their swords', on several occasions, all to no effect. According to Johnstone, however, the Jacobites came to 20 yards from their enemies. Eventually they retreated, noting what had happened elsewhere.[84]

These attacks may have been designed as feints, to provoke their enemy into firing ineffectually at long range. Then the Highlanders would have been able to charge without being blasted at short range.[85]

Taylor, whose unit was on the right of the first line, later wrote: 'But our Gunners galling their Lines, they betook them to their small Arms, Sword and Pistol, and came running on our Front-Line like Troops of Hungry Wolves, and fought with intrepidity.'[86]

The left wing of the Jacobite army may have been reluctant to fully commit themselves to battle, because their flank was unprotected and thus vulnerable to the troops of dragoons on the regulars' flank.[87]

The right and centre units of the Jacobite army were rather more determined. They also had the advantage that they outflanked Barrell's battalion, which was on the extreme left of the regulars' front line and they had a lesser distance to charge. It is probable that the Jacobites fired at the regulars – an officer of Munro's later wrote that he had been shot at six times, though probably ineffectually (the officer in question was unhurt).[88] According to Henderson, 'in a stooping Posture, with their Targets in their left hand, covering their Head and Breast, and their glittering Swords in their Right, they ran swiftly upon the Cannon, making a frightful Huzza'.[89] For all his faults, Murray was at the head of his Atholl men.[90] The charging Highlanders were met with volley fire from Barrell's and Munro's battalions. This was deadly, as Hughes noted, 'the King's men did not fire till near close upon them . . . that dropt them down as fast as they came on'.[91] A volley of musketry, delivered at 30 yards and cannon firing cannister were murderous.[92] According to Linn, the volley fire of the infantry lasted about a quarter of an hour, but this is certainly an exaggeration.[93]

Linn gave a graphic description of this part of the battlefield:

> they came up very boldly & very fast all in a Cloud together, Sword in hand; they fired their pieces & flung them away, but we gave them so Warm a Reception that we kept a Continuall Closs [volley or salvo] fireing upon them with our Small arms; besides, 2 or 3 of our Cannon gave them a Closs with grapeshot which galled them very much & so in ane instant they retreated & our Cannon & a few Royalls [mortars] sent them a few small bomb shells & Cannon balls to their farewell.[94]

According to Lord George Murray, the possession by the regulars of the walls was crucial, writing on the following day that 'they with their front fire and flanking us when we went upon the attack destroyed us without any possibility of our breaking them, and our Atholl men have lost a full half of their officers and men'.[95] This was despite Murray's courage: 'Lord George behaved himself with great gallantry, lost his horse, his periwig and bonnet, was amongst the last that left the field, had severall cutts with broadswords in his coat, and was covered in blood and dirt'.[96] It is ironic to note that Murray had eschewed manning these walls and his men paid dearly for this error.

It was the Jacobite chiefs and their officers, charging at the front of their men, who suffered disproportionately from such fire. McGillivray of Dunmaglass, colonel of the Mackintosh regiment, was killed, as were all the officers, except three. Cameron of Lochiel (*c*.1700–48) was wounded by grapeshot in both ankles and had to be carried off the field. Macdonald of Keppoch was killed by two musket balls. Colonel Maclachlan was killed by a cannon ball.[97] These casualties would have played havoc with command and control of the units on the field.

Such losses were not enough to stop them all, however. According to Elcho, 'The centre join'd the right, and in a Sort of a mob, without any order or distinction of Corps, mixt together, rush'd in and attack'd the Dukes left wing, and broke the regiments opposite to them in the first line.'[98] One account states the attackers were fifty men deep.[99] Hand-to-hand fighting ensued. 'There was scarce a soldier or officer of Barrell's or Munro's which engaged, who did not kill one or two men each with their bayonets or spontoons'. Of Barrell's, it was said 'After the battle there was not a bayonet in this regiment but was either bloody or bent.'[100] An officer from Munro's later wrote that 'Our lads fought more like Devils than Men'. A colleague in Barrell's wrote:

> the old Tangerines [Many of the men had served in Tangier] bravely repulsed those Boarders with a dreadful slaughter, and convinced them that their Broadswords and Target is unequal to the Musket and Bayonet, when in the Hands of Veterans who are determined to use them.[101]

It was here that the regulars took their heaviest casualties of the battle. Of Barrell's battalion, seventeen were killed, including Lord Robert Kerr, a captain, and 108 wounded (about a third of the total). Munro's men were not as badly affected, but even so, fourteen were slain and another sixty-eight injured – about a fifth of the total. Eleven officers were killed or wounded. This is an indication of the severity of the combat.[102]

This was the climax of the battle. Henry Hastings wrote 'if they could have broke through it might strike such a panic in the rest as to make the day their own'.[103] Yet the stout resistance by Barrell's and Munro's could not entirely stem the Jacobite onslaught and the outnumbered soldiers had to give ground. Two guns were overrun.[104] But those Jacobites who did manage to break through the battalions of Barrell's and Munro's, were met by Sempill's and Bligh's battalions of the second line. Wolfe's battalion also came up in support of Barrell's. According to Hastings, 'The Duke immediately with great presence of mind ordered Huske with three regiments to flank them and three others to the left, who make great havoc of 'em, and the greater for them being (unusually) fifty deep.'[105] The fire poured on the Jacobites by these battalions was devastating. William Oman, a soldier in either Bligh's or Sempill's battalion, wrote of 'The perpetual fire of our Troops made for five minutes'.[106] They 'beat them off, and obliged them to turn their backs and run away'.

Battlefield of Killiecrankie (1689). *Author's collection*

Scene of the massacre of Glencoe (1692). *Author's collection*

Statue to Charles Edward Stuart at Glenfinnan. *Author's collection*

Edinburgh Castle *Author's collection*

Monument at Prestonpans, 2007.
Author's collection

Gravestone at Clifton, 2005.
Author's father (Mr David Oates)

Blair Castle, *c.*1910.
Author's collection

Charles Edward Stuart, 1720–88.
Richard Sharp's collection

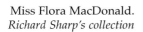

Miss Flora MacDonald.
Richard Sharp's collection

William Augustus, Duke
of Cumberland (1721–65).
E. Charteris, (from William
Augustus, Duke of
Cumberland, 1913)

Thomas Pelham-Holles, Duke of
Newcastle (1693–1768).
Author's collection

egular soldier, 1745. *Author's collection*   Jacobite re-enactors at Culloden, 2007.

Culloden Moor, looking
west towards the Jacobite
lines, 2007. *Author*

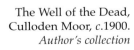

The Well of the Dead,
Culloden Moor, *c*.1900.
Author's collection

Cairn and graves of the
clans, Culloden Moor, *c*.1910.
Author's collection

Culloden Cottage, Culloden
Moor, *c*.1910.
Author's collection

House in Inverness where
wounded regular soldiers were
taken after Culloden, 2007.
Author

Church in Inverness where Jacobite prisoners were taken, 2007. *Author*

Ruin of Glengarry castle, Loch Oich, *c*.1900. *Author's collection*

An artist's impression of soldiers searching for Jacobite sympathizers. *Taylor Library*

Isles of Rhum and Eigg
c.1910.
Author's collection

Isle of Skye, *c*.1910.
Author's collection

Fort George, 2007.
Author

During the struggle, some Jacobites were at a disadvantage as they had thrown away their targe shields on the march and so were more exposed to their enemies' bayonets.[107] The fighting was not all one-sided. Bligh's and Sempill's battalions took the second highest casualties, totalling thirty-five in all.[108]

The Jacobites had been repulsed. One observer wrote, 'These wretches were so smartly repulsed, that in a transport of rage truly barbarian, finding that their efforts to surround our flanks were vain, they pickt up stones and dirt and threw them at our men as they fled.'[109]

The flight of the Jacobites then began in earnest. According to Johnstone: 'What a spectacle of horror! The same Highlanders, who had advanced to the charge like lions, with bold, determined countenances, were in an instant seen flying like trembling cowards in the greatest disorder.'[110] The MacDonalds on the left of the Jacobite front line, who never engaged the regulars in direct combat, saw the retreat of the Athollmen, the Camerons and the Appin Stewarts on the right and began to fall back too.[111]

Meanwhile the Argyll men and Murray's Highlanders, perhaps four companies strong, had already pulled down two little stone walls to the left of the regulars' front line, by orders of Hawley, in order that the Jacobite army could be outflanked. Furthermore, as one observer noted, they 'gave distinguished marks of their courage and good conduct during the whole action'. Another stated they lined the walls, opened fire on the Jacobites and 'kill'd and destroy'd great numbers of them', before charging them and pursuing them for a short time. Among those killed in return Jacobite fire was Captain Campbell of Ballimore.[112] The broken walls enabled those cavalry on the left wing of the army to move forward and threaten the Jacobites. Yet they could not immediately advance as units from the second line of the Jacobite army, including Lord Lewis's Gordons, Fitzjames and Elcho's tiny cavalry units and Avochies's infantry were hastily marched to defend this otherwise vulnerable flank. The cavalry did not advance because their enemy's strength was concealed by them being behind a ridge – the battlefield sloping uphill northwards from the river and so an attack could have been risky.[113] It was only when 'the Rebels began to give way and the fire of the Foot slacken'd' that the cavalry advanced. Wolfe, who was with them, thought that this should have happened earlier in order to have had an even more devastating effect on the Jacobites.[114]

On the right of the regulars' front line, the cavalry advanced against the fleeing MacDonalds, Linn writing they 'pursued with Sword & pistol & Cutt a great many of them down So that I never Saw a Small field thicker of Dead'.[115] According to one writer, 'The Duke of Kingston's Light Horse broke in and then followed an universall root which ended in a dreadfull slaughter for half an hour without giving any quarter.'[116]

Cumberland's infantry did not move forward, but instead stood their ground and dressed ranks.[117] An officer of Munro's related that his men killed fifty of their opponents in their flight, but an officer from Wolfe's claimed they 'took a great number of prisoners'.[118] However, Oman claimed that there was some attempt at a chase: 'We made our pursuit, but could hardly march for dead bodies, sure never such slater was made, in so short a time'.[119]

Some resistance continued. The French units of the Royal Scots and the Irish Brigade, having not taken part in the battle to date, were well formed and were able to deter potential attackers. In 1793 an elderly Glengarry officer recalled that the French fired three volleys, but William Home wrote, only a year before, 'as to the French auxillaries, they did not fire a shot. I never thought much of them.' But they too were forced to fall back, albeit in good order. Stapleton was mortally wounded and died on the following day. The retreat was also facilitated by a cannon which had been brought up during the battle and moved to the Culloden enclosure on the left of the Jacobite line. It 'played on Kingston's Horse and favoured the retreat of the left wing'.[120]

Charles made good his escape. It is debatable whether he tried to rally his troops or not. According to Elcho, as soon as the left wing began to give way, he 'turn'd about his horse and went off . . . and never offer'd to rally any of the broken Corps'.[121] However, other accounts state that he tried to rally what units he could, though without success, and had to be led from the stricken field, protected by a bodyguard of Fitzjames's Horse.[122] Most of the fleeing Jacobites fled south to Badenoch and Ruthven, towards the Western Highlands, where many of them lived. A few, including the Frasers and the French troops, went northwards to Inverness and then to Ross shire. That town was later secured for Cumberland by the grenadier company of Sempill's batallion, and the French and Irish troops surrendered to him.[123]

Lord Ancrum (*c*.1712–75), who commanded the cavalry on the right wing, led the pursuit of the fleeing Jacobites. This was very effective. 'Ancrum was order'd to pursue with the horse as far as he could; and did it with so good effect that a very considerable number was killed in the pursuit.' One account states 'Major General Bland [in command of the left wing] also made great slaughter'. The pursuit was so rigorous that it was said that the streets of Inverness ran with blood, though Kingston's Horse ceased the pursuit a mile from the town.[124] One contemporary historian claimed that the troopers of Kingston's Horse slew ten to twelve men each.[125]

The pursuing officers and men went about their work willingly. According to Colonel Henry Conway (1718–84), our cavalry on the left coming up almost unperceived upon their left flank, put their right in entire confusion and made vast slaughter . . . our cavalry did their duty very well in the pursuit, sparing very few that came in their reach.

He referred to the enemy as 'vermin'.[126] Colonel Yorke wrote:

The remembrance of former wrongs, the barbarity with which our prisoners had in general been used, and the glorious desire of recovering lost reputation, infused such spirits in the breasts of all, that had not fear added wings to their feet, none would have escaped the edge of the sword.[127]

The troopers were all too willing to attack the Jacobites if the letter of Enoch Bradshaw of Cobham's dragoons is to be believed. He wrote on 11 May to his brother thus:

These rapacious villains thought to have destroyed their prisoners, and by their orderly books, had they got the better, we were to have been every soul of us cut off, and not have had one prisoner, and for the Duke he was to have been cut as small as herbs for the pot, thus they said their books declare. But, God be praised, he would not suffer such inhumanity and barbarous villains to thrive.[128]

The road to Inverness from Culloden is downhill – excellent for pursuing cavalry and terrible for their luckless foes. Whitefoord later wrote of the pursuit and was regrettably suitably vague: 'You know the pursuit was bloody and are no stranger to the other circumstances that followed.'[129]

It was customary for cavalry to pursue a defeated foe and the result was inevitably bloody unless there was any formed resistance against them. It was also during the rout that most casualties were inflicted on the losers. Elsewhere, the picture was grim. As a contemporary letter observed, 'The moor was covered with blood; and our men, what with killing the enemy, dabbling their feet in the blood, and splashing it about one another, looked like so many butchers.' Others were killed far from the site of combat, as Alexander Tough, surgeon to the Scots Fusiliers noted, 'whom we suppose in their flight to have at last languished of their wounds lamenting Charley's fate'.[130] The aftermath of any battle is not for the squeamish and Culloden was not an exception to the rule. The Jacobite victory at Prestonpans had presented a similar spectacle.

The battle was over in about half an hour, or less, from the first cannonade to the rout of the Jacobites; though Whitefoord thought it was only fifteen minutes from the Jacobite charge to their rout. As an officer of Munro's noted, it had been 'the bloodiest Battle with the Rebels that was ever fought in the Memory of Man'.[131]

The Aftermath of the Battle

Cumberland congratulated his victorious troops. According to Linn, 'after it was over he Rode along the Same Line & Returnd us a great many thanks for our good behaviour & he Said he never Seed better ordered or well done'.[132] He later wrote, 'I have the Satisfaction to say that all the General officers & the Corps did their utmost in his Majty's Service, & all strove to shew their Zeal & Bravery on this Occasion'.[133] An anonymous observer agreed that the soldiers had all behaved well. 'Not a man in the whole army behaved ill. On the contrary an uncommon spirit appeared through the whole of them.'[134] The soldiers cheered, 'Flanders! Flanders! We'll follow your royal highness against any enemy!'[135] Cumberland's behaviour also gave satisfaction to the observer who wrote 'The Duke behaved as usuall, led on his men on foot in a plain soldier's coat with a common gun and bayonet.'[136] Oman wrote of him being 'Our gallant Hero' and 'His Royal Highness' behaviour was like his noble predecessors, viz., with great calmness, and Bravery'.[137]

Some of the credit for the victory must go to the Duke. Fawkener wrote:

> His Royal H. gave Life & Spirit to the Army. He settled all the Marches, & by His activity got together the necessary Fund of pro-visions for putting the Army onto Motion towards this barren Country, & He provided so well, that we have not wanted any thing. The Disposition of the Army for the Action as well as the Directions for the Execution were also entirely owing to His R. Hs.[138]

Cumberland sent Bury to London with the news of the victory. Travelling by sea, he arrived at the court on 24 April.[139]

It is when the casualties of the battle are discussed that matters become controversial. After any battle, the reported number of casualties on both sides tend to be unreliable. Suspiciously round numbers are always given and each general will underestimate his own losses, and maximize those of the enemy. Culloden was an exception, because Jacobite estimates of their own dead tend to be as high as those numbers put forward by their enemy. It is possible that the aim was to exaggerate the brutality of the victor. There is no doubt that Jacobite casualties were high and those of the victorious regulars were low, though this is only to be expected. However, the disparity at Culloden was greater than at most battles in this era.

Reported numbers of Jacobite dead are highly disputed and can never be properly ascertained. One published account states 500 were killed on the battlefield and 500 in the flight; a later account from the same journal gives a total of 2,000. It also claimed that the Jacobites put their losses at 4,000, which would mean that about 80 per cent of their army was slain – a fantastic figure.[140] Marchant notes that 2,000 Jacobite dead were buried, which sounds more realistic, though it is still a very high proportion.[141]

Losses in Cumberland's army are easier to be certain about. The regular army put its losses at 50 dead, 259 wounded (of whom some later died) and one man missing. Most of the casualties were from Barrell's and Munro's battalions, unsurprisingly so.[142] Anecdotal evidence supports this low figure, Linn writing 'We lost very few men of our Army, only a few wounded; our loss is about 200 men Wounded & Killed. Thank God we lost not one man of our Regiment, only a few Wounded; we never had Such good Luck befor.' Such differences in casualty figures between a victorious and a badly beaten army are not uncommon. At Naesby the Royalist dead perhaps numbered 1,000 and their enemies lost about a fifth of this number.[143]

The French troops at Culloden surrendered and were made prisoner, to the number of 222. One officer wrote that they had the 'hope for everything which is to be expected from the English generosity'.[144] Of the rank and file of Jacobites, 326 were taken prisoner, though almost half of these were prisoners taken from the skirmish on the previous day. After the battle, more were found and brought in, many of whom were wounded. Apart from the human losses, the Jacobites lost all their artillery and baggage, which amounted to 22 cannon, 2,500 muskets, 27 barrels of gunpowder, 22 ammunition carts, 1,019 cannon shot and 500 weight of musket shot.[145] Noble and gentry prisoners included the Earl of Kilmarnock (1705–46) and Sir John Wedderburn (1704–46) on the field of battle, Lady Mackintosh and other Jacobite ladies at Inverness.[146] However, Charles and many of his senior officers escaped the field.

As to the wounded Jacobites on the field of battle, they met with mixed responses. Jacobite accounts are full of dreadful tales. Elcho wrote: 'Everybody that fell into their hands gott no quarters except for a few who they reserved for publick punishment; the Earl of Kilmarnock and Colonel Farquharson.'[147] This is probably an exaggeration. Johnstone wrote in a similar vein:

The Duke of Cumberland had the cruelty to allow our wounded to remain amongst the dead on the field of battle, stripped of their clothes, from Wednesday the day of our unfortunate engagement, till three o'clock in the afternoon of Friday, when he sent detachments to kill all those who were still in life. A great many, who had resisted the effects of the continual rains which fell all that time, were then despatched. He ordered a barn, which contained many of the wounded Highlanders, to be set on fire and the soldiers stationed round it drove back with fixed bayonets the unfortunate men who attempted to save themselves, into the flames, burning them alive in this horrible manner, if they had not been fellow-creatures.[148]

Jacobite propaganda which appeared in late 1746 showed this incident and Jacobites thereafter were convinced that the burning building atrocity happened. Later in the century, 'a gentleman of great veracity who was a captain in Ogilvy's first battalion' who was 'very young' and 'full of knowledge of it' gave an account to a younger man. Yet the latter could only write: 'I have tried to find out what wounded gentlemen were burnt next morning [presumably the morning after the battle] in a house near the field, but I can only get authenticated five, but there were many more in the house.'[149] Sir John Wedderburn (son of the above named gentleman) in 1792 recounted how 'Menzies of Suen and Stewart of Rynachan, wounded, were in the house that was ordered to be burned next morning with the wounded people in it'.[150] There seems to be some doubt when this incident occurred – some claiming it was on 18 April, others that it occurred on 17 April.

How reliable were these memories, recorded over forty years later? Even the sympathetic Wedderburn had to record, 'It is surprising with what Difficulty I have got any intelligence to be depended upon . . . their memory very good but some mistaken as to numbers.'[151] The veracity of this is questionable, since neither Elcho nor Johnstone were eye witness to these events, having fled the battle after it was lost. Perhaps they were relating second-hand accounts given by fellow Jacobites. Stories later collected refer to soldiers bayoneting or clubbing wounded Jacobites to death. Some of these are exaggerated or questionable at least. Certainly the incident of the barn which was set afire is not proven. The Revd Thomas Birch was given 'an absolute confutation of this most improbable story' from two men who were at the battle.[152] Captain Kinnier of Munro's, who had been injured in the battle, told what he knew:

He avers that to his certain knowledge none of the wounded rebels were carried to that house, that only a few of the common soldiers of the Rebels were there and two sergeants, but not one ensign, nor any of the superior rank. He adds that not one of these had received any hurt and that they did not remain in the house above two hours.[153]

The building where this was supposed to have taken place was 'the Red Barn' Yet this building was built after Culloden and there is no archaeological evidence to suggest an atrocity. Although the incident described may have taken place elsewhere, the case for it ever having happened has not been proved.[154]

For what it is worth, Charles Edward Stuart, who was also not present as an eye witness, was credited with the following view:

> He seemed unwilling to give credit to the horrid narrative of men being massacred in cold blood, after victory had declared for the army commanded by the Duke of Cumberland. He could not allow himself to think that a general could be so barbarous.[155]

It is worth noting that one atrocity story is certainly false. Cumberland is alleged to have ordered an officer to kill one Charles Fraser, a wounded Jacobite:

> The gentleman lying on the ground was young Inverallachy. It was told by the sogars that one officer of distinction and then another were ordered by C-d to shoot that man, which they refused to do, C-d inquird a common sogar if his gun was chargd. He replying it was, C-d ordered to shoot that man, which he did.[156]

A later version names the officer in question. Here Cumberland orders, 'Wolfe, shoot me that Highland scoundrel who dares looks on us with such contempt and insolence.' The future conqueror of Quebec is alleged to have answered thus, 'My commission is at His Royal Highness' disposal, but I never can consent to become an executioner.'[157] A few points can be made here. First, to disobey a direct order on the field of battle was a grave military offence and would have been taken before a court martial. Wolfe was not court martialled. Secondly, Wolfe makes no reference to this incident in the letters he wrote about the battle and has nothing but praise for his commander. In the following years, Wolfe rose to the rank of Major-General, which, had there been any animosity between him and the Captain General of the army, would have been very unlikely. Thirdly, the latter story dates from 1794 and from an unknown provenance.

A Highland officer in the Duke's army when asked about alleged atrocities said 'he never heard of the rebels being thus killed in cold blood, which, being a thing very uncommon, he thought his men could not miss to observe and tell him of it'.[158]

Yet there is clearly some truth in the Jacobite statements, which are backed up by those on the opposing side. According to Henderson, a Whiggish historian:

> The Field was clear, and the victory being Compleat, the soldiers, warm in their Resentment, did Things hardly to be accounted for; several of the wounded Men were stabbed, yea, some who were lurking in Houses, were taken out and shot upon the Field, tho' others were saved, by those whose Compassion was raised at the sight of so many Victims.[159]

Henderson explained this conduct partly by attributing it to the 'No quarter orders' allegedly given to the Jacobite army, but also to the troops' rage at the Highlanders for previous atrocities. He wrote:

> the Rebels had enraged the Troops, their Habit was strange, their Language still stranger, and their way of fighting was shocking to the utmost Degree: The Rebellion was unprovoked, and the King's Troops had greatly suffered by it; the Fields of Preston [pans] and Falkirk, were fresh in their memory, they had lost a Gardner, a Whitney, a Munro besides other officers . . . their mangled corpses could not but stir up the soldiers to revenge. Therefore, if, when they found Vengeance in their Power; they violated the stricter Rules of Humanity, some allowance ought to be made for the Passion they were inspire with at that time.[160]

An officer in Munro's wrote 'Our Regiment had ample revenge for the loss of our late colonel [Sir Robert Munro] . . . not one that attack'd us escaped alive.'[161]

In a similar vein, Hughes wrote: 'This Rebel Host had been deeply in Debt to the Publick for all their Rapin, Murder and Cruelty; and since the Time was now come to pay off the Score, our people were all glad to clear the Reckoning, and heartily determined to give them a Receipt in full.'[162] Wolfe wrote 'as few prisoners were taken of the Highlanders as possible'.[163]

A contemporary journal added:

> it will be remembered, that a considerable sacrifice was made of

common lives in that heat of Vengeance which could not be prevented in Troops that had so much Reason to be enrag'd.[164]

It is also worth pointing out that even wounded enemy soldiers still pose a potential danger to the victors. The latter were taking no chances. Furthermore, the stress of combat and the sight of their comrades being killed often leads troops to savage acts, especially if their enemies have been resolute in the fight. Killing instincts are not simply turned off.[165] As one contemporary noted 'the obstinacy of the Rebels, who, as they lay wounded on the Ground, fired many pistol-shots at the soldiers as they passed by them, which obliged the latter for their own security, to dispatch them out of the way'.[166]

Bystanders, perhaps not so innocent, were also caught up in the pursuit. Hughes later wrote: 'many of the inhabitants, not doubting of success, who came out of curiosity to see the Action, or perhaps to get plunder, never went home again to tell the story; for their being mixt with their own people, we could not know one from another'.[167]

There is no doubt that the soldiers were exasperated at their foe. Linn wrote, 'We waded to the knees in Mud & Dirt through the Moor Severall times that day with a good will to be att them, & no Wonder, considering the fatigues we have undergone this Winter by hunger & cold & Marching, night & day, after them.'[168] Some soldiers were angry about the deaths of their comrades and senior officers in this and other battles in the campaign; Oman referred to Lord Robert Kerr, of Barrell's battalion, 'being among the slain at Culloden'.[169] A contemporary historian notes 'Our Troops . . . embraced this Occasion to revenge their late disgrace at Preston Pans and Falkirk'.[170]

There was another alleged reason for the killing after the battle was over. One controversy was the 'discovery' in a pocket of one of the Jacobite prisoners of the following order:

It is his royal highness' positive orders, that every person attach himself to some corps of the army, and remain with the corps night and day, until the battle and pursuit be finally over, and to give no quarter to the elector's troops, on no account whatsoever. This regards the foot as well as horse. The order of battle is to be given to every general officer and every commander of a regiment or squadron.

It is required and expected of each individual in the army, as well officer as soldier, that he keep the post he shall be allotted, and if any man turn his back to run away, the next behind such man is to shoot him.

No body, upon pain of death, is to strip the slain, or plunder until the battle is over. The highlanders to be in kilts, and no body to throw away their guns.

Sign'd

Geo. Murray, Lt. Gen.

In another version of this order, the 'no quarter' sentence is omitted.[171] This document was given wide publicity, being printed in most newspapers, but was it genuine?

It was certainly believed to be so by those in the victorious army. Wolfe, who was on Hawley's staff, later wrote, 'The Rebels, besides, their natural Inclinations, had orders not to give quarter to our men. We had an opportunity of avenging ourselves for that and many other things; and indeed we did not neglect it.'[172] Oman wrote a week after the battle, 'Some of their orderly books being found their mock Prince gave out in orders not to give Quarter to the English, which [would] have caused a great many lives to be taken, they were positively sure of the victory, and regretted nothing.'[173]

Arthur, Lord Balmerino (1688–1746), a Jacobite, when on the scaffold for high treason in August 1746, attested:

I think myself bound upon this occasion to contradict a report which has been industriously spread and which I never heard of till I was a prisoner, 'That orders were given to the prince's army to give no quarters at the battle of Culloden' . . . I do declare that it is without all manner of foundation; both because it is impossible it could have escap'd the knowledge of me, who was Captain of the Prince's Life-guards . . . but still much more so because it is entirely inconsistent with the mild and generous nature of that brave Prince . . . I believe rather that this report was spread to palliate and excuse the murders they themselves committed in cold blood after the battle of Culloden.[174]

A contemporary historian declared: 'But if such a cruel order was ever given, it is scarce possible it could be known so soon after the battle'.[175]

Lord Bury, who had been sent by Cumberland to inform the King of the news, was put to task on this matter. According to Hastings:

He was attacked last Thursday at the masquerade by several masks who asked him questions in broad Scotch. Did the Duke make order that no quarters should be given? To which he answered, No, but, that, their men knowing the day before the action the orders of the rebel generals, [he] believed they gave the rebels no quarter; and that for his own part as long as he wore a sword he never would give quarter in the field of battle to a rebel.[176]

A Highland officer asked some sergeants about this order; one claimed he had heard of it, but others had not, and the officer 'found less reason to believe there ever was any such order'.[177] According to Walpole, Lord Kilmarnock was asked,

> 'do you know anything of the resolution taken in our army, the day before the battle of Culloden, to put the English prisoners to death?' He replied, 'My Lord, I was not present; but since I came hither, I have had all the reason in the world to believe that there was such an order taken; and I hear the Duke had the pocket book with the order.'[178]

The Jacobite troops were certainly given an order which was very similar, as one later wrote, when preparations for the night march were being made:

> We were likewise forbid in the attack to make use of our firearms, but only of sword, dirk and bayonet, to cut the tent strings and pull down the poles, and where we observed a swelling or bulge in the fallen tent there to stick and push vigorously.[179]

During a night attack in the American War of Independence, Captain Patrick Ferguson wrote: 'It being a night attack, little quarter could be given, so there was only five prisoners.'[180] Clearly, the Jacobite army's command had had no qualms about contemplating a massacre of their foes, which sheds a more sinister light on their method of making war.

It is probable that the order refers to the action that the Jacobite troops should make when they reached Cumberland's camp on the night march, as it is unlikely that such orders would have been written on the hectic morning of the battle. But they would not have become known to the regular troops until after the fighting was over. They may serve as a retrospective excuse for the actions of some, but could not be a motivating factor in those actions. Henderson's explanation of the soldiers' behaviour is probably close to the truth.

Yet there is more controversy. On the following day, Cumberland issued the following order:

> A Capt[ain] & 50 men to march immediately to the field of Battle & search all cottages in the neighbourhood for Rebels. The officer &

men will take notice that the publick orders of the Rebels yesterday were to give no quarter.[181]

This is capable of two interpretations. It could mean that Cumberland was giving his men the wink that they were to do to the Jacobites what they would have done to them. An anonymous letter published by the Revd Forbes states, 'parties were ordered to go and search for the wounded in houses in the neighbourhood of the field, to carry them to the field, and there to kill them, which they did'.[182] Yet we do not know who wrote this and what his authority was. Or it could have been a warning to his men that they were facing a dangerous and deadly foe who had yet to admit defeat. Yet one letter written after Culloden claimed 'A day or two after the battle, large detachments were sent out, who killed some and brought on several prisoners.'[183] It is also worth noting that to send troops back to a battlefield was not uncommon. Johnstone recalled returning to the battlefield of Falkirk on the following day, for instance.[184]

Wedderburn recounted another story, the veracity of which is regrettably ambiguous:

> Captain Grossett on horseback met an officer and party going next morning with orders to put to death all wounded men in the field, & upon hearing their business said he would go with them, accordingly being higher than them he showed them some wounded men laying among the heather, one of which called to him for water, upon which Grossett called a soldier to bayonet him. The wounded man, on seeing what they were about lifted up a gun lying there and shot Grossett. I wish this story could be authenticated.[185]

One Ranald MacDonald was among the wounded. He later recalled:

> They were just presenting their firelocks to his own breast when he was saved through the clemency of Lieutenant Hamilton who, if he remembers, belonged to Cholmondely's regiment, and took him to a neighbouring country house.[186]

According to Hughes, other orders were made directly afterwards. One was to make 'strict search in houses for arms' and Lieutenant-Colonel Cockayne was sent with 500 soldiers 'in quest of them that should be found lurking after the battle'.[187] Yet it is not certain that widespread indiscriminate slaughter occurred. Linn makes no mention of it and although he wrote 'we send out every day Strong parties of foot & horse', he added '& they bring in great heaps of prisoners every day'.[188]

The wounded were not neglected. An order of the day read 'A Detachment of a subaltern & 20 men per Regt. To go with the empty carts to ye Field of Battel & bring in ye wounded men and arms'.[189] On the following day, Findlater gave '12 guineas to the men that were wounded yesterday in the Battle, which is to be laid out by the surgeon of the hospital in providing to them both'.[190] On 18 April, the wounded were seen to. A lieutenant and thirty men were to scour the battlefield concerning the 'wounded men in that neighbourhood'. A sergeant and six men were to 'take up all the wounded men'. Others were to visit all the houses and bring the wounded from them and into the hospitals.[191]

It has been argued that the killing of wounded Jacobites was the work of the 'Vestry Men'. These were not regular soldiers, but criminals or unemployed men pressed into the forces by magistrates. There is no evidence that they were responsible for such actions. In fact, if such activity did occur, it was more usual for it to be the work of veteran soldiers who were used to harsher conditions of warfare, and certainly most of Cumberland's troops had such experience.[192]

Historians have also contrasted the humanity of the Jacobites after Prestonpans towards the wounded regulars with the 'merciless' treatment meted out to the former when the tables were turned. We need to remember that, as campaigns become longer, both sides become more ruthless and the earlier chivalry is rarely seen. The Jacobites are not known for their clemency towards their defeated enemies after Falkirk, for instance. Too many disappointments and too much blood had already been shed for that.

The lesser crime of looting from the defeated took place. Clothing from the dead Jacobite officers was taken and worn by some of the victorious troops. A letter from Inverness noted 'Soldiers, who are strutting about in rich laced waist coats, hats, &c.' Men were given a shilling for each sword they brought in, two shillings and six pence per musket and sixteen guineas for each Jacobite standard.[193]

It has sometimes been argued that Culloden was not a decisive battle and that what killed off Jacobitism as a political force were other factors, such as the moral degeneration of Charles Stuart, the weakening of the clan system, the disinclination of France and the English Jacobites to support the cause and the accession of George III. Undoubtedly all these long-term factors played a part, though they would not be obvious to contemporaries. But it can hardly be doubted that Culloden was the most important battle of the Forty Five as it destroyed the Jacobite field army and persuaded its leader that the campaign was at an end. Notably, the final Jacobite schemes of restoring the Stuarts, which occurred in the 1750s, centred around England, not Scotland.

Cumberland was in no doubt about the battle. On 18 April, he wrote:

> I had the honour to acquaint His Majty. The 16. by Lord Bury of the compleat Victory we gained that Day over the Rebels; I must own I never expected They would have had the impudence to risk a General Engagement, but they having burnt down Fort Augustus the day before, convinced me They intended to stand.[194]

His soldiers agreed with him. Private Taylor was writing on the day after Culloden,

> so compleat a victory . . . We are now here encamped and I hope soon to be South again, most of our work now been over, except among the Highlands and taking them that have escaped . . . And it is my opinion his Royal Highness will use Lenity to all, but Nonjurant Episcopal Ministers who all thinking parts of Scotland must own to be the Nursers and Formers of this and all Rebellions since the Revolution.[195]

Bradshaw agreed, writing, 'In short, 'tis mine and every bodies' opinion no history can brag of so singular a victory.'[196] Colonel Yorke wrote 'I flatter myself that this is the last time blood will be shed in the field by fellow subjects of this island'.[197] According to Richard Webb, 'they have not had such a threshing since the Days of Old Noll [Oliver Cromwell]'.[198]

Conclusion

Culloden was unusual in battles of this era (the defeat of Charles XII's Swedish army at Poltava in 1709 by Peter I's Russians, the surrender of the Jacobite army at Preston in 1715 and the defeat of Monmouth at Sedgemoor in 1685 are other examples) because it was so conclusive. Even Marlborough's dazzling victories in 1704–9 had not resulted in a decisive allied victory. One army had not only defeated its opponents in the field, but had routed them and had also been able to inflict such heavy casualties on the fleeing enemy that it ceased to exist as a fighting force. The regulars not only outnumbered the Jacobites but their firepower was far more deadly and their morale, unlike at Prestonpans and Falkirk, held. The Jacobites had very little, if any, chance of victory at Culloden. Yet the only alternative to battle was the break-up of the army because of the supply crisis.

But what happened after the battle? Although the pursuit of the cavalry and their hacking down fleeing Jacobites was deadly enough (and probably accounted for most of the Jacobite casualties), it was no more than routine work for cavalry once an enemy broke and ran. Often, of course, cavalry were prevented from this by having an enemy who left the field in good order – as Cumberland's army did at Fontenoy. But here, the cavalry who had seen little action were fresh and their enemy tired and all but defenceless. The victorious Jacobites at Prestonpans and Falkirk had felt no compunction in doing the same, it should be remembered. Nor is it likely they would have been more merciful had the night march before Culloden succeeded.

What is more controversial is what happened to the Jacobite wounded. Certainly not all were killed. Some were taken prisoner, but the total was only about 154 (perhaps a tenth or less of total Jacobite casualties), excluding the French prisoners of war. Some of the wounded were certainly killed by the regular infantry after the battle ended. How many were slain in such a manner is impossible to know. Although there was no known order from Cumberland to do so, and indeed, he makes no reference to it, nor did anyone else (except Jacobites), he did not do anything to stop it. Soldiers such as Wolfe seem to have had no qualms about dealing thus. As Henderson remarked, the soldiers were angry and exasperated by their foes and took this opportunity to have their revenge. This was bloody, but it is not impossible to understand it, though it did give the Jacobite propaganda machine wonderful ammunition.

Chapter 6

Operations around Inverness, April–May 1746

*I cannot but be affected with great Grief and Concern, when I observe
that the Jacobites appeared to be no ways dismayed or humbled by the
late Defeat of the Rebel army.[1]*

The battle of Culloden was over, but did that spell the end of the campaign?
The contest was not yet quite done with. Cumberland had to ensure that the
Jacobite army ceased to exist as a fighting force, that it was dispersed and
disarmed and that its members surrendered. He also needed, as far as possible,
to take steps to prevent the outbreak of another insurrection.

An immediate observation was made by Private Linn, 'I hope by the
Assistance of God almighty that the heart of the Rebellion is broke & that they
will not be able to rally any more.'[2] A month later, on 22 May, Newcastle wrote
to Viscount Irwin in Yorkshire:

> As to our public affairs I thank God they go tolerably well everywhere
> but in Flanders . . . His Royal Highnesses' unexampled conduct and
> bravery has retrieved the honour of our troops and restored peace to
> this kingdom. We must now endeavour to make such use of this great
> event by regulating affairs in Scotland and punishing the rebels as
> may prevent the like rebellion in the future.[3]

The army's work, though, was not at an end. Cumberland had already
remarked to Newcastle before Culloden that two strategies were needed to
stamp out Jacobitism. He now told him on 23 April:

> I really believed that a month or 6 weeks will inable me to do all that
> will be necessary to the military & I would to God that I could be in
> town *to explain a number of things that cant be explained by writing*
> [original emphasis]. If we had destroyed every man of them, such is

the very soil that rebellion would sprout out again if a new system of government is not found out for this country . . . I believe the greatest blow to the Jacobites in this country would be to move the judiciary courts from Edinburgh to Glasgow for the former is the heart of rebellion.[4]

Could the italicized phrase imply that Cumberland either had or was contemplating a massacre of Jacobites? Some historians have implied that this was so, but it is far from certain and must remain another mystery. As was noted in Chapter 4, Cumberland had no qualms about writing his mind to Newcastle, so this comment probably does not have any sinister connotation. He may felt discretion was necessary in case the letter was seen by political foes. He also seems to have believed that judicial and administrative change was the key, not mass slaughter.

He certainly thought that firmness was crucial. A week later he told Newcastle: 'The Jacobite rebellious principle is so rooted in this nation's mind that this generation must be pretty well wore out, before this country will be quiet'.[5] The means to this end were explained to General Campbell on 13 May: 'What remains will be to distress the rebels by all the ways & means possible to bring them to a total submission to His Majesty's mercy.' Campbell was instructed to 'make incursions into the country of those which have not brought in their arms'. In particular, the focus was to be on the Camerons, the first significant supporters of Charles.[6]

Although the Jacobite army had suffered a decisive defeat at Culloden, this did not automatically mean that the struggle was over. As we have seen, perhaps about 2,000–3,000 Jacobite soldiers were absent from the battle. Charles Edward Stuart and some of his senior officers had escaped the stricken field. But, as Elcho remarked, perhaps with the wisdom of hindsight, 'they should have arranged a rendezvous in case of defeat'.[7] Colonel Yorke agreed with this assessment that there were no contingency plans as to what the Jacobite army should do after the battle, whatever the result.[8]

However, the fight had gone out of their leader. According to Johnstone, Charles was 'in a state of complete dejection, without the least hopes of being able to re-establish his affairs . . . and had abandoned every other project but that of escaping to France as soon as possible'.[9] Others were not so downcast. According to Johnstone, Elcho

represented to him that this check was nothing, as was really the case, and exerted himself to the utmost to persuade him to think only of rallying his army, putting himself at its head, and trying once more the fortune of war, as the disaster might be easily repaired. But he was sensible to all his Lordship could suggest, and utterly disregarded his advice.[10]

Charles and a number of cavalry and officers had gone to Stratharick, where 'he order'd them all to go to Ruthven of Badenoch, where he would Send them orders'.[11]

Yet, according to O'Sullivan, Charles had not entirely given up the struggle at this point. Not only does he not refer to any of the despair which Johnstone emphasizes, but on 17 April he went on the road towards Fort Augustus

> where he expected to make a head, & yt the most part of those yt country wou'd joyn or assemble. But having waited near Forte Augustus till about two hours of day, & not finding a soul, nor meeting any mortel yt cou'd give him any accts, went to Glengarry's house.

Yet he soon afterwards 'foresaw there cou'd be no considerable body of the army assembled to make a head any where'.[12]

Johnstone was of the opinion that further resistance was possible. Apart from the need for fearlessness and firmness in misfortune, he pointed to other factors. Because many men had not been engaged in the battle, the Jacobite army could recover. Cluny's McPhersons, some 500 strong, and other Highlanders, gathered at Ruthven. Johnstone was convinced that in eight days' time, their strength would be recovered and they would be able to defeat Cumberland's forces.[13] Johnstone later wrote 'I am morally certain that, in the course of ten or twelve days, we should have been in a condition to return to Inverness and fight the Duke of Cumberland.'[14]

He also considered the possibility of 'partisan warfare'. Johnstone believed that in the Highlands, a small number of men could hold off far larger numbers. Secondly, he argued that the number of cattle in the Highlands would be enough to supply these guerrilla fighters. He could not understand why this method of continuing the struggle was not tried, believing in no compromise: the Jacobites had to 'conquer or die'.[15]

The Jacobites at Ruthven included the wounded Perth and Lord George Murray, but despite initial hopes – John Daniel wrote 'At first we had great hopes of rallying again' – orders to the contrary arrived.[16] Charles sent Thomas Sheridan with orders 'that they might disperse and every body Shift for himself the best way he Could'.[17]

Charles was advised by Lord Lovat 'not to quit the Country, but Stay and gather together again his Scatter'd forces'. But according to Elcho, he was convinced that the Scots would betray him and so, on 17 April, sent away his escort and disguised himself as a servant. His long wanderings in order to escape Scotland had begun, but even so he had hopes of his followers gathering together, in his absence, to 'defend the Country as long as possible, until Succours came to him from France', and wrote letters to his supporters to this effect on 24 April.[18]

The letter (dated 28 April) was shown by Sheridan to a number of Highland chiefs, including Lochiel. It stated:

> the only thing that can be done, is to defend your selves till the French assist you. To effectuate this, the only way is to assemble in a body as soon as possible, and then take measures for the best, which you [the Scots Jacobites] who know the Country are only Judges of. This makes me be of little use here, whereas by my going to France instantly, however dangerous it be, I will certainly engage the French Court either to assist us effectually and powerfully, or at least procure such terms as you would not obtain otherwise.

He suggested that a council of chiefs should command and that Perth and Murray would stay with the army to the last.[19] If he really believed this could work, then he was indeed an optimist. France had already sent some help to the Jacobites but only when they had a field army; now they had none, any aid was extremely unlikely. Charles had concluded that his presence was superfluous and abdicated his leadership. Yet he held out optimistic promises that the cause was not lost, even in the foreseeable future. He could not guarantee that these promises would be fulfilled, and indeed they were not, as France's attention was focused on the Continent, not on Britain. What was needed was success and this had not materialized. In a later rebellion, substantial French aid was only forthcoming after the American rebels had succeeded in defeating a British army.

It is also worth pointing out that hopes for a successful guerrilla campaign rested on two conditions. One of these was that the army had enough supplies with which to continue the struggle. As noted, the Jacobites had to fight at Culloden because the supply system had collapsed. As Napoleon allegedly remarked, 'An army marches on its stomach'. Secondly, it was dependent on the fact that the regular troops would be unable to penetrate the Highland strongholds of the Jacobites. As we will see, neither of these hopeful scenarios was tenable.

There was some succour to the Jacobites in May. Two French ships landed stores, ammunition and gold at Arisaig.[20] This amounted to 35,000 louis d'or.

Considerable controversy surrounds exactly what happened to this money. Much of it was taken by Cluny of McPherson; some by John Murray, some was taken back to France by Charles and some was stolen.[21]

How effective would a prolonged struggle have been? The Jacobite army had lost its military supplies and its food supply. Nor was there any money to pay the troops. In these circumstances, it seems very unlikely that an army could have been kept together. Even if French aid was forthcoming – a very unlikely circumstance – it would take some weeks or months to arrive. The military prospects seemed bleak, at best. Yorke thought there could be no refuge in the mountains, writing:

> The truth of all this they will find it difficult to make good when our Red Coats appear in the heart of their county; nor will all my Lord Lovat's absurd cunning . . . be able to prove our absence when our bayonets glitter in their eyes, or are buried in their bodies. They have no meal for love or money in the country; their only support is cattle, the blood of which dried they make use of as bread.[22]

Even so, there was concern that the Jacobites were still in armed bodies and so dangerous. Bland wrote on 12 May, 'It is incumbent on us all to be alert, and not suffer ourselves to be surprised'. He thought that the Jacobites' only hope was to surprise the regulars.[23] Ferguson thought the danger not insignificant, 'the Rebels have gathered in a body again to the number of 4,000 and are in great spirits with their Prince at their head'.[24] Lord Glenorchy of Taymouth, writing on 3 May, informed Yorke that this was the case. According to him,

> 200 Macgregors went through in broad daylight, to my great mortification, that I did not expect it nor had arms to oppose so many. They went . . . into their own country of Balquhidder where they . . . endeavour to conceal themselves . . . They ought to be extirpated from thence, being the most pernicious race of mankind in being.[25]

Fletcher retailed the news on 19 May that 'They talk of assembling at Strontian, in Lunart, & to keep a body moving, to harass our troops, in hopes to obtain terms & try to persuade the people that the Pretender's son, is to return with a greater force, but yt gains no credit even among the rebels themselves.'[26]

There were other Jacobites in Lochaber. As Ray wrote, 'The Rebels being now dispersed all over the Highlands, and skulking in secret corners.'[27] Glengyle had 120 armed men at his back, retreating from Sutherland, and aiming for Balquhidder. Lord Pitsligo and some of the infantry were at Buchan, seeking passage to France. Charles himself, with Perth and Cameron of Lochiel, was thought to be at large in the latter's country. There was talk that the McLeans were planning to assemble at Strontian and harass the regulars from there.

Unknown by the loyalists, plans for further resistance were being formed among a number of Jacobite chiefs, probably encouraged by the arrival of the French gold. On 8 May, at Murlaggan in Lochaber or Badenoch, the following resolution was reached:

> We, subscribers, heads of clans, commanders and leaders, do hereby unanimously agree, and solemnly promise forthwith, with the utmost expedition, to raise in arms for the interest of His Royal Highness Charles Prince of Wales, and in defence of our country, all the able-bodied men that all and every one of us can command, or raise, within our respective interests or properties.

Their next step was to meet on 15 May at Achnacarry in the braes of Lochaber. Those to meet included the Camerons, MacDonalds, MacLeods, MacKinnons and the Appin Stewarts. They were to keep their plans to themselves and not to reveal them to any subordinates. Meanwhile, the Frasers, MacGregors, Menzies, Glenlyons were to assemble at Rannoch and the Atholl men were to go to the braes of Mar. Pitsligo and the Farquharsons were to meet and agree on a suitable rendezvous with the others. Cluny of MacPherson was to tell the Mackintoshes of the resolution to continue the struggle. They were all to raise their men and organize them into regiments and corps, and to enforce strict discipline by hanging deserters.

The final resolution was:

> We further promise and engage ourselves each to the other, to stand and abide by these our resolutions, for the interest of His Royal Highness, and the good of our country, which we apprehend to be inseparable, to the last drop of our blood; and never to lay down our arms, or make a separate peace, without the general consent of the whole. And in case any one engaged in this association sh'd make separate terms for himself, he shall be looked upon as a traitor to his Prince, and treated as an enemy.[28]

Cameron of Lochiel was one of the principal leaders. He wrote to Cluny on 13 May to tell him 'We are preparing for a summer campaign, and so hope soon to join all our forces'. He instructed Cluny to send along any stragglers from Lord John Drummond's regiment or any men from any other regiments which he found in his country. Any money should also be sent. But there were the same difficulties which had presented themselves before Culloden, as Lochiel observed, 'I have scarcely a sufficiency of meal to secure myself and the gentlemen who are with me, for 4 days, and can get none to purchase in this country.'[29] Thus, several weeks after Culloden, the military threat from the Jacobites still existed.

Captain Scott, at Fort William, had an inkling of what was afoot, and told Colonel Napier that the Jacobites were gathering – Camerons, Frasers and MacPhersons – and were sending messages for others to join them; threatening any who did not help.[30] Meanwhile, Cumberland received a free hand over what he should do next. To give a field commander discretionary powers in a fluid situation was not unusual; Wade had been given similar instructions in the previous year. Newcastle, who had absolute trust in the King's son, told Cumberland on 23 May:

> I have nothing to command from His Majesty to suggest to your Royal Highness, relating to the disposition of the Regular Troops, or the Highland Companies, His Majesty being convinced, by experience, that your Royal Highness needs no Directions, to enable you to do what is most for His Majesty's Service.[31]

There was no shortage of advice as to how to deal with the Jacobites. An anonymous correspondent was convinced that the Jacobites were 'fully persuaded that an opportunity will soon be afforded them, to push their affair with greater success, than they have hitherto had'. He suggested that Episcopal meeting houses should all be shut unless King George was explicitly prayed for there. This, after all, was in the terms of the Toleration Act of 1712 which allowed their existence only if the reigning monarch was acknowledged. Any minister who did not pray thus should be dismissed, as 'all these meetings are nurseries of Jacobitism'. Again, this was not an unreasonable observation as most Jacobite clans were Episcopalian. Estates of Jacobite clans should be sold and the power of the clans diminished, and with it, Highland language and dress.[32] These were to form the basis of the legislation eventually passed in the next few years.

A contrast is usually made between Duncan Forbes, an alleged 'moderate', and the 'brutal' Cumberland. An oft quoted remark from a Jacobite source is:

> When his lordship [Forbes] was paying his levee to the Duke of
> Cumberland at Inverness, he thought fit (as it well became his char-
> acter and station) to make mention of the laws of the country, etc. To
> which the Duke of Cumberland was pleased to say, 'The Laws of the
> Country, my Lord! I'll make a brigade give laws, by G-D!'[33]

Cumberland's authentic correspondence ran rather differently. Indeed, he
wrote of Forbes:

> We are vastly fond of one another, but I fear it wont last as he is as
> arrant Highland made as Lord Stair, or Crauford, he wishes for lenity
> if it can be done with safety, which he thinks but I don't, for they
> really think, that when once they are dispersed it is of no more con-
> sequence than a London mob.[34]

He also wrote of Forbes, 'he has given such convincing proofs of his affection,
and zeal, diligence and activity'.[35]

Forbes wrote of the Duke, some weeks later, 'his patience, which surprises
in such Years, is equal to his fire, & in probability will do very great service
to the public'.[36] Forbes's comments on how to deal with the Jacobites are also
worth noting. Although he did argue 'Unnecessary severitys create pity . . .
nurse to disaffection', he also observed:

> No severity that is necessary ought to be dispensed with. The omit-
> ting such severitys cruelty to the kingdom . . . No reasonable person
> can think that the punishment of the leaders of this fierce and
> desperate rebellion sever, since the abuse of the lenity shewn in the
> prosecution of the last rebellion aggravates their guilt.[37]

The reality was that Cumberland and Forbes had more in common than has
sometimes been portrayed.

Cumberland may have recalled the precedent of the rebellion of 1715,
where there had been no final decisive battle and the Jacobite army melted
away shortly after James Francis had departed for France. Cumberland was
concerned that Jacobitism in Scotland had not been expunged then and while
its adherents had retained their arms, the danger remained. Therefore, to
disarm the clans was a step of paramount importance, though such steps had
been ineffectually attempted in 1716. As a proclamation given at Inverness on
1 May stated:

It having been represented to me, that numbers of the rebels, after the overthrow they met with in the late battle of Culloden, have dispersed themselves over the country, and returned to their respective homes, or to near neighbourhood of their former habitations, where they presumptuously and insolently remain in possession of those arms, with which they attempted the overthrow of the government, without having given the least marks of quitting the traitorous disposition, by which they have formerly been guided . . . [38]

Cumberland told Newcastle, 'I have also taken the liberty to make use of the power granted me by His Majesty, in issuing a proclamation for the seizing of rebels and arms . . . I shall send to all the shires and counties.'[39] His answer was to instruct the civil officers of Scotland; the sheriffs, stewards and their deputies, the magistrates of the boroughs, the justices of the peace and all other law officers, to search for all those involved in the rebellion who had not given up their arms, as per the previous proclamation of February, and have them arrested. They were to work in conjunction with the ministers of the Church of Scotland, who had been involved in the previous proclamation. Anyone who harboured Jacobites was also to be seized for later trial.

Many Scots did indeed take advantage of the chance to surrender their arms and to receive a pardon. According to *The Gentleman's Magazine*:

Upon the 13th Inst., Alex. McDonald of Glenco surrendered his arms, and those of all his people who were at Glenco, to Maj. Gen. Campbell, submitting himself to His Majesty's mercy: Appin's people who were at home, have also followed his example, and both he and Glenco have given notice thereof to such of their men as are absent, ordering them to return to their own country.[40]

Apparently, the clan chief had written thus to Campbell,

I do informe you that I am nowe very sensible of my folly and great error in taking up arms against His Majesty and resolve never to do the like while I have life and so surrender up myself as your prisoner, depending on His Majesty's clemencie and pardon.[41]

According to a contemporary newspaper:

Rebels coming in daily and laying down their arms and submitting to the King's mercy. It is particularly said that the MacDonalds of

Glengarry, and the Glencoe men, have been so wise to act that part . . . Several of the people of Badenoch . . . who were seduced and compelled by the rebels to rise in Arms with them in the present unhappy Rebellion, came to this place, conducted by the Rev. Mr William Blair, Minister of Kingussie, and John McPherson of Benchar, and delivered their arms to the Hon. Brigadier Mordaunt, and he permitted them to return home in the same manner. It is to be hoped that this precedent will be imitated by others in the same situation, that themselves and families may be saved from destruction.[42]

An anonymous volunteer with the army wrote: 'the rebels came in by hundreds daily giving up their arms (which were few, and bad enough that they brought us) and receiving protections'.[43] The Lord of Col gave up sixty-eight muskets and sixty-two bayonets.[44] Yet one Archibald Grant expressed some cynicism over such surrenders on 23 April, writing 'Great numbers of each sort are certainly hid under ground'.[45]

An exception to this rule was to be found in the case of the Grants of Glenmoriston. They did not receive such pardons. Instead, after they surrendered their arms, some of their number were shipped to London. Grant told Cumberland, 'Here are in a Number of Men come in with their Arms, who would have submitted to none in Britain but to me.' Cumberland replied, 'No! I'll let them know that they are my Father's Subjects, and must likewise submit to me.'[46] According to a Jacobite source, this was 'owing altogether to a pique the Duke of Cumberland entertained against the Laird of Grant for not raising his men in the service of the Government'. Grant had apparently tried to raise his men as a loyalist corps, but the men had refused to march unless it was to join the Jacobites. Possibly Grant was now acting thus in order to ingratiate himself with Cumberland. There were sixty-nine men, of which some were banished and others died in captivity.[47] One letter, however, suggests that Grant gave the men no such terms, telling them to go to Cumberland or have their houses burnt; this was double-checked by an officer and Cumberland concluded that the men were prisoners of war.[48] Such results, though, were not usual.

Apart from the surrender of weapons, Cumberland sought to capture Jacobites. Indeed, the emphasis after Culloden seems to have been on taking live prisoners, not killing them. Wolfe wrote to Captain Hamilton on 19 May, 'His Royal Highness . . . desires you will continue that assiduity in apprehending such as have been in open rebellion or are known abettors, and that you will be carefull to collect all proofs and accusations against them, and deliver them to Major Chaban.' He later wrote, 'if you think the attestation of

Mr Watson's warrant a sufficient proof of his having acted in a treasonable manner, you are to make yourself master of his person, and confine him at Montrose with the rest'.[49] Webb looked forward to ending the rebellion by bringing 'their Nobles in Chains and their chiefs in fetters of iron'.[50]

Such a policy certainly bore fruit. According to Ray, 'all the Gaols were soon full of Prisoners, notwithstanding the great Number that was shipped off to Newcastle'. Prisons at Montrose, Stirling, Perth and Aberdeen were also filled.[51] Fawkener attributed this large haul of prisoners to the fact that 'those who have surrendered themselves have done it merely to avoid the fatigues, hardships & continual terrors of skulking and hiding'.[52]

Prisoners were therefore an important matter to be dealt with. A general order of 20 April instructed officers to note the details of each prisoner, for these would be needed by the Judge Advocate, Mr Bruce. They were to 'goe round ye Prisoners wth him & take particular notice of each man'. Soldiers had to ensure that prisoners were put on board ships and that no man be allowed to escape.[53] Clearly matters were to be conducted legally; hence the gathering of pertinent information about the men taken.

Newcastle told Cumberland on 5 May that lists of prisoners had to be made, along with evidence and witnesses against them, as a prelude to their subsequent trials. Cumberland had already been paying attention to the matter. Fletcher was working on this matter, 'I have reason to expect that very long lists will be sent me.'[54]

The government in London did not begin to make official decisions about the prisoners until 12 May. Newcastle told Cumberland that he should

> give immediate Directions for transmitting hither, as soon as possible, an exact list of the names of the several officers and persons of note that have been committed, by your Order, to any prison in Scotland or England, with an account of the proofs against that can be brought against them; together with the names of the private men that have been taken in arms against His Majesty.[55]

The prisoners endured grim conditions. Once in gaol, they 'were in a most miserable condition, being stripped of their cloaths when taken. They were sent to prisons, and some had not wherewith to cover their nakedness. No regard had to the cryes of the wounded or to the groans of the dying.'[56] Many were hungry or became sick and were refused medical attention. When they were placed on board ships for London, conditions worsened. Many died in the cramped and vermin-ridden environment. It was alleged that sailors killed prisoners by drowning on the pretence of clearing the vermin from them.[57]

Elsewhere, 'The misery and distress of the fugitive rebels was inexpress-ible, hundreds being found dead of their wounds, and thro' hunger, at the distance of 12, 14 and even 20 miles from the field of battle.'[58]

It is worth noting that conditions in prisons were not the fault of Cumberland. Eighteenth-century prisons were not designed to house large numbers of prisoners, but small numbers. In the exceptional circumstances of the Forty Five, they were crammed full to overflowing and so conditions were even more miserable for those within their walls. It should also be clear that massacring Jacobites was not the main goal – capture was of paramount importance.

Apart from the Scottish Jacobite prisoners, there were several hundred French troops who had surrendered after Culloden. Their officers wrote a note, in the 'hope for every Thing which is to be expected from the English Generosity'.[59] They were shipped from Inverness to Newcastle on 28 April. Charles's French servants, which included a Negro, were also released from captivity.[60] These men were not deemed to be rebels, but prisoners of war and civilian servants, who were to be treated in a civilized fashion.

It was another story for those Jacobites who resisted. They were to be dealt with as if they were still at war. Wolfe told Hamilton:

> You know the manner of treating the houses and possessions of rebels in this part of the country. The same freedom is to be used where you are as has been hitherto practiced, that is seeking for them and their arms, cattle, and other things that are usually found. Those that have submitted to His Royal Highness' proclamation are to be treated as you have mentioned. The list is to be kept and their arms are to be taken from them.[61]

As previously stated, both Wolfe and Hawley believed that this meant helping themselves to their unwilling hosts' possessions, though Cumberland is not known to have personally partaken in such activities.

There had been no formal cessation of hostilities, nor could there be as the Jacobites were not viewed as being a legitimate army, but as rebels and crim-inals. Therefore, Jacobites who had not been taken already had to be captured. On 30 April, Yorke wrote 'Since the battle our time has been taken up in hunting out the Rebels who made their escape from our fury that day.' This included Charles himself. Yorke added 'When we move, we shall do our best to ferret him out, and if we can't send him to his long home, endeavour at least to rid the island of him.'[62]

After Culloden, Cumberland therefore dispatched troops against the Jacobites who had fled the immediate vicinity. Lord Sutherland and Lord

Reay employed their Scots soldiers in taking over 100 prisoners.[63] They were to be rounded up and their arms were seized.

Much use was made by Cumberland of the Scots clans loyal to the government. In late April, the Grants were sent to Mackintosh country. They had already arrested Lord Balmerino. Sutherland and his 900 men were sent to the Frasers' country. Lord Loudon and his forces, 1,300 strong, were ordered from the Isles of Skye to the Glenranalds country and to march up to Fort Augustus, where they were told to 'drive the cattel and burn the plowes of all those that either are or have been out in the rebellion and to distress them in every other way and to burn the houses of their leaders'.[64] On 8 May, Loudon's forces (eighteen companies) marched to Fort Augustus, in advance of Cumberland's main force. Bland then went with three battalions of infantry.[65]

Regular troops were also active against properties of Jacobites which were close to Inverness. The property of high-ranking Jacobites was particularly at risk. Colonel Cockayne and 500 men were sent to Lady Mackintosh's house – she was a prominent Jacobite. A number of Jacobites found there were shot, 400 cattle were taken and the lady herself captured. Mordaunt was sent with 900 men into Fraser country on 18 April, 'to attack all the rebels he may find there'. Ashe Lee wrote to Henry Fox (1705–74), Secretary at War, to tell him that they left at three in the morning of that day 'to destroy the Frazers' country, which we affected, plundered and burnt Lord Lovat's house and those on his estate'. His salmon weir was also destroyed. Anything which could be moved, including 300 bolls of oatmeal, 1,000 bottles of wine, his library valued at £1,400 and his stores of malt, were taken back to Inverness. Lee added 'We made a few prisoners'.[66] Oman wrote, without comment, 'We have burnt Lord Lovat's house and made one day's forage for the whole army, upon his ground.'[67]

Cobham's dragoons were marched to Montrose, Borve and Stonehaven in order to watch the coast there. Trooper Bradshaw looked forward to success, writing, 'We are guarding the coast that Charles may not get off. I pray God I had him in this room, and he the last of the Stuart race; it wou'd be my glory to stab the villain to the heart.'[68] Likewise Ancrum took Kerr's regiment to watch the northern coast, in particular, to Banff, Elgin and Peterhead.[69] Patrols searched villages and towns on the coast in order to locate any escaping Jacobites. All masters of merchant vessels were forbidden to receive passengers without a passport to attest their not having fought with the Jacobite army.[70]

There were diverse methods of interpreting these orders. According to Ancrum, 'Lord Strathmore has been particularly liberal in granting protections there'. Anyone with a certificate signed by a JP had been allowed to go on board ship. Ancrum took a different view on the certificates, 'to which I have taken upon me to order no regard to be had'. He also disapproved of Jacobite prisoners being allowed out on bail if they were ill – 'if these things are allowed they will soon take care all to be ill'.[71] Meanwhile, in May, transport ships were found for the Hessian troops, who were returned to Flanders.

Tough measures were to be adopted if there was any resistance. On 29 April, Cumberland wrote to Ancrum to take three regiments of dragoons to Invernesshire.

> You are to seize the persons, arms ammunition, etc., of all those who have been actors or abettors in the present Rebellion, & to cause regular Dispositions to be made against them when secured. If you should have intelligence of any Parties in arms you are to draw together such a force as you shall judge sufficient & should you meet with any Resistance, you are to put them to the sword.[72]

Another target was the Episcopal churches, whose ministers had largely supported the Jacobite cause. As an anonymous officer wrote from Aberdeen on 3 May:

> The people of the episcopal church here are all Jacobite; they pray for the pretender, and are confirmed by bishops appointed by the pretender at Rome. His royal highness, therefore, has judged very properly in suppressing all those Episcopal meeting houses, except where the clergymen appointed by English bishops have leave to officiate.[73]

Ancrum informed Newcastle on 9 May, 'Since I left Inverness I have burnt two Roman Catholic Meeting houses and five Episcopal, not forgetting the librarys of popish Jacobite books in the house of one Gordon, a priest.'[74] Elsewhere, as in Presshome in Banffshire, a priest's library was seized and taken to Cullen, where it was burnt in the market place.[75]

The Lord Justice Clerk wrote to Fawkener approvingly on 4 May on this matter:

> His Majesty took great notice of what you mention relating to the Non Juring Episcopal Meeting houses, which have for several years [been] overlooked and connived at in Scotland, and as they are generally the nurserys and schools of Jacobitism and disaffection, His

Majesty thinks it highly proper, that the laws should be put into
execution against all such Episcopal Meeting houses, where His
Majesty and His Royal Family are not prayed for according to the
usage of the Church of England.[76]

He added that the laws would be put into operation against such places.[77]

Cumberland knew that the army could only do so much, as he reiterated in
a letter of 23 April: 'It will be absolutely necessary that the new laws take place
before His Majesty's forces quit this country; and I flatter myself that within
a month or 6 weeks at longest, we shall have done all that can be done by the
military.'[78] On 19 May he wrote about 'the honour His Majesty has done me
by his approbation of the measures I have taken for the total suppression of
this unnatural rebellion & that the King's ministers have it now under their
consideration to prepare proper Bills, this session for preventing the like
mischief'.[79] Yorke agreed, writing

I long to hear you have begun to make some laws for this country,
which absolutely till this time have been without any, or governed by
the imposition of the Highland scoundrel chiefs. You must never
expect to see a total end to the rebellious spirit of this country till the
Highlanders are unclanned, undressed, effectually disarmed and
taught to speak English.[80]

There was talk of the transportation of Jacobite clans. This has often been
held against Cumberland, but this view is too simplistic. This idea was far
from novel – it had first surfaced in the aftermath of the 1689 rebellion and
Forbes wrote in 1746: 'If any method can be fallen upon, at the expence of
pardoning the least mischevious of the commons of the Highland clans, to
transport the most dangerous and active to America.'[81]

A writer in a contemporary journal argued that 'the transporting scheme
might not be amiss for some of the most guilty and obstinate among the
common people', but also that 'as to rooting out or removing a whole nation
which might be made of use in their native country, I think it would be equally
cruel and impolitic'. After all, mass transportation to the American colonies
might lead to 'the spirit of resentment remaining they may possibly be more
serviceable to the French [who held Canada], and dangerous to us, than in the
Highlands'.[82]

Chesterfield had mentioned the same idea in the previous year, 'And if I
were to direct, I would have a short Act of Parliament for the transporting to
the West Indies every man concern'd in the rebellion, and give a reward for

every one that should be apprehended and brought to transportation.'[83] A writer in one newspaper claimed 'I think they should do more, and that they [Glengarry's MacDonalds] should be sent to visit some of our Plantations.'[84]

It was therefore hardly original for Cumberland to pass on these suggestions, on 8 May, telling Newcastle:

> It is wish'd here by the well affected that some whole clans could be transported, not as slaves, but to make them colonies in the West Indies, because it is feared, & I believe with great reason, that while they remain in this island their rebellious & thievish nature is not to be kept under without an army always within reach of them.[85]

Newcastle was interested in the idea, replying thus, 'His Majesty would be glad to know in what manner it is proposed, that that should be done, whether by trial and condemnation, or by an act of Parliament for that purpose.'[86]

Cumberland replied, suggesting that the Camerons and MacDonalds could be sent across the Atlantic:

> This scheme might be put in execution, either by a citation to any individual in these clans to appear, under penalty of outlawry (as the most open Act of Treason might be proved against every one of them) or by a law passed for their being transported as there formerly was one, against all of the name of McGregor for I am sorry to say that it is my opinion was there the least occasion, they should rise again.[87]

Cumberland last referred to this issue on 27 May, but this plan was not put into operation; possibly because of the cost, possibly because many transported men might return and so render it a dead letter. It is important to note that though Cumberland considered the scheme, he was neither its originator – the Scots were – nor alone among loyalists to think it worth serious consideration. There was clearly a lack of enthusiasm among the elite for this suggestion.

We now turn to the soldiers in Cumberland's army. Once Cumberland reached Inverness over 200 prisoners taken by the Jacobites and held in unpleasant conditions were released. Other former soldiers had no cause to be happy. Linn writes, unfortunately without comment, 'We have about 100 of our Deserters that Deserted from our Army in fflanders taken prisoners that fought against us in the Battle & they are all to be hanged, & they are a hanging of them every day.'[88]

Yet Linn exaggerated. A number of army deserters who had joined the Jacobites and had been taken after Culloden were tried by court martial at Inverness and thirty-six were hanged between 20 April and 13 May. This was almost a third of those men hanged for participation in the rebellion. Desertion was a capital offence under the Articles of War, so this is hardly surprising. After the battle of Preston in 1715, four officers were executed for having deserted and joined the Jacobites.[89]

Yet the majority of deserters were not hanged. Twelve were transported, ten were released or discharged, about twenty-two were probably returned to their units.[90] This magnamious – or pragmatic – approach was probably due to Cumberland. According to Henderson, 'When his Highness came to hear of these frequent executions, he interposed his authority, and commanded that a report should be made to him before executing the sentence.'[91] Trained soldiers were not to be squandered without good reason. Once an example had been made of some, the others could be, and were, reprieved in order to fight the King's enemies in another campaign.

Apart from Jacobites and deserters, the soldiers themselves had to be kept under control. A string of orders was issued at Inverness to this effect in the following weeks. These were particularly necessary because parties of soldiers had to be sent out against the Jacobites, for whom they felt little love. For instance on 19 April, the following order was issued, 'It is His Royal Highness' orders yt no man goes above a quarter of a mile out of camp, several outrages & disorders having been committed which he will not permit on any account.'[92]

Loyalist and Jacobite estates and property were equally in danger. On 17 April there was a general order stating 'The Estate of Lord Provost Forbes in this Neighbourhood not to be damaged, specially the King's Mills' and on the following day, a sergeant and twelve men were sent to the King's Mills 'to prevent any further disorders'. Yet another order ran to a similar effect on 25 April, officers being responsible that 'neither plundering nor disorders are committed & avoid Forageing the corn belonging to the Lord President, or other loyal persons'. Country people bringing supplies in to the army were not to be molested.[93] A distinction was made between Jacobites and non-Jacobites, Loudon telling General Campbell that Cumberland 'would have you for the present not to disarm those countries which belong to the King's friends, but only such as are possessed by rebels'.[94]

Fletcher had been told by some 'known to be well affected to His majesty' that four quartermasters from St George's dragoons had in early May 'threatened to dispossess [them] . . . & turn the cattle off the Grounds and put their horses in their place'. The petitioners' cattle would suffer if they were taken off their present grazing grounds and alternative pasture could have been found for the dragoons' horses.[95]

In order to avoid plundering, the troops had to be kept together in camp. An order of 17 April stated: 'The men to be kept together in camp . . . no plundering on any account except by order & in Presence of an officer'. No man was to be outside the camp after nine and patrols were to 'prevent disorders and to take up all stragglers'. There were also instructions about not gambling. These were not merely words. When men from Pulteney's battalion and a Campbell were discovered plundering several days later, they were court martialled. Men returning to the camp had to be searched. On 2 May,

> The battmen & officers servants of every regiment that foraged yesterday are to be searched immediately & if any bedding, bedclothes, wearing apparell, or anything else that has the appearance of plunder to be found on any if them, they are to be confined.

On 3 May, Roger Weigh of Wolfe's battalion was ordered to receive 1,200 lashes 'for morauding & stealing of meal'. Thomas Webb and Caleb Shaw of Sackville's received 500 each for stealing meal, and several other men received similar sentences for theft. Officers could also be punished by having their pay stopped for making false returns about men being absent from camp.[96]

As time went by, senior officers were feeling frustrated and wished to return to 'real' campaigning on the Continent. Hawley wrote on 30 April, 'this Rebellion is, I think, quite crushed and His Majesty's enemys quite dispersed for some few years, at least, and not the least prospect of any more military action & since a different scene is now going to be acted here, in which I am not at all well versed'.[97] Likewise, a fortnight later, Cumberland wrote 'Tis impossible to express the impatience I am in to hear from Flanders.'[98] But despite such wishes, their work in Scotland was not yet over.

Preparations were under foot to shift the centre of operations to Fort Augustus. Cumberland intended to go there with the Argyll militia, eleven battalions of infantry and Kingston's Horse. Boats on Loch Ness were sought. He left for Fort Augustus on 24 May.[99] This was certainly in order that the Jacobites still in arms could be dealt with. A more severe part of the campaign was about to begin.

It is worth pointing out that Cumberland had the full support of the government. Newcastle, with whom he had been in constant communication, wrote to him on 12 May:

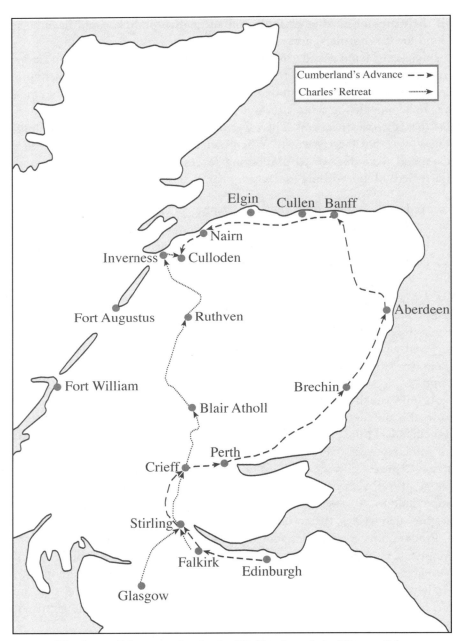

The focus of the campaign in the Highlands and the Western Isles,
May–July 1746

I have now the Honour to acquaint your Royal Highness with His Majesty's entire Approbation of the measures your Royal Highness is taking for completing the good work you have so successfully begun, by the total suppression of this unnatural rebellion and the re-establishment of the peace and tranquillity of the kingdom.[100]

It is also interesting to note that, on about 20 May, a memorandum was sent to Cumberland with the following ominous message: 'No severity that is necessary ought to be dispensed with, the omitting such severity, is cruelty to the King and the kingdom.'[101]

The armed struggle between the regulars and the Jacobites had only reached a lull in the weeks immediately following Culloden. There were still a number of Jacobites who were determined enough to fight on and were based in the Western Highlands under Cameron of Lochiel. Elsewhere, Jacobites were surrendering and their arms were being taken in. Troops were being directed to these ends, but work was also undertaken by loyalist Scots forces, both military and civilian. This part of the campaign was not particularly bloody.

Chapter 7

Operations around Fort Augustus, May–July 1746

*A Letter to the Journalist suggests that the severities practised against
the Highlanders, in destroying their habitations and killing their cattle,
are become necessary and justifiable.*[1]

Cumberland arrived at Fort Augustus on the evening of 24 May with eleven battalions of infantry and Kingston's Horse. A bloodier phase of the campaign was about to begin, as Cumberland was determined both to root out the active Jacobites and to capture Charles. Yet many of the less violent activities that had been initiated already continued. Many of the operations which were to occur in the Western Highlands and in the Isles, although ordered by Cumberland, were not supervised by him personally, because they could not be. The exact handling of these orders was very much the responsibility of the subordinate officers: majors and captains. The question of course is how much weight is upon him who gave the overall orders.

Some troops arrived ahead of him. On Thursday, 24 May, Cumberland had sent Haughton's battalion to Fort William, in order to relieve Guise's men who had formed the garrison there.[2] It had been a grim march from Inverness, as an officer related, 'On the 24th, we made a long and very tedious march of many miles, without seeing more than 2 men and 6 houses all the way, but mountains upon mountains, some of them very high, and all very bleak and barren.'[3]

Meanwhile, on 14 May, Loudon with his Highlanders and some of Howard's troops had been sent against the Camerons and MacDonalds, who were in arms and 300 strong, having helped to coerce the men of Moidart into helping them. The loyalists marched against Lochiel's mansion at Lochaber at the west end of Loch Arkaig in a pincer movement. The Jacobites dispersed once they saw advance parties of troops being sent against them, 'after firing a few shots across a river'.[4]

According to Lochiel, his men marched to Achnacarry and were surprised to find regulars there:

> upon which we advanced, thinking to make them halt; but their numbers were so much superior that it had no effect, and we were almost surrounded by a party that came by the moor on the side of Loch Arkaig, who actually took an officer and two men of mine, which made us retreat for twelve miles; and there, considering our situation, it was thought both provident and proper to disperse, rather than carry the fire into your country, without a sufficient number, as was expected.

Although Lochiel thought dispersal best, he still advised his fellows to 'keep their arms, as we have great expectations of the French doing something for us'. Yet on 25 May he concluded:

> I have advised all my people to do as the best and safest course, and the interest of the public; yet some of them have delivered up their arms without my knowledge, and I cannot take it upon me to direct in this particular, but to give my opinion, and let every one judge for himself.[5]

Lochiel told his men to escape the best they could. They then sent a man to ask if they could submit to royal mercy by surrendering their weapons.[6] On 26 May, 140 MacPhersons surrendered their arms. The Camerons had, on the previous day, said that they would have done likewise, and earlier, had it not been for their chief.[7]

This was the end of all formal resistance to the regular army as the Jacobites finally realized that continued warfare was impossible. The regulars, of course, were not to know this. Indeed, their searches in the forthcoming months resulted in the discovery of substantial caches of arms and ammunition. The conclusion which could be logically drawn from these finds was that the contest was still not at an end. For the Duke and his men, the conflict was ongoing.

Stockpiles of arms and ammunition were discovered by troops throughout the Highlands, if the reports in *The London Evening Post* are to be believed. Captain Ferguson found 150 weapons and gold at MacNeil of Barra's house on the island of Barra in May. He found 800 muskets and sixteen barrels of powder in a cave on the western coast later that month. In early June, on the coast of Moidart and the Island of Raasay, 1,000 muskets, thirty barrels of powder, twenty barrels of shot and French brandy were located. Eight cannon were found in Loch Shiel, with nineteen barrels of powder and thirty-two chests of arms buried nearby.[8]

These seizures probably prompted the following order, one of Cumberland's last whilst in Scotland, in early July:

> all houses where Arms of any kind shall be found for the future shall be burnt to Ashes, and that as Arms have been found, buried under Ground, that wherever they can be discovered, the Field, and adjacent Fields, shall be laid waste and destroyed as well as the Houses.[9]

There was other evidence that the rebellion was not yet at an end. Skirmishes between regulars and the Jacobites continued. In late June, a Jacobite detachment was on the hill of Minniegrigg, but was soon dislodged. In July there were exchanges of fire on the braes of Angus and near Garramuir wood. Possibly these Jacobites were groups of men raiding for food, as one report said they 'have no subsistence but what they pilfer'.[10]

Because of activity such as this, there were further sweeps of the country-side by detachments of regular troops. On 5 June, Lord George Sackville (1715–85) and Major Wilson took 500 infantry to Bernera and then were to march southwards along the coast until they reached the head of Loch Arkaig. Lieutenant-Colonel Cornwallis was to meet them here with 300 troops and then they would proceed through the counties of Moidart and Knoydart, to destroy Lochiel's house. Captain Scott would meet them from the south. General Campbell would scour the land around Castle Mingary with the Argyllshire militia. Their aim was to disperse any scattered bands of Jacobites.[11]

Small ships of the Royal Navy were also employed against the Jacobites at this time. On 28 June, a detachment from the garrison at Fort William under Captain Millar was sent aboard the *Furnace* and *Terror* sloops. These two ships had 90 regulars and 120 Argyll militiamen in them. They searched the coasts of Knoydart and Arisaig. One of these raids led to the capture of Lord Lovat, hiding in a tree trunk.[12]

But there were other reasons for such troop movements, which were not stated in the public prints. First, on 5 June, Cumberland was uncertain about the whereabouts of his cousin, thinking that he had already left aboard a French vessel, but knowing that some Highlanders thought otherwise. Constant searches by both regulars and militia were made for Charles himself. O'Sullivan noted that there were seven warships between Barra and South

Uist on 20 June in order to try and capture Charles.[13] In mid-July, 2,000 men, divided into sixteen parties, were hunting for him.[14] Cumberland told General Campbell that Charles should not be offered a pardon even if he lived in exile.[15] He sent one Captain Hodson to accompany Campbell 'that I may be the better informed how he be taken or killed'.[16] Colonel Conway with 500 regulars and the Argyll militia searched Skye, with orders to let no one escape and Ferguson's men searched South Uist and Barra.[17] Soldiers were posted from Loch Huren to Loch Nevis, on the assumption that Charles was at the latter. Despite this, Charles managed to slip through the net and escape.[18]

As to the second reason, Cumberland wrote:

> The Reason why I have sent such a force into that country, are to convince them that it is as much in His Majesty's power to march his forces into that country which they have hitherto boasted is inaccessible . . . to disperse the small remains of the rebels which may be got together, & to be certain whether the young man is still amongst them.[19]

The regulars were certainly able to operate in the Highlands. As a letter pointed out,

> They [the Jacobites] are greatly surpriz'd to find our soldiers climb over their rocks and mountains full as nimble as they can themselves, and to bring cattle down from places they deem'd inaccessible to us, In short, we have detachments at present in all parts of the highlands; and the people are deservedly in a most deplorable way, and must perish either by sword or famine – *A just reward for traitors.*[20]

It should be recalled that one of the conditions for a successful Jacobite campaign was that the regulars would be unable to penetrate the Highlands. This line of thinking was clearly fallacious.

The spirit of the officers and men towards the Jacobites was a very sour one. There was little sympathy for the foe. Some of Cumberland's officers were becoming exasperated with the Jacobites. One wrote from Fort Augustus on 5 June:

> After the battle of Culloden, his royal highness began with the rebels in a gentle, paternal way, with soft admonitions, and a gracious promise of pardon and protection to all the common people, who should bring in their arms, and submit to mercy. Some took this

opportunity, and were dismiss'd in peace with protection to their habitations. But great numbers, especially the Camerons, MacDonalds, Grants and Frasers, were perfidious, often promised to surrender, appointing their own time, and as often as not, broke their words; which has oblig'd his royal highness to lay the rod more heavy on them, by carrying fire and sword thro' their country and driving off their cattle, which we bring to our camp in great quantities, sometimes 1000 in a drove.[21]

Cumberland wrote on the same day 'the obstinacy of the Highlanders is inconceivable'.[22]

Yorke shared this animosity against the Jacobites, writing on 26 May:

We get great quantities of cattle and burn and destroy some of the country, but I hope we shall destroy much more; was it left to me I would not trust one of the Highlanders . . . we are in the heart of the vile race.[23]

The fact that the regulars were able to penetrate the Highlands led to the capture of many Jacobites, who, according to Yorke, 'chose rather to be taken than lead that miserable life any longer'.[24]

He was convinced that Cumberland's policy was the correct one. 'This is a truth they never experienced before, because nobody but one of the Duke's rank and honesty could, or would stand the clamour that a just severity must raise against him.' Yorke was certain that such severity was due to the stubbornness of the Jacobites who refused to admit defeat, 'it must be confessed that these rascals die hard and force even-handed justice to return the ingredients of their poisoned chalice to their own lips with more rigour than might otherwise have been their lot, had they made their submissions in due time'.[25]

Lee agreed that such destruction was necessary and that Cumberland had been lenient hitherto. He wrote on 31 May, 'Such is the obstinacy of some, that they choose to starve rather than surrender themselves and their arms. His Royal Highness wearied with this abuse of his lenity.'[26]

Those Jacobites who did surrender their weapons to either Presbyterian ministers or army officers were allowed to remain at home until the King's pleasure was known. In fact, such handovers were 'chiefly to be ascribed to the vigilance and good Advice of the Ministers of the Church of Scotland'.[27] According to Yorke:

Such as do not submit on these conditions, are pursued and put to the sword as rebels in arms, their cottages and husbandry gear burnt and all their cattle drove away and disposed of. Numbers have endeavoured to get off by giving in a few old arms and shuffling from day to day, in hopes that as the army might be called away and leave 'em: but they found to the contrary, for as a day has been limited to most of 'em for their submission, in failure of that time, military execution has been enforced.

Glengarry for example, promised that the clan would surrender its arms, 'which was granted him and his own behaviour winked at; but as his promise was not fulfilled in due time, his house was burnt to the ground and his estate laid waste'. Glengarry was later obliged to hand in the arms.[28] His reluctance to do so was to cost him dear. Lee wrote 'Glengarry's house and country is this moment blazing, for he broke his word, in not bringing in the remainder of his men within a limited time.'[29]

A contemporary account of the reality of the 'fire and sword' policy in late May was as follows:

Two days since Glengarry's house was burnt, with all the little huts on his lands; for they don't deserve the name of houses; and Yesterday Lochiel's house and lands were served the same way. Our men have brought in all the cattle they can find upon these grounds, which is a vast number, so that in a week's time the villains will have nothing left to subsist them.[30]

Michael Hughes gave a similar description of the burning of Lochiel's manse:

his fine chairs, Table, and all his cabinet Goods were set afire and burnt with his house. His fine Fruit garden above a mile long was pulled to pieces and laid waste. A beautiful summer house that stood in the pleasure garden was also set on Fire, and everything valuable burnt or destroyed.[31]

Hughes further described the work of these parties:

From thence the Party marched along the Sea Coast through Moidart, burning of Houses, driving away the cattle, and shooting those Vagrants who were found about the mountains. Lord George Sackville was in another way with 480 men. We camped in a valley

12 miles from the Isle of Mull, and detached parties about their sheils and glens, who did great execution among those who were still in arms, obstinately refusing to submit and accept of Pardon.[32]

A contemporary historian relates tales of destruction:

A volunteer present in this expedition owns, the Devastation was so great, that for the space of 50 miles neither House, Man, nor Beast was to be seen . . . All these different corps ranging their country, carrying fire and Desolation as they passed, shooting the vagrant Highlanders in the Mountains, and driving off the cattle, with which they returned to camp.[33]

Writing on 16 June, Hawley estimated that there had been 'about seven thousand houses burned allready', but added 'all is not done'.[34] Elsewhere, houses at Ruthven belonging to the MacPhersons, except for a public house, were burnt by troops.[35]

The men of Moidart refused to hand in their weapons and General Campbell, on 29 May, sent 150 soldiers there to search the houses, drive off the cattle, but not to burn any houses. However, the Jacobites learnt of this plan and drove off their cattle beforehand. When the troops arrived, Kinloch Moidart's house and the small cottage nearby were burnt. More soldiers were sent for, and soon after the Moidart men surrendered their arms.[36]

None of these observers thought such actions unduly harsh, nor did they blame their commander for such actions. Yet some thought that the effects were punishing enough. Tales of suffering began to circulate. A contemporary history refers to 'Several poor people, especially women and children, [who] have been found dead in the hills, supposed to be starved' and 'vast numbers of the common peoples' houses or huts are likewise laid in ashes; all the cattle, sheep, goat, &c are carried off'. A loyalist Scottish clergyman wrote on 21 June about how the families of Jacobites suffered:

As most of this parish is burnt to ashes, and all the cattle belonging to the rebels carried off by His Majesty's forces, there is no such thing as money or pennyworth to be got in this desolate place. My family is now much increased, by the wives and infants of those in the rebellion in my parish crowding for a mouthful of bread to keep them from starving; which no good Christian can refuse notwithstanding the villainy of their husbands and fathers to deprive us of our religion, liberties and bread.[37]

Some of the loyalist Highlanders suffered with the Jacobite. In early June, Major Forrester took 700 soldiers into Glengyle. At Corryarclet and Letterewe, houses were burnt and all horses, cattle and sheep were taken to Glengyle, 'without distinction'. Robert Graham, who had supported the government's cause, lost twenty-five bullocks, seven horses and twenty-eight sheep. A tenant of his lost eight cattle and had his house burnt down. He had not been a Jacobite. James Stuart had twenty-four cattle stolen and yet had been able to produce a certificate from his minister that he had not been in the rebellion. All these sufferers were tenants of the loyalist Duke of Montrose (1712–90). Curiously enough, at Stronachlachar, the troops had 'there burnt down the miln & all the other buildings about it except that house possessed by the said Robert Graham . . . who having a certificate from the minister, that he had never been in the rebellion'.[38]

Mungo Graeme, who had written about these matters, wrote again on 12 June to relate that these burnings were 'without the least Distinction of Persons, whether they had been in arms, or not . . . No regard was held thereto, but were told they might follow after their cattle to Crieff or Perth, & there make their claims.' John Blair, another tenant of Montrose, who lived at Craignchty and 'well affected to the government', had his inn set ablaze by a sergeant and sixteen soldiers. Although his wife and children tried to save the furniture, it was taken from them and burnt. Cattle and other foodstuffs were also taken by the soldiers. Although Blair's house had been used by an Episcopal preacher, it had been in a room hired for the purpose, and the man had been an Episcopal Whig, so to destroy the place was unduly harsh. Those in Monreith were alarmed at the approach of the troops and moved their cattle to a safer place.[39]

Newcastle responded to these complaints on 3 July, which had been raised by Montrose. He claimed that the soldiers acted without Cumberland's orders and contrary to his wishes. A strict inquiry would be made into the matter.[40] Cumberland did indeed investigate, writing:

> I immediately ordered an account to be drawn up of the proceedings of the King's troops in those parts where the Duke of Montrose complains that undeserved and unprovoked injurys have been offered to his tenants and I have ordered it to be done. I take it for granted there will be more applications of the same kind.

Yet Cumberland put the blame elsewhere, arguing

> if his factors had, in any shape, done their duty, as I am sure he would have them, they would have saved great Trouble & Mischief, both to

their master & many others; for the Duke of Montrose is in the too common case of well affected persons of rank, whose factors have not made use of their influence of their masters to serve the common cause.[41]

Cumberland was not directly to blame, but rather it was the men on the spot who must shoulder much of the responsibility. A Scottish observer noted, as regards the military expeditions, 'some mistakes I believe have happened, made by officers out on command' and another opined, 'Was there as much goodness in proportion to their rank in the other officers as their commander is possessed of, his stay at Fort Augustus would have been as agreeable a sojourn as any in the world.'[42]

Some officers certainly agreed. Forrester stated that 'if any such mistake was committed, and innocent people's houses burned, it was imputeable to Captain John Campbell', whose Perthshire volunteers knew the country and against whom the orders were to be carried out. Campbell was called to account and argued that 'everyone of ye persons whose houses were burned, had been concerned in the rebellion'. Forrester admitted:

> I could say no more about the matter than I had no proof of the people's circumstances or behaviour at the time, tho' on strict enquiry it appears that some of them were no ways concerned, and indeed its now pretty evident, that most, or rather all of them, were forced out and stayed very short time with the rebels having deserted with the first opportunity.[43]

Brigadier Mordaunt had, apparently found 'no sign of the country's laying down their arms & trusting to the King's mercy, but that they stood out, in defiance of every body'. He sent Forrester

> to reduce the country by force & destroy by Fire and Sword all such who should resist & the houses of the absent . . . or those who had been in arms . . . sparing at the same time such people and houses whom the ministers certified to have stayed quietly neutral at home, tho' no ways assistant to the King's forces.[44]

He added, when the matter of stolen cattle was raised:

> It would be absurd to spend time in answering the foolish and groundless complaints of those who pretended to have their cattle

drove away in the lands of the rebels because nobody will pretend to say that when cattle are feeding promiscuously on top of hills, it is possible to distinguish nicely between those that should be taken, and those that should not, particularly when it is notorious that any who have been so certified for & in consequence therefore lived un-molested, have made so bad use of that protection as to screen the cattle and effects of rebels.[45]

Forrester, 'a very distinct humane man', did not like the orders he had been given by Brigadier Mordaunt, but said 'they were such as no officer of the army could shun to obey'. He added 'he was already blamed for too much lenity in the execution' and had 'expressed the greatest reluctance and un-easiness at his being obliged to execute so undesirable an office'.[46] There were other complaints. As a contemporary history remarked, 'Even the well-affected in the rebellious counties are likewise sufferers.'

Yet this policy did not affect all the Highlands. Henderson wrote:

the people gladly came in, had certificates of their surrender given them, and these were always sustained. In these districts, not one house was burnt, except Castle Downie, the seat of the family of Lovat. I had the same account from the clergy of Abertarff, in which there was scarce a house burnt.[47]

After the raid which resulted in the destruction of Glengarry's house, in which cattle were taken to Crieff, 'Those belonging to people not in the rebellion, were, however, given back.'[48]

Cumberland did apologize where wrong had been done and did his best to restore stolen property. He wrote on 11 June that he was:

extremely sorry you should have any sort of reason to complain of injury or violence from those who were sent out with no other design than to annoy & distress such as are still in arms & acting maintenance & support of the wicked rebellion . . . I am, I assure you very much concerned it should have happened. Lord George Sackville tells me the cattle & other things taken have been returned, if anything yet remains, I will give the necessary orders about it & if I can do anything more towards repairing the injuries & loss your tenants have sustained, I shall be pleased with an opportunity of giving such proofs as may be most satisfactory of the just sense I have for the form attachment and zeal you have shewn on all occasions.

Cumberland added 'it did not happen from any mischievous purpose in the soldiers in the party to plunder all people indiscriminately, but from the indiscretion of some of the tenants who in their first alarm upon the appearance of troops amongst them, fired upon them and from hence the disorder took its rise'.[49]

Yet, even when efforts were made to restore property wrongly taken from non-Jacobites, problems arose. As one laird's factor put it, 'it was agreed that all cattle &c taken from innocent people should be restored', but how could claimants establish their right? Initially they were told that they needed to provide a certificate from their minister to say they had not been Jacobites and to have witnesses who could swear that the claimed property was indeed theirs. This was a cumbersome process, as the factor explained: 'This soon proved to be a tedious and difficult method of providence, which it would be necessary to abridge.' Eventually, the certificate and marks of witnesses were needed, but by that time, some of the cattle had been killed by soldiers for food or had been dispersed, and so, 'in none of these cases could any redress be obtained by the proprietors'.[50]

However, according to Jacobite sources, the activity of some subordinate officers was of a much different and of an even more unpleasant nature. According to a Jacobite source, 'While Cumberland was at Fort Augustus great liberties were taken by some of the officers sent on different commands, particularly Colonel Cornwallis, Major Lockhart, Monroe of Culcairn, Captain Scott and, Captain Grant, son of Grant of Knockando and Strathspey.'[51] It is, though, worth bearing in mind that these accounts are not substantiated from other sources, so their exact veracity is questionable. On the other hand, it is probable there is some truth in them.

According to one source, writing in 1750 from London:

> In several parts of the Highlands in Scotland the soldiery spared neither man, woman, nor child, particularly those under the command of Major Lockhart, Caroline Scott, etc. The hoary head, the tender mother and the weeping infant, behoved to share in the general wreck, and to fall victims to rage and cruelty by the musquet, the bloody bayonet, the devouring flame, or famishing hunger and cold! In a word, the troops sported with cruelty. They marched through scenes of woe, and marked their steps with blood.[52]

Captain Scott is said to have had three men of Slanes hanged after they surrendered to his troops, according to Captain Mackintosh, a militia officer. Apparently they were going to Fort William to hand in their weapons.[53] He had Ardshiel's wife's house ransacked and cattle taken, and had the house damaged. On the isle of Barra, he had a man hanged on suspicion, though he said he had not been in the rebellion.[54]

According to one informant, 'I have been told Major Lockhart came not short of Captain Scott in many of the like actions.'[55] Lockhart is said to have strung up three men and stripped another naked, though the latter's life was saved by a fellow officer (this sounds very much like the story retailed above – were the two based on the same incident?). There were reports of three women, one of whom was pregnant, being raped, though the assault on the latter was doubted.[56] In Lochaber, Captain Grant 'stripped men, women and children without distinction of condition or sex . . . He burnt and plunder'd as he marched.' Finding one Alexander Cameron with a gun, he had him shot dead. Cameron had said that 'he saw these who had submitted to the Kings mercy plundered as well as those who did not' and he had fled with his family. A beggar woman who would not tell, because she did not know, where Lochiel was was also shot.[57]

Lockhart took one Grant of Daldrigan, who was not a Jacobite, and had him bound and stripped and then put upon a gallows, together with three other men he had had killed earlier that day (this is probably the incident already referred to above). The hanging was prevented by one Captain Grant in Loudon's regiment. However, Lockhart went on to rape a pregnant gentlewoman, shoot a man accompanying a Presbyterian minister and rape another woman, leaving her for dead.[58]

An independent witness to such behaviour is vouched for by Jean Cameron, who wrote to Duncan Campbell on 16 June about her concerns:

> there is so many flyeing parties thro' the countrie . . . they not only burn houses take away cattle but strips weemen as children to the skin and use them in a most barbarous manner . . . it is not easie for a woman and new childing to sculk thro the hills.[59]

Some of the commanders of naval vessels also allegedly acted with similar cruelty, when landing on the Western Isles. Cumberland's orders to naval officers in early June had been rather vague, though it was standard practice to have such orders for no commander-in-chief can cater for all eventualities and some initiative must be left to the man on the spot. He told them that 'they are to land [on a number of named islands] from time to time, as occasions may offer & to enquire after & search for all strangers who may have resorted there since the Battle of Culloden, & to seize all such of them as they can lay hands on', before sending them to him. No damage was to be done to any

property belonging to Alexander MacDonald. In the case of an island shelter-
ing suspects, 'the people of that place should be menaced' and could be
'further proceeded against in the way of military execution' if they were hand
in glove with the Jacobites.[60]

Ferguson gave Cumberland an account of his campaign on the islands
towards the end of May. His expeditions involved landing a number of
soldiers and seamen. On 12 May he arrived at the isle of Raasay 'to search and
burn', with an officer and sixty sailors and an officer and thirty men of
Campbell's regiment. The orders were carried out and three prisoners were
taken. Having been joined by Commander Duff's sloop, *Terror*, on 18 May,
they arrived at the Bay of Moror, where 'We burn'd Moror's house & a small
village, meeting with little or no opposition.' On the following day, a house
which Charles had stayed at was burnt, along with two or three villages.
Prisoners and arms were taken. The laird of Moidart's house was later burnt.
On 30 May, they arrived at Eigg. Finding armed Jacobites there, Ferguson
had thirty-one men arrested, killed some of their cattle, seized arms and burnt
all their boats.[61] Two months later, he wrote, 'I have had some success in
distressing the rebels and seizing their persons, arms &c.'[62] Hardly a massacre.

There is another version of events, as related by Jacobites, in which further
activity is attributed to these expeditions. Duff and Ferguson (the latter being
described as 'a fellow of very low extract, born in the county of Aberdeen,
who, being naturally of a furious, savage disposition') arrived at Eigg with the
intention of assaulting the women there, but, forewarned, the latter escaped.
One woman, though, died in her escape. Later, at Caana, Ferguson
'committed several branches of cruelty upon the poor people'. At Eigg, Duff
burnt houses and seized cattle.[63] While Ferguson was conducting a search for
Charles at Kingsburgh, he was told 'Why sir, the world belies you if you be
not a very cruel, hard hearted man: and indeed I do not like to come through
your hands.'[64] Yet Ferguson's reputation was well earned. After he arrested
one of Lochiel's brothers, he 'would not allow him a bed to lie on, nor anything
else but ropes and cables'. The prisoner fell ill and, despite entreaties by
others, Ferguson refused to give the man any aid. He died. Yet when he
arrested Flora MacDonald (who played a crucial part in Charles's escape),
General Campbell 'ordered Miss MacDonald to be used with the utmost
respect'.[65] On another occasion, in his quest for Charles, Ferguson took one
John MacGinnis and 'he caused him to be stripped naked, tied to a tree, and
whipped with the cat o' nine tails till the blood gushed out at both his sides'.
Another man was threatened likewise but, once again, the presence of General
Campbell prevented him being mistreated.[66]

In May when Ferguson's sloop arrived on Raasay, the village was burnt, the cattle stolen or killed. The inhabitants surrendered their arms. During another expedition there, two months later, the inhabitants were questioned as to Charles's location. Donald Nicholson ran away – he was arrested and whipped. Two women were raped.

> This visit was infinitely worst than their first, as they slaughtered many more of their cattle of all kinds, excepting horses, than they at first did. They so robbed the whole inhabitants both of their bed close and even their body close, that I am certain there was not the value of two shillings sterling of close of any kind left to any of the poor familys upon the island.

In all, 280 cows, 700 sheep and 20 horses were killed. About 300 houses were destroyed. Together with losses of furniture, the total estimated value was 25,000 Scottish marks.[67]

How much truth is there in the above accounts of brutality towards civilians and their property? Some, certainly. As already noted, property was burnt and cattle were taken, as per orders from Cumberland. That much is certainly accurate, as accounts by loyalists also refer to such activity. Nor was it unknown for those captured to be further assaulted, if there was a perceived need for this. James Hamilton told the Duke of Richmond that a servant of Lord Lovat's had been found 'but he refus'd telling where his master was, the Capt. Ordered his boatswain to tye him to a tree and whip him. When he received about thirty lashes he begged to be untied and he would then tell them where his master was.'[68] Some who were killed may have been guilty of the crimes they died for. An unnamed man was hanged at Inverness in June, as a spy, and in early July, 'Three men were hanged here the other day, who were found in arms'. Nor were the Jacobites slow to kill those who had aggrieved them – John Catanach, who had informed on them, was murdered.[69] The references to rape, torture and murder are unsubstantiated. But, judging by the doings of some specimens of soldiery throughout the ages, it is difficult to believe that the Jacobite stories related above are entirely fabricated. The extent of their veracity is open to dispute, however. Given the known attitudes of officers and men towards the Jacobites/Highlanders (seen by some, incorrectly to be synonymous), it is hard to see how it could have been otherwise. Most armies have their quota of sadists and psychopaths, and these men are sometimes able to indulge in such appetites, authorized or not.

However, it seems odd, if Cumberland was indeed the butcher of legend, that his subordinates neglected to mention their brutality to him. Had he been of that kidney he would have relished tales of terror. Perhaps, if we assume that the Jacobite tales are true and Ferguson's letter is not, the reason why he was given a bowdlerized version of events was because he did not approve of the extreme lengths to which his subordinates were prepared to go.

Certainly, much of the military action taken in the Highlands was the responsibility of the men on the ground. Mungo Graham noted that the orders were to differentiate between Jacobite and non-Jacobite property. Yet, as he wrote on 23 June:

> the order for burning did not specify the particular persons who were the Rebels, whose houses were to be burnt, but it was left to the officers who were to execute the orders, to judge who were rebels, who not, what houses to burn and what not, and their officers burnt any house that was pointed at, by such sycophants as they brought along with them, who generally had it in view to avenge themselves on those whom they bore a grudge against.

One such informant was Sergeant McNichol of Perthshire, who was 'a notorious thief' and 'who avenged himself upon one whom had declared him for theft, by burning of his house in Cladock on Crown grounds, upon his information that the tenant had been in the rebellion'.[70]

A non-Jacobite account relates how Loudon had given protection certificates from Cumberland to some of the MacDonalds. He then states:

> But the Major [Lockhart] would pay no Regard to them; for when any such were shewn to him, his answer was, 'That because of their many wicked and inhumane Acts, both of a publick and private Nature, if they were to shew him a warrant from Heaven, it should not prevent him executing his Orders.'[71]

Lee wrote that Lockhart was sent against the Glenmorrisons on about 29 May 'to do military execution. He is just returned, killed about 17 (some of which are hanging by their heels in different parts, with labels expressing the reason of it), burnt above 400 houses, and drove home about 1,400 head of cattle'.[72]

Yet Lee was not critical. He wrote himself: 'Thirty houses are now burning in my view, Glorious Firework! More entertaining than any ever exhibited at Cuper's Garden . . . this heathenish Country, converting them to Christianity, and propagating a New light among them.'[73]

One extreme measure which was never adapted was suggested by Huske. He recalled to Yorke a policy used in Ireland in the previous century:

They were obliged to come to extremities by offering certain rewards for the head of a Raperie, I think it was £5, which brought in many a one and put an end to Rebellion . . . Such laws in this Country for a year or two, I believe you will agree with me, would do good; for without extremities I believe they will never submit, but continue as rebellious as ever.[74]

Huske was not alone in advocating such a policy. Hawley wrote on 16 June, 'if His Majesty would leave me the Foot here and the Parliament give the men a Guinea . . . for every rebel's head they brought in, I would still undertake to clear this country'.[75] Cumberland never seems to have even considered this possibility; more evidence that his subordinates were more ruthless than he.

The conduct of the soldiers was variable and it seems that Cumberland exercised a minimum of supervision over them. General Campbell (sometimes alleged to show little mercy) was a most compassionate man and when he found that Charles Stewart of Appin's family had suffered, he wrote on 25 May;

I know the brave Duke, under whose command and orders I act, to have as much humanity as any man on earth; from which, and my own natural inclination, I have taken the liberty of ordering back your milk cows, six wethers, and as many lambs . . . I have taken the freedom at the same time of ordering two bolls of meal, out of my own stores, to be left here for you, which I desire you to accept for the use of yourself and little ones.[76]

Another Scot who believed in Cumberland's humanity was Mrs Fraser of Achnagairn, Forbes's sister, who wrote, 'All these mischiefs is not to be laid at the Duke's charge but the vile informers which they are daily plagued with.'[77]

Jacobites were not always killed offhand when found. John Webb told General Campbell on 13 June, 'I returned last night from searching the north side of the Loch Shield agreeable to your orders, where I found nothing of great Consequence, only six Rebels in arms, who I send you by Lieutenant Campbell.'[78]

Although many senior Jacobites fled to France, John Murray was not among them. He was taken at Mr Hunter of Polwood's house by a sergeant and seven men of St George's dragoons. A number of other Jacobites surrendered. Mr Cameron of Dungellen brought his men and arms to General Campbell. The inhabitants of Morvern and Ardnamurchan did likewise.[79]

The Macgregors whom Glenorchy feared in late May were still causing concern on 8 June. He wrote that they 'had the insolence and folly to continue in arms to the number of about 200. They keep together in small numbers and wear white cockades.' They refused to disperse and surrender their weapons as Glenorchy requested. This was because their chiefs, who could not expect pardon, persuaded them otherwise, allegedly because a number of the House of Lords were objecting to the war on the Continent and so the government would be disrupted and in chaos. Glenorchy concluded, 'The poor, ignorant people gave entire credit to what was told them, and still continue in a state of rebellion.'[80] Soldiers were occasionally attacked – two men from Fort William had their limbs hacked off by Camerons whilst fishing in late May.[81]

Threats were used before action took place. For example, in order to recover arms taken from Loudon's men who had fled before the Jacobites earlier in 1746, an announcement was made that they should be delivered to the storehouse at Inverness. A deadline of a month was given – if they were not delivered by 1 August, 'the possessors, wherever they are found, whether civil or military, and of what rank soever, shall be prosecuted with the utmost rigour, as the law in that case directs'. Such measures were not always successful. When Ancrum had made declarations from Aberdeen concerning the surrender of arms, few, if any, were surrendered. Ancrum then gave orders to his troops 'that all houses where arms of any kind shall be found for the future shall be burnt to ashes, and that arms have been found buried under ground, that wherever they can be discovered, the field, and adjacent fields shall be laid waste and destroy'd, as well as the houses thereunto belonging'.[82]

Fawkener wrote about what happened to the recalcitrant clans.

> Our parties visit the clansmen who do not bring in their arms, and they have now their share in the mischief they so plentifully brought to others. Most of these people might be prosecuted for Robbers & I don't know whether that might not be a good way to mortifie their pride . . . the tenaciousness of these creatures of their arms is very remarkable, they have denied them against the menace of death.[83]

Yet, as he told General Blakeney:

> if any of the common people who have been in the rebellion, shall present themselves, to deliver up their Arms & submit themselves to His Majesty's mercy, you are to receive them & after they shall have put their hands to a declaration which I send you herewith a form, you are to dismiss them, giving each a certificate of that herewith.

Officers, though, were to be taken prisoner.[84]

Arms were still being delivered. Fletcher wrote on 30 May, 'The Rebels are every where delivering up their arms and submitting to the King's mercy, which even the Camerons have at length done.'[85] On 1 July, Lord Sutherland proclaimed that anyone who returned the arms that had been taken from his men in February before 1 August would be granted an amnesty. If they did not, they 'shall be prosecuted with the utmost rigour, as the law in that case directs'. Blakeney told Cumberland that, though many arms were given in, they were mostly of a low quality and old. He did list on 16 June that fifty-three muskets, thirty-nine swords, four pistols and nineteen dirks had been surrendered to him at Inverness. Five days later he related that 534 men had handed in a total of 275 muskets, 169 swords, 26 pistols and 45 dirks.[86]

There are many surviving lists of clansmen and the arms they surrendered. On 15 May, Glengarry brought in seventy-nine men, who delivered sixty-three muskets, twenty-seven swords, three pistols and four dirks to Lord Loudon. Two days later, forty-four Stratharick men gave up twenty-eight muskets, three swords, seven pistols and a dirk. On 7 June, sixty Mackintoshes gave Loudon thirty-five muskets, sixteen swords, three pistols and three dirks. All these men had their names recorded.[87] And there were many others: MacDonalds, Camerons, MacPherson, McMartins, Mackintoshes. On 2 June, Campbell reported that the Munroes had brought in their arms and submitted, 'so that I have used no violence having that country in my power'.[88]

Promises of help to collect arms were also made. One document of 30 May read 'We are the under subscribers do hereby oblige ourselves to appear and do all that lyes in us to be forthcoming to send in all ye arms we can find in this country knowing that consequence of any arms being taken then will be forfeiting every good intention.'[89] An undated document is a 'List of the gentlemen within the lordship of Badenoch who have been most active in bringing in the people to surrender'.[90] The minister of Alvie sent in lists of men in the parish who were not involved, forty-five in all; and also those twenty-three men who were forced into the Jacobite ranks, but who later surrendered their arms. There are many lists of parishioners who were active Jacobites, too.[91] Donald Fraser, minister of Kilcaimin made up a certificate for Kenneth McFarqquhon to state he was not an active Jacobite.[92] The Revd John Paul of Rothes sent lists of his parishioners, and in a covering letter noted:

> In obedience to the order of the Lord Justice Clerk communication to me . . . I send enclosed a list of ye parishioners who have not been concerned in this wicked and unnatural rebellion . . . I have the

pleasure to assure you that not one man in my parish did take up arms against His Majesty King Gorge.[93]

Cumberland was sceptical about the success of the policy of delivery of arms. He wrote to Newcastle on 29 May thus:

I hope His Majesty will not imagine that by these peoples laying down their Arms, the country is a jot safer from any fresh rising. For at this time almost every Highlander is possessed of 2 or 3 sets of arms, which are hid. But we are forced to take that or no satisfaction at present, they are all dispersed, & tho' I know that every single person in the country has been in the rebellion, yet unless I could get each person sworn against, there is no taking them up, so that in appearance all that can be done purely military is now over, therefore, I don't propose to stay here above a week longer.[94]

He added that 'The only effectuall method for disarming the Highlands appears to be by the proposed annual visitations & by *death or transportation* being the punishments inflicted on all whom may be found armed or have arms concealed.'[95]

Blakeney also cast doubt about the effectiveness of this policy, writing to Cumberland on 13 June, after noting that fifty-three men had handed in twenty-two guns, ten swords, three pistols and a dirk, 'I cannot help observing that the firearms they give in are very much out of order and that they don't care to part with their favourite broadswords, pistols, Dirks and Targets.'[96]

Yet Normand MacLeod, writing to Forbes on 11 June, put matters differently, 'The Duke is well enough pleased with the delivering of Arms in Brae Lochaber, Badenoch and MacIntoshes' Country.'[97] Campbell told Fawkener on 2 June, 'Several of the Munro people having brought in their arms and submitted to His Majesty's mercy. Others are coming in daily so that I have used no violence having that country in my power at any time.'[98]

Newcastle was also hopeful, writing on 5 June:

His Majesty is far from thinking that this sort of submission, and laying down their arms is a security to be depended on: But it is to be hoped, that the method that will be taken, if effectually executed, will be sufficient to disarm the Highlands and to secure the peace of that part of the kingdom for the future.[99]

Cumberland later admitted, 'The McPhersons have indeed acted honestly enough in bringing in their arms, but the rest are no way to be persuaded upon but by force.'[100]

Even those areas which had complied with the government's orders were not immune from trouble. Glenorchy told Yorke on 17 June: 'Several of the Rannoch people, who brought their arms to me, came here to-day complaining that, notwithstanding they had complied with all that was ordered them, the troops have carried away their cattle.' He told them that he had given them receipts for the arms, but had made no promises. The people told him that they expected mercy, not the prospect of starvation. Glenorchy said no more to them, but was sympathetic and told Yorke, 'In my humble opinion, the county would be sooner quieted if a distinction were made between those who produce certificates of having delivered up their arms and those who do not.'[101] This had some effect. On 10 June it was noted that from Morar, Arisaig, Mordaunt and the Isle of Eigg, 'the common people submitted to the government & brought in their arms & every person got a certificate'.[102]

There were few signs of active Jacobitism in Scotland and what little there was was soon stamped out. Major Chaban told Fawkener that James Stuart's birthday had been celebrated on 10 June on the links at Montrose. A number of lads had made a bonfire and no one had extinguished it. They were questioned and admitted the charge. Their parents were told that they must inculcate loyalty in their children and such should never be repeated. The parents, six men and three women, were gaoled until Cumberland's pleasure be known. He decided that the boys should be whipped through the town (a common enough punishment in the eighteenth century), the town crier proclaiming their sins and the parents being bailed for good behaviour.[103]

Further action was taken against episcopal meeting houses. According to Douglas, 'Several meeting-houses in the north, particularly about Strathbogie, have been pulled down by the soldiers. Some Non-Jurant Episcopal meeting houses have been likewise burnt and destroyed and they are generally shut up all over the kingdom.'[104]

Mindful of the morale of his soldiers, Cumberland provided entertainment for them which coincided with one of his own interests – horse racing. Contrary to the statements of some historians, these races were not competed in by naked girls, but as follows:

> the Duke's Presence which afforded Pleasure to every Soldier as often as they beheld him; and to divert their Melancholy, his Royal Highness and Officers frequently gave Money to be run for by Highland Horses, sometimes *without Saddles or Bridles* [doubtless the origin of the

confusion]: both Men and Women riding: Here were also many Foot-Races, perform'd by both Sexes, which afforded many Droll scenes.

These entertainments were 'necessary to entertain Life in this Manner, otherwise the People were in danger of being affected with hypocondrical Melancholy'. Exhaustion, poor weather and grim surroundings round Fort Augustus were resulting in many men becoming physically ill and having to be sent to Inverness. Those remaining often became mentally unwell.[105] This might account for some of the violence offered towards some of the Highlanders.

Plunder was seen by many as a soldier's perquisite in war. At Fort Augustus, there were sales of the cattle which had been confiscated by the soldiers. According to Ray, 'At this Time most of the Soldiers had Horses, which they bought and sold with one another at a low price, and on which they rode about, neglecting their Duty; which made it necessary to publish an Order to part with them, otherwise they would be shot.' Dealers far as far afield as Yorkshire came to buy these animals and the soldiers shared the profits.[106] There was even a fixed tariff of fees; on 4 July, captains received £26 4s 8d, lieutenants £14 2s 4d, sergeants £2 16s 5d, corporals £1 15s 3d and privates and drummers £1 8s 2 ½d.[107] Clearly Cumberland condoned such behaviour; he saw the interests of his men as being more important than those of the Jacobites and had taken much pride in his soldiers' victory at Culloden – such spoils of war were his men's rewards for a job well done.

Not all soldiers agreed with such a policy. Bland was one. He wrote 'We military men make very bad judges where property is concerned.' He noted that the goods of Scots, whether participants in the rebellion or not, were been taken out of hand by his colleagues. He added:

> I preached up the Doctrine at Aberdeen to some of my Brethren but it made little impression, and their example descended to officers of a lower station, and from them to the private men, which drew on all the licenticousness we have all seen, and which will cost the lives of several of our men before it is cured. I don't pretend to limit HRH power in particulars as he had an undoubted authority to lay the whole of the country under military execution when His Majesty's service requires it. We subordinate officers should never presume to do it but by express orders from him [Cumberland].[108]

Some soldiers certainly profited by the campaign. Ray wrote 'These sort of soldiers commonly plunder'd and burnt, so that many of them grew rich by their Share of the Spoil'.[109] Plunder in war is not uncommon; as previously said, it was usual during the English Civil War as well as on the Continent.

Yet there were limits. Indiscriminate plunder was ruled out, as it had been at Inverness. A general order of 24 May read:

> No plundering nor Moroding on pain of hanging. Patroles to goe instantly from the picquet during the Night & take up & search all soldiers they find out of camp. The three men Genl Howards taken up plundering to be tried immediately & the sentence brought before Genl Bland . . . the picquet around the camp & suffer no man on any pretence after Tatoo to goe out of the camp.

It was no idle threat. On 4 June four men were flogged for 'plundering under pretended orders from His Royal Highness the Duke'.[110]

There was also concern that some of the soldiers might have Jacobite sympathies, or acted in a negligent manner towards their enemy. On 12 June, two men were given 900 lashes each for allowing MacDonnell of Glengarry to escape. An order of 8 July read:

> if any soldier, soldier's wife or any other person belonging to the Army, is known to sell or give away any meal to any Highlander, or any person of the country, they shall be first whipd severely, for disobeying this order & then put upon meat & water in the Provost for as fourthnight.[111]

James Ray thought that the campaign had been a great success. When it was over, he wrote:

> The Work in the Highlands being mostly over, and I having the Pleasure of seeing and lending a Hand in reducing the Enemies of my King and Country to an unwilling obedience, had a Desire to leave these parts (so long harassed by the Highland Banditti, that it more resembled the habitation of Savages than the Residence of civilized Society) and to return to England.[112]

Fellow contemporary historian, Boyse, wrote:

> Thus were this fierce People subdued, when neither the Romans nor Saxons could reduce, and who had often bid Defiance to their Native Kings. They had rashly kindled a Flame, which after scorching

England, was now blown back on themselves, and consumes them to the vitals.[113]

Walpole agreed, writing on 7 July, 'The Duke is still in Scotland, doing his family the only service that has been done for them there since their accession.'[114]

Newcastle was certain that Jacobitism had been crushed and wrote on 9 July, 'there is no Room to doubt, but that the Rebellion is now totally suppressed, and that every thing has been done by Your Royal Highness, for His Majesty's cause, that could anyways render your presence necessary in Scotland'.[115] Yet Cumberland was uncertain whether his campaign had been successful. In July he wrote to his successor in Scotland, Albermarle, to state 'this country is in so unsteady a station'. He expected another rebellion and warned Albermarle to 'keep the whole in a Readiness to take to the Field at a day's Notice' should the Jacobites reassemble and try to march south.[116] He earlier wrote: 'I have nothing to say new from this country but that to my great astonishment I find them a more stubborn and villainous set of wretches than I imagined could exist.'[117]

Despite Cumberland's best efforts, Charles managed to escape. He was taken by a French schooner off South Uist on 17 September, for Boulogne, just over five months after Culloden. These months on the run, with only a small band of followers were Charles's finest hour – and it is due to this part of his life that he won his heroic and romantic reputation.

A critique of the pacification was penned by Duncan Forbes in either 1746 or 1747, in a draft document, which is in contrast to his sentiments as expressed in the previous chapter. He noted the difference between the government's approach in 1716 and that taken thirty years later:

> Upon the dispersion of the rebels in 1716 no orders were given for distressing the common highlanders. The country became instantly quiet; and tho' a small Spanish force landed on the coast of the Western Highlands in 1719 . . . they were not able to bring together above 10 or 1,700 Highlanders.

But as a result of a different policy in 1746:

> Tho the Jacobites who keeped out of the rebellion may (terrified by the fate of their friends that embarked) keep out of any new insurrection, yet if French should risqué a few troops with some provisions

in the course of the winter, ther is no doubt that so many of the rebels as are in Scotland and out of custody, would join them.

He argued that those Jacobites who were not killed or prisoners, were 'at the same time ther is no doubt that the Highland rebels, reduced to want will in all events plunder the adjacent Low Country'. Nor would transportation be effective as those transported could return without any difficulty.

What Forbes advocated was 'some indication of mercy'. As long as men were hunted and deemed rebels, they would harbour resentment against the government. What he suggested was 'If the common Highlanders who have escaped the dangers of rebellion are assured of mercy before France frame any schemes for formenting new commotions, the high probability is that they will with great gladness receive it and consider well before they imbark again on such a project.'[118]

As if to bear Forbes out, Cameron of Lochiel was still eager to embark on a fresh attempt to restore the Stuarts in February 1747, writing to his master:

> If we could return to the Highlands with artillery, arms and ammunition, and only 4 or 5 battalions of foot, we would not only relieved our distressed friends and save the remains of our country, but deliver the whole kingdom of Scotland from the slavery to which it is, or will soon be reduced . . . I hear from all hands, and have great reason to believe that all Scotsmen, not excepting those who are most distinguish'd in the government's service, are so inraged at the inhumanity with which the Elector has proceeded . . . that they only want an opportunity to show their resentment.[119]

Yet Hardwicke thought that Cumberland had acted correctly:

> I told H.R.H. that I had always been of opinion that there had been too much neglect in the management in Scotland after that Rebellion [of 1715], but that since the Rebellion in 1745 great attention and application had been used, both in making new laws to reform Scotland and in endeavouring to put them into execution.[120]

Cumberland arrived in London on 25 July, to much acclamation. 'As soon as it was known, all the bells in the cities of London and Westminster rung, and at evening were illuminations and bonfires, with continual firing of guns for several hours, and all other demonstrations of the greatest of joy from people of all ranks.' Cumberland's official rewards were for his annual revenue to be raised from £15,000 to £40,000 and he was made ranger of Windsor Great Park.[121]

Although outside the strict remit of this study, it is worth briefly mentioning the fates of the Jacobite prisoners. As noted, thirty-six deserters were shot. Trials of the others took place in York, Carlisle and London. The more socially exalted prisoners were tried in the latter. It was they and the officers (30) suffered the most, along with the officers and sergeants of the Manchester Regiment (24). Three Jacobite noblemen were beheaded. Relatively few of the Scots rank and file were executed. In total, 120 men were executed, 936 were transported to the American colonies, 1,287 were released or discharged (including 387 French and Spanish soldiers), 298 banished or given conditional pardons. At least 88 died in prison, 58 escaped and the fates of 684 are unknown. It is probable that some of the latter, too, died in prison. It had not been a bloody assize compared to that of 1685, but there had been more executions compared to the situation in 1715–16.[122]

Following Forbes's comments, an Act of Grace was passed in 1747. It pardoned anyone who was not still in arms against the government, excepting a number of senior Jacobites, such as Cameron of Lochiel. On the military side, a massive fortification, named Fort George, was constructed a few miles from Inverness, to house a permanent garrison, though was not completed until the early years of the reign of George III, when any further outbursts of Jacobitism seemed very remote. Whether it was an effective deterrent or an expensive white elephant is debatable.

After Culloden, legal and judicial changes were ordered which reshaped Highland society and politics, which had been untouched even after the Union of 1707. The two major pieces of legislation were the Disarming Act and the Act abolishing heritable jurisdictions. These made the bearing of arms and the wearing of tartan and kilts illegal. The second Act diminished the power of the Highland chief over his clan, by no longer enabling him to exercise jurisdiction outside the king's courts and made his former right to call out his clan in war illegal.[123]

Cumberland was clearly in favour of such legislation, as he had previously stated in his correspondence to Newcastle before Culloden. On 20 April, Hardwicke wrote to him about the proposed new laws. He told the Duke 'Your R.H. has been fully informed how deeply we are engaged in Scotch Reformation, which your indefatigable labours and glorious success on the day, which makes the date of this letter, has given us the opportunity of.' He told his son that 'I have endeavoured to pursue his sentiments, and should be very sorry to fail of his approbation.'[124]

Other factors led to fundamental change in the Highlands as well as this legislation. These included increased involvement with the Lowlands and England in commerce, manners, fashion, religion and politics, making the United Kingdom more of a practical reality than ever before. These changes had been taking place prior to 1745 and continued throughout the century.[125] Whether the laws mentioned above were necessary is a moot point – but certainly politicians at Westminster, without the benefit of hindsight, thought so.

It is hard to deny that aspects of the repression after Culloden had been harsh. To take cattle was to leave families in direst want. But it also served to deprive any potential Jacobites of the necessary supplies of food which were vital to any continued campaign. Whether there could have been continued resistance is another question. Certainly Cameron of Lochiel and others advocated it, as Cumberland was aware. He probably did not know how weak this movement was, but he was not one to take chances, therefore the Highlanders were to suffer. The loyal suffered as well as the Jacobites. Apparently, the loss of the Duke of Gordon's property totalled £46,215 6s 2d and, even allowing for some exaggeration, this was clearly a colossal sum.[126] Yet Cumberland had had the approval of the government, with constant correspondence with Newcastle.

Chapter 8

Contemporaries, the Duke and the Rebellion

Give me leave to interrupt you for a moment to congratulate you on this great event in Scotland. This brave young man [Cumberland] has done his country and family incredible service, and one cannot help envying the Father the pleasure he must receive from such a son.[1]

We have already looked at how historians have viewed Cumberland. How did his contemporaries see him? Biased or not, they were at least judging him by the standards of their age. The matter is more complex than merely supporting the government and opposing the Jacobites or vice versa. Supporters of George II might not necessarily advocate severe measures against the defeated enemy. Clearly anyone with Jacobite sympathies would condemn Cumberland regardless, since the forces under his command had defeated the Jacobite army in a decisive manner and so the prospect of a restored Stuart king was even more remote than ever. And there is the matter of knowledge. Most people did not have first-hand, or even second-hand, experience of what had happened in Scotland in 1746. With ignorance, there might follow prejudice. Then there is the issue of self-interest. Anyone who is ambitious or wishes to stand in the good favour of his superiors will hail the victor, whoever they are. Finally, we must also bear in mind that only a fragment of the evidence survives, and that which does may not necessarily be a fair sample, though since that is all there is, it must be used.

In England there was much thanksgiving and celebration when the news of Culloden arrived a few days after the battle was over. These were often communal events, sponsored by a town or city's corporation. They could also be religious, with clergymen preaching triumphal sermons. Or they could be more private, with thoughts being exchanged in correspondence, or most intimate of all, in diaries. It is also important to note that there were at least two phases of these celebrations – in the immediate aftermath of the battle and on 9 October, the day appointed by the government as the official thanks-giving day for the defeat of the rebellion.

Contemporaries wrote to one another about Cumberland's success. Christopher Melfield of York wrote to Sir Rowland Winn: 'I have the plea-sure to tell you, that the Duke of Cumberland gained a complete victory over ye rebels'.[2] John Tucker wrote from London to his brother: 'I congratulate you most heartily on the glorious and happy Exploit of our young Hero who entirely defeated the Rebels near Inverness the 16th inst . . . I wish you health to enjoy the tranquillity of which I promise myself this Event will prove the foundation of.'[3]

Comments from diaries were meant for the diarist's eyes only. We can therefore expect them to be reliable indicators of the diarist's thoughts and what they saw or heard. James Clegg wrote on 21 April 1746, 'Great rejoic-ings for the Dukes victory' and on 29 April, 'We have good news from Scotland . . . Blessed be God.'[4] Likewise, Richard Kay wrote on 27 April, 'We have had a Thanksgiving Service on Account of the Duke of Cumberland having defeated the Rebells at Culloden . . . We are hearing of very good news.' Three days later he wrote, 'spent the Evening here with some Neighbouring Friends in rejoicing at this good News from Scotland, the Defeat of the Rebells who of late have been very much the Disturbers of our Peace'.[5] Gertrude Saville wrote: 'The joyfull news came of the Duke's having intirely defeated the whole Rebell army'.[6] And later:

> What cause have we to be thankfull to the Lord of Hosts, the only Giver of Victory . . . We were most unworthy of this great deliver-ance . . . O let us not be so again least some worse ill befall us! . . . Great Honour and thanks are due to him who thou was pleas'd to make thy Instrument, the young Duke, whose Courage and Conduct were extraordinary.[7]

Public celebrations were widespread in Yorkshire, as William Jessup noted:

> I hear there is very good news. The Duke hath killed and taken most of the Rebels and they were ringing the Bells and making great rejoicing in Leeds yesterday, having received expresses of the Victory which was gained with a very inconsiderable loss on our side, and they were ringing the Bell and made a Bonfire at Honley. Great rejoicings ringing of Bells &c. at Cawthorne, Penistone &c. A great Bonfire on the Sudill . . . There was great rejoicing at York. They had the Pope, Pretender and a Child in a warming pan.[8]

In London, there were great celebrations once the news of Culloden was heard:

> The Guns at the Tower and Park were fired twice. At night such rejoicing, so many Bonfires, such illuminations were never seen. Scarce the meanest house that had not some candles – nay, some Hackney Coaches and Chairs, Cellars and Bulks [shopfronts and stalls]. Some Houses had flamboys on the outside as well as Candles. 'Twas a Glorious sight.[9]

It was not only in England that there were celebrations. According to Henderson, 'The City of Edinburgh was not behind in testifying her Joy.'[10] Likewise, in Glasgow, on 21 April, there was music and bells ringing, a bonfire at the cross, dignitaries drank loyal healths to the King, Cumberland and the Prince and Princess of Wales. Windows were lit up at night. In fact, 'The Night concluded with the highest Expressions of Joy and Loyalty to His Majesty, and the greatest demonstrations of Joy.'[11] Fletcher wrote from Edinburgh, 'God be thanked our tedious Trouble is now drawn to a speedy and happy conclusion . . . this is very great news and a Glorious day to be remembered with joy and thankfulness'.[12] Ludovic Grant wrote on 18 April, 'It gives me no small pleasure to hear of the Duke of Cumberland's success against the Rebels.'[13] Civic rejoicings occurred elsewhere in Scotland – in Stirling, Dundee, Dumfries, Perth, Irvine, Montrose, Brechin and Linlithgow.[14]

There was also praise directed towards Cumberland himself. This was most prevalent when he returned from Scotland to London in July. Herring was eager to demonstrate his loyalty at York in July, where there was a civic and diocesan reception. Miss Saville wrote 'there was Bonfires and Illuminations all over the Town – more than upon the account of his Victory'. Herring also referred to him as 'our Hero'.[15] The loyal address of the University of Cambridge, sent in May 1746, referred to Cumberland's 'admirable Conduct and Heroick Bravery . . . gained immortal Honour to himself'.[16]

Clergy poured praise on Cumberland in their sermons, some of which were printed. Thomas Maddox of Liverpool's thanksgiving sermon included the line, 'We can never sufficiently admire and praise the unparalleled bravery and Conduct of His Royal Highness, the Duke of Cumberland'.[17] The Revd William Wood, a Yorkshire clergyman, likened Cumberland to Joshua, Israel's deliverer, and told his congregation that the Duke had been inspired by God.[18] On hearing the news of Culloden, Herring wrote to Cumberland:

'Give me leave to interrupt you for a moment to congratulate you on this great Event in Scotland. This brave young man has done his country an family incredible service and one cannot help envying the father the pleasure he must receive from such a son.'[19] Official recognition included the granting of the Freedom of the City of London and of York and the granting of an annual additional revenue of £25,000.[20]

The University of Oxford sent a glowing address to the court:

> We the Chancellor, masters and scholars of the University of Oxford, beg leave to approach your royal highness, with hearts full of the sincerest joy, to congratulate your majesty on the signal victory obtain'd over the rebels, thro' the blessing of God, by your majesty's forces under the command of his royal highness the duke; no part of your majesty's subjects being more deeply sensible of the extreme misery to which their kingdoms must have been reduced, had this most wicked rebellion, in favour of a popish pretender, have finally succeeded.[21]

It is worth noting that Oxford was one of the centres of Jacobitism in England and always returned Tory candidates to the Commons in this period. The thanksgivings were not, therefore, merely restricted to the natural supporters of the government.

Panegyrics about Cumberland were common. One read:

> William, in short, had a Sweetness of Disposition, an innate Courage, a Fund of Good-Sense and Good-Nature, which made him ador'd by the Soldiers and esteem'd by all others, with a noble love of Glory, which he pursued only in the Paths of Virtue and Honour. His chief Ambition was to command the Head of Armies, there to signalise his Military Virtue, as the Scourge of Tyranny and unrighteous Power.[22]

On the day appointed for national thanksgiving, Clegg wrote: 'This was the thanksgiving day for the defeat over the Rebels. I preached to a pretty full Congregation.'[23] Likewise, Kay wrote, after noting the occasion, 'I heard Mr Braddock preach at Bury Chapple . . . We hope the rebellious Crew are now suppressed, and that the Crown is established in the Protestant Line of Succession.'[24]

Parish churches the length and breadth of England rang their bells for the victory at Culloden and on the day appointed for national thanksgiving on

9 October. This is recorded in churchwardens' accounts and is important for it is evidence of popular support for the victory of the status quo at the lowest level of national administration. For example, at Kirkham in Lancashire, the accounts read that the bells were rung for two days at the cost of 12 shillings 'at News of the Duke's Victory'. At Halifax, money was spent on the celebration of 'the Glorious Victory obtained over the Rebels'.[25]

Corporations also bestowed their thanks on the Duke. York City referred to 'the late glorious success over rebellious savages'. They welcomed Cumberland after his return from Scotland and presented him with the freedom of the city in a gold box.[26] Newcastle upon Tyne also granted him the freedom of the city and local corporations such as the Merchant Adventurers' Company and Trinity House honoured him similarly.[27]

Some Scots in London were as happy as any Englishman. Dr John Mitchell wrote on 17 May to Professor Charles Mackie thus:

> I heartily rejoice with you and all sincere well-wishers to liberty (civil and ecclesiastick), religion, property and staunch revolutionary principles, upon the great and glorious deliverance God hath been yet again pleased to work for us from popery, slavery and desolation . . .
> I perfectly agree with you as to the praises due to the Duke of Cumberland as the instrument, and am fully satisfied that without his presence another defeat had been our lot.[28]

It is also worth noting that commentators in England had very little to say about the suppression of the rebellion and the punishment of captured Jacobites. The exception was the trials and executions of the Jacobite lords in London in the summer of 1746 and, to a far lesser extent, the trials of the common men. But even then, there was little comment, only statements of fact.[29] None of the diarists refer to activity in Scotland and had very little to say after the Jacobites returned to Scotland in late December, despite the reporting of activity in Scotland in the press.

Those who did comment included the senior figures of the political elite. They wholeheartedly approved of what had happened, and they rejoiced in it. Most harboured anti-Scottish prejudices and believed that the time was not yet ripe for mercy. For them, Jacobitism had to be crushed in its heartlands. Cumberland had performed a great service for them.

Walpole approved of Cumberland's actions: 'The Duke is still in Scotland, doing his family the only service that has been done for them since their accession.'[30] He also wrote 'The Duke behaved very bravely and humanely' and 'All the letters are full of the Duke's humanity and bravery'.[31]

Richmond was another who was pleased at the decisive nature of Culloden, writing on 27 April, 'most joyfull it is to thinke that so many of those villains are destroy'd, & indeed the Rope must finish those that have escaped with their lives & are taken, else wee shall all deserve to have all this over again'.[32] He was convinced that

> depend upon it the moment the Duke leaves Scotland the rebellion breaks out again. & so it will at any time if wee have ever less than eight thousand men in that country. For it is now evident beyond contradiction that nothing butt force will ever keep that stinking corner of the Kingdome quiet; & since I am on that Toppick I wonder to hear nothing of the Tyralls of those Peers or any of the rebels. I hope that untimely compassionate argument of their having still some of our people prisoners does not prevail, for if it did all these villains would escape unpunish'd which I am sure every honest English subject would have butt too much reason to cry out loudely upon.[33]

Richmond was not in favour of mercy, writing on 30 November, 'the very great lenity, & in my opinion ill timed mercy, to so many notorious rebels, will certainly bring about another rebellion'.[34]

A correspondent of Richmond's who was with the army in Scotland wrote of the trials of the Jacobites in London, but probably had the bigger picture in mind, too:

> I am extreamly glad to find ye tryalls of the Rebells go on so glibly, as I am convinced the Clemency of '15 was ye chief cause of the Rebellion of '46 and I firmly hope that every one, that came before ye House will meet ye same fate, for they are the Roots of that damned affair, and never was a people more proper to make examples of.[35]

Herring thought likewise. On 30 July, he wrote 'I am not a sanguinary man but surely ye proper time for mercy is, when ye Rebels have delivered up their arms, which they have not done or shown any disposition to.' He was also to write: 'It grieves me to hear of friends of the government saying clemency will bring down another rebellion.' Herring claimed that most people were 'universally chagrined' at the idea of mercy shown to the defeated enemy, and though they specifically meant the three lords being tried in London, they may have inferred the same about other Jacobites.[36]

Writers in journals published in the summer of 1746 discussed whether mercy ought to be shown to the defeated Jacobites. One alleged, 'Pity to the rebels now under the censure of law, that they may be the objects of mercy, is the cry of those and only those, who wish well to the rebels' and that this was actuated by 'Cruelty committed by the king's forces under the command of the duke at the battle of Culloden, is another cry actually propagated by them'. However the writer argued that pity was misplaced because the Jacobites were criminals:

> their crimes being of the blackest dye, as murder and robbery, and those the means to introduce and establish tyranny and popery. When a common malefactor is to suffer for murder or robbery, no reasonable man can so pity as to hope that the criminal may be received to mercy, because the law which preserves society and property has given the criminal up to punishment, as a satisfaction due in justice to the breach of the law.

The rebellion had, after all, cost the lives of hundreds of soldiers, destroyed property and hurt commerce.[37] Cumberland, therefore, was lauded as the 'Conquering Hero' by a wide cross-section of British society. They approved of his actions wholeheartedly.

There was some Jacobite comment against Cumberland and celebrations for Culloden, though it was very minimal. One Revd John Rooke of Willian, Hertfordshire, was accused of obstructing such celebrations. An anonymous letter accused him of refusing permission for the bell ringers to ring to mark the occasion. Others wished to build a bonfire instead, but apparently Rooke 'was so much disgusted at this Proceeding' and told the constable to disperse the crowd. Rooke also threatened legal action against one of the crowd who tried to light the bonfire. Yet this tale might have only been concocted by someone with a grudge against Rooke, as no action seems to have been taken against him and Rooke's behaviour in the previous year was certainly loyalist.[38]

Some genuine English Jacobites did express criticism of Cumberland. In June 1746, Richard Waring of Chipping, a flax dresser, said 'God damn the Duke and the King too. The Duke is a heretick.' Likewise, Henry Welborn, a labourer of Coniston, in Yorkshire, said 'God damn the Duke of Cumberland he never did good in his life'.[39] Then there was a Jacobite verse found in York Minster on 9 October 1746. It read:

What mean these vile and idle pranks?
To murder men and then give thanks

Stop preacher, and go no further
God ne'er accepts thanks for murder.[40]

It is unknown whether these remarks refer to events in Scotland or to the recent execution of Jacobite prisoners at York.

The most famous remark is that retailed by Horace Walpole in a letter of 1 August:

> the Duke, who has not so much of Caesar after a victory, as in gaining it, is for the utmost severity. It was lately proposed in the city, to present him with the freedom of some company; one of the aldermen said aloud, 'Then let it be of the Butchers!' [41]

And so the epithet of 'the Butcher' was born. Some of the City aldermen were known to have Jacobite sympathies, and it is difficult to know what lies behind this comment. What is certain is that Cumberland's enemies now had a convenient label for him, which has stuck to him evermore. Herring related how the King had had a paper put into his hands stating 'Recall that bloody tyrant from Scotland'.[42] Walpole had little time for such comments, writing that 'the Scotch, the Jacobites, and his brother's jealousy never rested till they had . . . entirely lost him the hearts of the nation'.[43]

Likewise, according to Johnstone, Cumberland

> was held in contempt by all respectable persons in England, even by those who were in no manner partisans of the house of Stuart. Ever afterwards he was known in London by the appellation of 'the butcher'.[44]

Yet this was an exaggeration, perhaps unsurprisingly so, given Johnstone's Jacobite views.

There were many Jacobite propaganda verses written about the Duke. One features Cumberland with Hawley, Huske and Lockhart, shortly after Culloden:

> Hawley: 'Now we soldiers now we've put 'em to rout
> Kill all the wounded see their latest breath
> And let them feel our mercy by their Death'.
> Cumberland: 'You heard me then I hope I was obeyed
> Canst be the heat who for these wretches plead'.
> Lockhart: 'With joy I did obey your just commands

And seventy eight were finished by my hand'.
Cumberland: 'Well done, my Lockhart worthy of thy self . . .
For thy reward I give thee this command
Go burn and plunder all the northern land
You'll not be moved by wretched women's cries . . .
First burn their houses put themselves to flight'.[45]

There were a number of prints published of the Duke in 1746. Most were highly complimentary. But at least two were not. One print showed him thus:

holding a bloody axe, and standing by a leafless tree; below him appear the crown falling from a plant, which is perhaps a turnip [the Jacobites taunted the Hanoverians with this symbol], a lamb endeavouring to escape from a wolf; beyond a head and arm lie on a blazing altar, and several bodies are suspended from a gallows.

Another was even more grotesque:

the Duke of Cumberland, who is symbollised by this figure of an ox standing on its hind legs; and an epaulette, the latter is formed of butcher's hooks, butcher's sleeves, apron, &c. a candle is stuck in his small cocked hat; in one hand is a bloody cleaver, in the other a slaughterer's axe. On his breast is a butcher's tray. In the background are a house in flames, with soldiers preventing the inmates from escaping, a gallows and flames for the execution of the rebels.

The latter is dated 9 December 1746. It is interesting to note that the alleged atrocity of the burning house at Culloden finds its way into this print.[46]

Fortune is fickle. Cumberland's popularity, so high in 1746, waned in the years after Culloden. With the Jacobite menace, once seen as extremely dangerous, over, his services in its suppression were overlooked. As Henry Lowther wrote to Irwin on 28 March 1752: 'The person who anno 1745 was styled our deliverer is now become the hatred of men of all ranks and conditions.'[47] Another reason for this change was the death of Frederick, Prince of Wales. Now the new heir to the throne of the elderly George II was the young Prince George (1738–1820, from 1760, George III) and there was suspicion that if there was to be a regency that Cumberland might assume power. Cumberland was likened to the 'wicked uncle' of evil memory, Richard III (another much maligned man).

Horace Walpole noted in 1751: 'The morning the Parliament met, great numbers of treasonable papers were dispersed by the Penny Post . . . levelled chiefly at the Duke, whom they compared to Richard III'.[48] Fears of the Duke's politics were allied to his military actions and Walpole added that 'whatever despotism he had a mind to establish might be grounded in the appearance of law'. Finally, 'he had taken every step to make himself unpopular both with the people and the army'.[49] This was because of his attempts to make the army more professional (which was objected to by some of the officers), and the fact that the mere existence of the army in peacetime was viewed by civilians with suspicion. Although he was honourable and dutiful, and disdained political intrigue, 'In other respects he was not much to be esteemed'.[50]

There is no evidence that Cumberland was capable of cruelty in his military career after returning from Scotland in July 1746. The change in how the Duke was seen is probably due to the changing political circumstances. When the Jacobites were a danger, his role in their suppression was applauded – he was the national saviour. Yet when this danger was over and safely in the past, he was fair game for political malice. Defeat in battle at Lauffeldt in 1747 and at Hastenbeck in 1757, though his troops were outnumbered in both, put paid to his military career and he never held a commission thereafter.

Yet the wheel of fortune changed again. Cumberland's reputation recovered in his last years. As Ranger of Windsor Great Park he had the Virginia Water constructed by former soldiers, and there is an obelisk there in his memory. He helped to found the Jockey Club. Finally he played his part in politics in the construction of the Rockingham administration in 1765, which led to the repeal of the odious Stamp Act on the American colonies (for which he was feted in the colonies). In the same year, on 31 October, he died aged 44 and was buried at Westminster Abbey. Walpole wrote 'He would have made a great King, but probably too great a king for so corrupt a kingdom.' He also noted, 'In London, the Duke's death was deeply felt . . . the middling and lower people almost universally went into the closest mourning with weepers, and wore it for the whole time that had been customary before the consternation enjoined in the last reign.' Yet, despite a subscription to raise money for a statue, insufficient funds were forthcoming.[51]

It is also worth noting that, in the 1750s and 1760s, Englishmen referred to the Duke as 'the Duke of Cumberland', not as the Butcher or by any other derogatory reference.

James Wooodforde (1740–1803), then an undergraduate at Oxford, refers to the Duke thus in his diary for 1761.[52] Similarly, a few years earlier, in 1756, Thomas Turner, a Sussex shopkeeper, made the following reference in his diary, 'Heard this day that the Duke of Cumberland is a-coming into Sussex to view the seacoast'.[53] Others described him similarly – Richard Lyttleton in 1754, Lord Dacre in 1756 and Henry Grenville in 1757.[54] Had they thought that he had been the bloody monster of Jacobite legend, they could have used the epithet referred to by Walpole above. The term 'butcher' was one employed by the Duke's enemies; whether Jacobites or Tories; it was not a term universally used by contemporaries. It was a deliberately loaded term, though one that has unfortunately stuck.

An elegy on his 'much lamented death' included the following lines:

> Ye grateful Crouds, who can so well express
> Great William's Bounty in your deep distress . . .
> Much belov'd . . .
> Much too soon remov'd . . .
> And at Culloden's sharp and bloody Field,
> He made the Rebels and their Leader yield.[55]

Certainly a contemporary's opinion of the Duke depended on his politics. Lord Marchmont observed, in 1747, in conversation with George II:

> I was the loudest in vindicating the conduct of His Royal Highness the Duke . . . [who] had conducted himself with great ability; and that all the complaints if the army were in themselves nothing . . . *it was the malice of His Majesty's enemies*. . . . He said 'his son did not go there to please them; *they naturally would be angry at him*'. I said 'that country had infinite obligations to the Duke'[emphasis added].[56]

Debate continued after Cumberland's death. James Boswell, who was sympathetic towards Jacobitism, recorded in 1775 that Dr Johnson saw 'a man who was very furious, and who, while beating his straw, supposed it was William, Duke of Cumberland, whom he was punishing for his cruelties in Scotland in 1746'. On the other hand, Boswell noted 'My honourable friend, General Sir George Howard, who served in the Duke of Cumberland's army, has assured me that the cruelties were not imputable to his Royal Highness.'[57]

In Cavendish Square a statue to him was erected. Although it was taken down in 1869, the inscription on the plinth still remains and reads:

William, Duke of Cumberland
Born April 15 1721. Died 31 October 1765
This Equestrian Statue
Was erected by

Lieutenant General
William STRODE
In Gratitude
For His Private Kindness
In Honour
To His Publick Virtue
November the 4 Anno Domini 1770.

As for Charles Stuart, despite winning popularity in France after Culloden, and living until 1788, his life after Culloden was one of failure, disappointment and alcoholism. The year 1746 had been the high point in the lives of both these two young men. Despite marriage, Charles had no legitimate heirs. His brother Henry had become a cardinal and died in 1807, the last of the heirs of James II.

Conclusion

His Royal Highness had strong parts, great military abilities, undoubted
courage, and had gained the victory of Culloden, which saved this
country. But his popularity ended with the rebellion; his services were
immediately forgot, and he became the object of fear and jealously. The
severe treatment of Scotland, after the defeat of the rebels, was imputed
to his cruel and sanguinary disposition; even the army had been taught
to complain of the unnecessary strictness of his discipline . . . All his good
qualities were overlooked, all his faults aggravated: false facts were
advanced against him, and false conclusions drawn from them.[1]

Having read the evidence so far, the reader may have reached their own
conclusions. What follows is not the final word, but the author's own conclusion, much of which should already have been implicit, at least, in his
comments to date.

What is certain is that Cumberland must be cleared of the grossest charges
that have been laid against him, often in very recent years by some who
should know better. He was certainly not an exponent of genocide against the
Highlanders. There is not a single known order by him commanding his
troops to murder unarmed men, women or children. Yes, some civilians
were killed in Scotland after Culloden by regular troops under his overall
command. But we must use the word 'civilian' with care. As far as
Cumberland was concerned, or his men for that matter, anyone carrying
arms and who was prepared to use them against them was an enemy. These
people were no different to the Jacobite 'rebels' they had been fighting
against.

Yet, even if we discount those Highlanders who continued the struggle in
various forms, there were almost certainly other civilian casualties. These
were those people killed on the direct orders of Captains Scott and Ferguson.
As terrible as these individual stories are, they do not constitute genocide.
Whether Cumberland was aware of them is another question, and certainly
neither subordinate was explicit about their alleged misdeeds in their corres-

pondence. He certainly did nothing, as far as is known, to reprimand these two if he did know. In any case, there are few wars, if any, in which some civilians or prisoners of war are not killed out of hand by small parties of troops. It is also worth noting that some officers, such as General Campbell and Major Forrester, were completely unlike junior officers such as Scott and Ferguson, as regards the Highlanders. Yet it is the activities of the latter two, not the former, which have received more attention from Jacobite historians and this has coloured views on Cumberland.

Then we come to Culloden, that battle allegedly so notorious that it is not mentioned in regimental honours of the British army. The fog, or rather, shroud of sentiment, must be rent aside. Stories certainly emerged afterwards from Jacobite sympathizers about atrocities which followed the rout of the Jacobite army; most notably the massacre of Jacobites in the cottage. Yet, as we have seen, there is considerable doubt as to whether this occurred. Archaeological evidence is inconclusive, at best, on the point. Even elderly Jacobites were unsure. No non-Jacobite mentions it, except one, and then only to discount it.

The Jacobite howls of horror about the dragoons who cut down fleeing Jacobites after Culloden also need to be treated cautiously. That fleeing troops were hunted down with zeal by the cavalrymen is not in any doubt. Yet this was not a war crime. It was conventional military practice which happened after any eighteenth-century battle in which one side was in full rout and the other had faster troops who were in a position to pursue. One might well recall the luckless regulars who were slain by triumphant Jacobites after Prestonpans, to which even Jacobite writers attest.

Staying with Culloden, we can turn to other events after the battle. Some of the wounded were indeed killed where they lay. How many, we know not. Who, if anyone gave the orders, is another unanswerable question. It may well have been officers in the front-line battalions. Certainly no one mentions Cumberland giving any such order, though of course nor did he restrain them from this action. These actions may seem despicable to the modern reader, or indeed anyone sitting comfortably away from the hostilities. They have not just risked their lives in a bloody battle against an enemy that had bested their comrades twice already, which had taken them away from the proper soldiering of fighting the French and had led them to campaign in the winter. Some men wanted recompense – revenge – for such; others may well have been frightened by these strange-looking enemies who may not all have been as helpless as they seemed. And if knowledge of the Jacobite night march and the Jacobite orders to show no mercy towards them had become common knowledge at any time, their anger would have been doubled.

We now come to the order made by Cumberland to send a party of fifty men to the battlefield on the following day. This is certainly ambiguous. Yet, as we have seen, Cumberland was not a man to mince his words. There was no reason why he should not have written orders, as the companies of Campbells had been given in February 1692, 'to put all to the sword' at Glencoe. He was backed by both King and Parliament and was at the peak of martial triumph. It is unlikely he was thinking long term about historians and others who would subsequently criticize his actions. In any case, it was conventional military wisdom to send troops to a battlefield in its aftermath, to collect weapons, standards and anything else which might be of use.

In the months following Culloden, the main imperative was to disarm the Highlands as much as it was possible to do, and to take prisoners. Cumberland did not think the latter measure would be successful, but, leaving genocide apart, there was not much else that could be done immediately. And prisoners were taken. Over 3,000 of them all told (the largest number taken after any conflict in Britain for over half a century), a number that overcrowded gaols and prison hulks could not comfortably contain – leading to many unintended deaths.

Rather, Cumberland had always seen the long-term solution to be in legislation. He had discussed this with both Newcastle and Hardwicke, two of the three senior politicians in charge of the government. Power needed to be removed from the Highland chiefs and the military aspects of the clan system demolished. Demilitarization was the key, not bloody massacre. For a young soldier, as opposed to a mature statesman, this was astute thinking.

Yet there was suffering in the Highlands after Culloden; indeed it had been set in motion beforehand, too. Parties of soldiers, sailors and militia had burnt property and stolen cattle – how much it is impossible to compute, but the North-West Highlands seem to have suffered grievously. Both Jacobites and loyal Scots suffered.

Part of this was certainly the result of policy as ordered by Cumberland. He was convinced that the Jacobite war machine had to be smashed, but then no one loyal to George II would have doubted this. Apart from the Jacobite field army, which had to be beaten in battle, the sinews of war – supplies – had to be attacked, too. The Jacobites needed food supplies and in part these were supplied by the products of the Highland economy, which was chiefly agrarian. Cattle were taken away and sold in the Lowlands and England, for no fighting force of any size could operate for long with a lack of food. Even after Culloden, there was the fear that the clans might reform for another campaign, though after the end of the May there was no realistic chance of this.

Yet, whilst Cumberland ordered such a policy, he was not wholly responsible for its execution. First, much was down to the men on the ground who had to implement this. Some were Scots and had their own grudges to settle; some were greedy for plunder and some had to rely on local informants, with the usual risk that they were out to ingratiate and enrich themselves. It should also be recalled that Cumberland did investigate some abuses and in some cases had goods returned to their owners.

Compared to some of his subordinates, Cumberland's behaviour seems favourable. Unlike Hawley and Wolfe he is not known to have personally indulged in plundering. Unlike Hawley or Huske he did not advocate giving a bounty for soldiers decapitating enemies. And loyalist Highlanders such as General Campbell and Forbes gave him credit for his humanity.

One thing which Cumberland did act against was looting. Any soldier or officer who was found to be guilty of theft was summarily punished, either by being discharged or by being executed. Was this unnecessarily brutal? Conventional military discipline did allow for this, so Cumberland was hardly extraordinary in ordering its application. Furthermore, it did offer some protection for civilians against depredations from the military.

We should also recall that many Jacobites, especially the rank and file, went unpunished for their part in the campaign. Many took the opportunity to surrender their weapons (or at least some weapons) and had their part taken by their priest. Many were pardoned and then let alone. We do not know their number, but the sixty-nine Grants of Glenmoriston who were transported were in the minority; their fate only known because they were dealt with harshly, and they are often held to be representative of the whole, rather than as exceptions to the rule.

Cumberland did not like the Highlanders (excepting soldiers in his army and Presbyterian ministers) as a whole, but then nor did the majority of the English whose opinions we know of, and these were shared by some Lowland Scots, too. His prejudices were commonplace. This makes him no better nor any worse than most of his generation. His opinions, though, were sharpened because, for him, this campaign was personal. The Jacobites had attempted to deprive his father of the crown, and he had been urged by his dying mother to do all he could to support his father.

We should also recall the charge of 'ethnic cleansing'. Cumberland did consider the idea of deporting whole Jacobite clans to the American colonies. The idea, though, came from others, mostly Scots. In any case, he did not press it home.

Another charge laid against Cumberland was that he was unreasonably cruel towards his own soldiery. This is nonsense. Men who ran from the battlefield of Falkirk and were to be hanged by Hawley were reprieved by him. Deserters found among the Jacobite prisoners after Culloden had mixed fates – some were executed, but the majority were not. Desertion followed by enlistment with the enemy was a heinous military crime anyway. Cumberland's troops seem to have had a high opinion of him throughout, and this cannot be said for those serving under other senior officers during the campaign.

The Jacobites, incidentally, were not always the heroes of romance. They were hard-headed soldiers who aimed to win. In trying to do so, some of their methods were not ones of which their admirers like to be reminded, but they should be stated. Supplies were often exacted from those who were unwilling by threats of fire and sword. In some case, these measures were applied, doubtless to encourage the others. Had the Jacobites surprised the regulars on the night march before Culloden, it is probable that a massacre would have ensued. That this did not happen is not the point – the intention was there, and ordered by Lord George Murray, who is still seen as a hero by some. This was not a struggle between black and white, but rather between shades of grey.

Cumberland did not act in a political vacuum. He was not head of state, as Cromwell had been. Instead, he acted with the full approval of the government, through its chief spokesman, the Duke of Newcastle – not usually known as a specimen of inhumanity. The young soldier's policy was never censured by his political masters; indeed, he had their applause, and so it was clearly agreeable to them. Yet Newcastle is never termed the 'red duke'. To him, and many others, the Jacobite menace, which had lasted since 1689, should be rooted out, in order to secure the safety and stability of the kingdom (and their own political supremacy). Cumberland cannot, therefore, be singled out. If there is blame, then the responsibility was shared.

The Duke of Cumberland has been harshly judged by historians, applying to him standards that were not those of his age, as well as by those who were and are Jacobites. It is only if all his actions and words, much of which are ambiguous, are seen in a 'Jacobite' light that he can be properly termed 'the Butcher'. Of course, he was not the 'whiter than white' hero (Sweet William) believed by loyalists in 1746, either. Rather he was a soldier who was defending his father's crown and was determined to stamp out the enemies ('Rebellious Scots to crush', to use a line from the contemporary National Anthem) which threatened it, if possible forever. Such measures did cause great hardships for some in the Highlands of Scotland. Innocent people suffered, some far more than others. This was due chiefly to the loss of property and cattle – not, except in a few cases, murder. It is hard to see how it could have been otherwise. Cumberland could not exercise total control over all his subordinates. Did he know – or care – about the murders carried out by Scott and Ferguson? This question is impossible to answer. It is probable that he knew that war does lead to atrocities and accepted them as inevitable. On the other hand, he did take steps to control unauthorized looting and many former Jacobites were left unmolested. His actions and those of his troops were, though, those of his times. Those termed 'rebels' by eighteenth-century governments were not deemed to be honourable foes, such as other regular troops (whom Cumberland, of course, dealt with fairly). Cumberland's campaign was, certainly in part, ruthless, though perhaps necessarily so, but he was not the butcher of Jacobite myth.

Notes

Introduction
1. *The Annual Register* (1765), p. 1.
2. J Tey, *The Daughter of Time* (1951), p. 141.
3. Horace Walpole, *Memoirs and Portraits*, ed. M. Hodgart (1963), p. 14.

Chapter 1
1. F McLynn, *Bonnie Prince Charlie* (1991), p. 557.
2. C Duffy, *The Forty Five* (2003), pp. 547–8.
3. A Henderson, *The History of the Rebellion* (1748), preface.
4. J Ray, *A Compleat History of the Rebellion* (1754), pp. v, ix.
5. Ibid., pp. ix–x.
6. Henderson, *History*, pp. 116–17.
7. Ray, *History*, p. 338.
8. A Henderson, *The Life of the Duke of Cumberland* (1766).
9. J Marchant, *History of the Present Rebellion* (1746).
10. F Douglas, *History of the Rebellion* (1755), pp. 231–4.
11. 'Miscellany', IV, *Scottish Historical Society*, 3rd series, 9 (1926), 117.
12. W A Speck, *The Butcher: The Duke of Cumberland and the Suppression of the '45* (1981), p. 1.
13. J Maxwell, *Narrative of the Expedition of Prince Charles Stuart* (1841), pp. 168, 170.
14. The Chevalier de Johnstone: A Memoir of the Forty Five, ed. B Rawson (1970), p. 130.
15. J Forbes, *Jacobite Memoirs* (1834), p. xviii.
16. J Barrett, *Cavaliers* (2000), p. 193.
17. A Ewald, *The Life and Times of Prince Charles Stuart* (1883), pp. 168–9.
18. C Petrie, *The Jacobite Movement* (1932), p. 178.
19. Ibid., pp. 214–16.
20. Ibid., p. 215.
21. D Preston, *The Road to Culloden Moor* (1995), p. 14.
22. J Prebble, *Culloden* (1963), p. 10.
23. Preston, *Road*, pp. 195, 239.
24. J Roberts, *The Jacobite Wars* (2002), pp. 176–90.

25. R Houston, 'The Ten Worst Britons', *BBC History Magazine* (Jan. 2006), 16–17.

26. A I Macinnes, 'The Aftermath of the '45', in R C Woosnam-Savage (ed.), *1745: Charles Edward Stuart and the Jacobites* (1995), pp. 107–8.
27. B P Lenman, *The Jacobite Risings in Britain, 1689–1746* (1980), pp. 259, 261.
28. J Black, *Culloden and the Forty Five* (1990), p. 201.
29. Ibid., pp. 177–8.
30. McLynn, *Bonnie Prince Charlie*, pp. 159–60.
31. Duffy, *The '45* , pp. 523–4.
32. Ibid., p. 528.
33. M Barthorp, *The Jacobite Risings, 1689–1745* (1982), pp. 15–16.
34. E N Williams, *Dictionary of British and European History, 1485–1789* (1980), p. 151.
35. J Plumb, *Eighteenth Century England, 1714–1815* (1960), p. 107.
36. P Langford, *A Polite and Commercial People: England, 1727–1783* (1997), p. 199.
37. L du Garde Peach, *Bonnie Prince Charlie* (1975), p. 42.
38. Speck, *Butcher*, p. 6
39. Ibid., p. 4.
40. Ibid., p. 95.
41. Ibid., p. 141.
42. Ibid., pp. 148–9.
43. Ibid., p. 201.
44. E Charteris, *William Augustus, Duke of Cumberland* (1913), p. vii.
45. Ibid., p. viii.
46. R Whitworth, *William Augustus, Duke of Cumberland* (1992), p. 1.
47. Ibid., p. 2.
48. Ibid., p. 93.
49. J Fortescue, *History of the British Army*, vol. 2 (1910), p. 146.
50. Ibid., p. 148.
51. S. Reid, *1745: A Military History of the Last Jacobite Rising* (1996), preface.
52. S. Reid, *Culloden* (2005), p. 106.
53. Ibid., p. 112.
54. Ibid., p. 113.
55. J. Sadler, *Culloden: The Last Charge of the Highland Clans* (2006), p. 256.

Chapter 2

1. J R Hartley, *The Go-Between* (1958), p. 1.
2. J H Plumb, *The First Four Georges* (1956), pp. 14–15.
3. British Library, Additional MSS, 35589, fo. 79r, 35598, fo. 164v.
4. J Black, *Eighteenth Century Britain, 1688–1783* (2001), p. 186.
5. Ibid., pp. 188–92.
6. *The Gentleman's Magazine*, 15 (1745), 51, 219, 385, 387.
7. 'The Great Diurnall of Nicholas Blundell, 1712–1719', ed. F Tyrer, *The Record Society of Lancashire and Cheshire* (1970), 40, 126–7.

8.   The Letters of Private Wheeler, 1809–1828, ed. B H Liddell Hart (2000), p. 196.
9.   C E Whiting (ed.), 'Two Yorkshire Diaries', *Yorkshire Archaeological Society Record Series*, 117 (1952), 108, 109.
10. A Saville (ed.), 'Secret Comment: The Diaries of Gertrude Saville, 1722–1757', *Thoroton Society*, 41 (1997), 261.
11. Whiting, 'Diaries', pp. 109, 110.
12. 'The Diary of Dr Richard Kay, 1716–1751', ed. W Brockbank and F Kenworthy, *Chetham Society* (1968), 102.
13. 'The Diary of James Clegg, II', ed. V S Doe, *Derbyshire Record Society* (1979), 558.
14. Leeds Archives, NH2875/7.
15. Whiting, 'Diaries', p. 113.
16. Ibid., pp. 114, 116.
17. Saville, 'Secret Comment', p. 263.
18. Clegg, 'Diary', ed. Voe, p. 559.
19. Bodleian Library, Ms Donc. c.107, fo. 174v.
20. W B Blaikie (ed.), 'Origins of the Forty Five', *Scottish Historical Society*, 2nd series, 2 (1916), 181.
21. Whiting, 'Diaries', pp. 113, 117.
22. Northumberland Record Office, ZRI/27/4/66.
23. J Ray, *The Compleat History of the Rebellion* (1754), pp. 354–8.
24. Ibid., pp. 363–4.
25. J Bate, *A Parochial Letter to the inhabitants of St. Paul's Deptford, Kent* (1745), p. 9.
26. J Hill, *False Zeal and Christian zeal distinguish'd or the essentials of popery described: A Sermon* (1745), pp. 25–6.
27. *The Gentleman's Magazine*, 15 (1745), 579, 653, 547; 16 (1746), 16.
28. E Burt, *Letters from a Gentleman in the North of Scotland*, vol. 2 (1754), 175.
29. Daniel Defoe, *A Tour through the Whole Island of Great Britain*, ed. P Rogers (1971), 676.
30. Anon., *A Journey through part of England and Scotland* (1746), pp. 94–5.
31. S Johnson and J Boswell, *A Journey to the Western Islands of Scotland and The Journal of a Tour to the Hebrides*, ed. P. Levi (1984), p. 65.
32. *The Diary of Dudley Ryder, 1715–1716*, ed. W Mathews (1939), pp. 88, 227.
33. *The Correspondence of the Dukes of Richmond and Newcastle, 1724–1750*, ed. T J McCann (1984), pp. 204, 236.
34. *The Correspondence of Horace Walpole*, ed. W S Lewis (1955), vol. 30, pp. 96, 287.
35. BL, Add. MSS, 35598, fos. 71r, 89r, 127r, 149r, 154r, 164r, 64v.
36. Royal Archives, Cumberland Papers, 10/275.
37. Ibid., 17/51.
38. BL, Add. MSS, 35598, fo. 74r.
39. Ibid., fo. 81r.

40. Ibid., fos. 70v, 89r.
41. West Sussex Record Office, Goodwood 111, 261.
42. R Patten, *The History of the Rebellion* (1717), p. 185.
43. D Szechi, *1715: The Great Jacobite Rebellion* (2006), p. 159.
44. T Royle, *The Civil War* (2005), pp. 331, 349.
45. J Falkner, *Great and Glorious Days, Marlborough's Battles, 1704–1709* (2002), p. 42
46. Ibid., pp. 42–3.
47. Ibid., pp. 50–1.
48. S Reid, *Wolfe* (2000), pp. 144, 180–1.
49. 'Peter Clarke's Journal', ed. H Paton, *Scottish Historical Society Miscellany*, 1 (1895), 520–1.
50. *Letters of Private Wheeler*, p. 196.
51. E Hathaway (ed.), *Costello: The True Story of a Peninsular War Rifleman* (1997), p. 175.
52. J Black, *European Warfare, 1660–1815* (1994), p. 231.
53. A Starkey, *War in the Age of the Enlightenment, 1700–1789* (2003), p. 5.
54. Ibid., p. 149.
55. Ibid., pp. 16–18.
56. L and M Frey, *Societies in Upheaval* (1987), pp. 105, 52–6.
57. Starkey, *War*, pp. 141, 142, 155.
58. R Clifton, *The Last Popular Rebellion: The Western Rising of 1685* (1984), pp. 219, 230.
59. Ibid., pp. 230–43.
60. J Prebble, *Glencoe* (1965).
61. T Harris, *Revolution: The Great Crisis of the British Monarchy, 1685–1720* (2006), p. 473.
62. Szechi, *1715*, pp. 168–9, 200–8.
63. *The Annual Register* (1798), p. 131.

Chapter 3

1. *The Correspondence of the Dukes of Richmond and Newcastle, 1724–1750*, ed. T J McCann (1984), pp.103–4.
2. ODNB, vol. 59, p. 105.
3. HMC Egmont, vol. 1, p. 16.
4. A Henderson, *The Life of the Duke of Cumberland* (1766), p. 15.
5. ODNB, vol. 59, pp. 105–6.
6. *Lord Hervey's Memoirs*, ed. T Sedgwick (1963), p. 246.
7. *The Gentleman's Magazine*, 10 (1740), 356.
8. *The Gentleman's Magazine*, 9 (1739), 382; 10 (1740), 356.
9. HMC Egmont, vol. 2, p. 437.
10. Ibid., vol. 3, p. 4.

11. Ibid., pp. 49–50.
12. *Correspondence of Horace Walpole*, ed. W S Lewis (1955), vol. 19, p. 52.
13. HMC Egmont, vol. 2, p. 235.
14. Whitworth, *Cumberland*, pp. 31–2.
15. *Walpole*, ed. Lewis, vol. 18, pp. 258, 268.
16. Ibid., p. 279.
17. Correspondence, ed. McCann, pp. 103–4.
18. *Historical Memoirs of his late Royal Highness, William Augustus, Duke of Cumberland* (1767), p. 5.
19. Reid, *Wolfe* (2002), p. 58.
20. R Whitworth, *William Augustus, Duke of Cumberland* (1992), pp. 47–9.
21. *The Life of Lord Chancellor Hardwicke*, ed. P Yorke (1913), vol. 1, p. 393.
22. Ibid., p. 399.

Chapter 4

1. BL, Add. MSS, 32707, fo. 14r.
2. B P Lenman, *The Jacobite Risings in Britain, 1689–1746* (1980).
3. *Hardwicke*, ed. Yorke, vol. 1, p. 435.
4. *Walpole*, ed. Lewis, vol. 19, p. 104.
5. Henderson, *History*, pp. 8–9.
6. Home, *History*, pp. 40–5.
7. *Walpole*, ed. Lewis, vol. 19, p. 105.
8. BL, Add. MSS, 32705, fo. 93r.
9. Ibid., fos. 113r, 114v, 131r, 155r.
10. Home, *History*, pp. 69–73.
11. Henderson, *History*, pp. 30–1.
12. Elcho, *Short Account*, p. 272; Home, *History*, pp. 87–8.
13. Ibid., pp. 90–4.
14. *Walpole*, ed. Lewis, vol. 19, pp. 116–18.
15. *The Private Correspondence of Chesterfield and Newcastle*, ed. R Lodge (1930), p. 69.
16. Ibid, p. 74.
17. J. Oates, 'The Responses in the North East of England to the Jacobite Rebellions of 1715 and 1745', Reading University Ph.D. (2001); Oates, *The Jacobite Invasion of 1745 in North West England* (2006); *The Gentleman's Magazine*, 15 (1745), 552.
18. *Hardwicke, ed. Yorke, vol. 1, p. 455.*
19. *Private Correspondence*, ed. Lodge, p. 73.
20. 'Memorials of John Murray of Broughton, 1740–1747', ed. R E Bell, *Scottish Historical Society*, 18 (1897), 231–4.
21. Home, *History*, pp. 99–100; R C Jarvis, *Collected Papers on the Jacobite Risings* (1971), vol. 1, pp. 175–94.

22. Home, *History*, pp. 111–14.
23. Oates, *Jacobite Invasion*, pp. 50–3.
24. *Private Correspondence*, ed. Lodge, p. 86.
25. *Walpole*, ed. Lewis, vol. 19, pp. 179–80.
26. Ibid., p. 174.
27. Henderson, *History*, p. 60.
28. *Private Correspondence*, ed. Lodge, pp. 87, 93.
29. Ibid., p. 95.
30. *Walpole*, ed. Lewis, vol. 19, p. 180.
31. C Duffy, *The '45* (2003), pp. 300–13, Oates, 'The Crisis of the Hanoverian State?', *JSAHR*, 81 (2003), 328.
32. J Ray, *The Compleat History of the Rebellion* (1754), p. 177.
33. Royal Archives, Cumberland Papers, 8/6.
34. Oates, *Jacobite Invasion*, pp. 81–2.
35. Home, *History*, pp. 107–9.
36. Henderson, *History*, p. 66.
37. *Hardwicke*, ed. Yorke, vol. 1, p. 486; HMC Egmont, vol. 3, p. 312.
38. A and H Taylers (eds), *1745 and After* (1938), p. 110.
39. Elcho, *Short Account* (1907), p. 350.
40. G C Mounsey, *Carlisle in 1745* (1846), p. 149.
41. NA, SP36/78, fo. 271r.
42. 'The Lyon in Mourning', ed. H Paton, *Scottish Historical Society*, 1 (1975), 29.
43. NA, SP36/78, fo. 282r; Merseyside Maritime Museum, DX594, fo. 31r.
44. *Private Correspondence*, ed. Lodge, p. 98.
45. Home, *History*, p. 110.
46. *Walpole*, ed. Lewis, vol. 19, p. 193.
47. *Private Correspondence*, ed. Lodge, p. 93.
48. Ibid., p. 123.
49. Ibid.
50. Ibid.
51. Ibid.
52. Ibid, p. 130.
53. Ibid, p. 135.
54. Ibid, p. 100.
55. Duffy, *The '45*, p. 416.
56. NA, SP54/27, fo. 29a.
57. Ibid., fo. 29b.
58. G Bailey, *Falkirk or Paradise! The Battle of Falkirk Muir 17 January 1746* (1996), pp. 128, 162.
59. *Walpole*, ed. Lewis, vol. 19, p. 204.
60. NA, SP54/27, fo. 48.
61. NA, SPS54/27, fo. 55a.
62. National Archives of Scotland, GD103/2/387.

63. *Hardwicke*, ed. Yorke, vol. 1, p. 493.
64. Ibid., p. 494.
65. NA, SP54/28/4.
66. NA, SP54/28/9.
67. NA, SP54/30/2.
68. RA, CP11/82.
69. RA, CP12/83.
70. RA, CP13/152.
71. National Library of Scotland, MS3734, fo. 308r.
72. Ibid., fo. 285r.
73. Ibid., fo. 343r.
74. Ibid., MS3735, fo. 514r.
75. Ibid., MS 3734, fos. 296, 313.
76. Ibid., fo. 432r.
77. Ibid., fo. 436r.
78. Ibid., fo. 430r.
79. RA, CP12/85.
80. NAS, GD1/90/1.
81. NAS, GD16/34/344.
82. RA, CP12/76.
83. RA, CP12/14.
84. RA, CP12/353.
85. RA, CP10/168.
86. NLS, MS 3734, fo. 430r.
87. RA, CP12/15.
88. RA, CP13/74–5; Whitworth, *William Augustus*, p. 100.
89. NLS, MS16621, fo. 91r.
90. RA, CP10/74; *The Newcastle Courant*, 2722 (15–22 Feb. 1746).
91. RA, CP13/3.
92. *The Newcastle Courant*, 2728 (29 March–5 April 1746).
93. *The Newcastle Courant*, 2728 (29 March–5 April 1746), 2729 (5–12 April 1746); *The Newcastle Gazette*, 95 (9 April 1746).
94. *The Oxford Gazette or Reading Mercury*, 19 (24 March 1746).
95. RA, CP10/132.
96. NLS, ADV.MS. 82.1.4/3.
97. NLS, ADV.MS. 82.1.4/2.
98. NLS, ADV.MS.82.1.4/23.
99. NLS, ADV.MS. 82.1.4/6.
100. NAS, GD103/2/387.
101. NLS, MS 3734, fo. 260r.
102. NA, SP54/27, 1a.
103. Ibid., 29/28, 32e.
104. RA, CP10/124.

105. NAS, GD248/48/4/23.
106. RA, CP11/323.
107. Ibid., 12/206.
108. NAS, GD128/69/14/7.
109. Elcho, *Short Account*, pp. 389–95.
110. BL, Add. MSS, 32706, fo. 234v-r.
111. RA, CP 10/293.
112. BL, Add. MSS, 32706, fo. 234v.
113. Ibid., fo. 258v.
114. Ibid., fo. 148.
115. Ibid., fo. 234v.
116. *The Newcastle Courant*, 2729 (5–12 April 1746).
117. S Reid, *1745: A Military History of the Last Jacobite Rising* (1996), pp. 81–90.
118. Ray, *History*, p. 269.
119. Oates, 'Hessian Forces Employed in Scotland in 1746', *JSAHR*, 83 (2005), 335.
120. Ibid.
121. Ibid.
122. NA, SP54/30, fo. 108r.
123. NA, SP36/81, fos. 149r–150v.
124. NLS, ADV.MS 23.3.28, p. 195.
125. Elcho, *Short Account*, pp. 409–10.
126. Ibid., pp. 414–15.
127. Ibid., pp. 416–19.
128. NA, SP54/30/2.
129. BL, Add. MSS, 32707, fos. 13r–14r.
130. Ibid, 32706, fo. 260r.
131. RA, CP10/162.
132. BL, Add. MSS, 32706, fo. 325r.
133. Ibid., fos. 325r–326v.
134. NA, SP54/30/2.
135. NA, SP54/29/27a.
136. RA, CP13/45, 104, 148.
137. Ibid., fo. 121.
138. Ibid., fo. 152.
139. *The London Magazine* (1746), 195.
140. Blaikie, 'Origins', p.157.
141. Ibid., p. 156.
142. Henderson, *History*, p.116.
143. NA, SP54/29/32A.
144. Ibid.
145. NA, SP54/29/2a.
146. *The Gentleman's Magazine*, 16 (1746), 235–6.

147. NAS, GD1/90/3.
148. NA, SP54/29, 32a; 30/143r.

Chapter 5

1. *The Gentleman's Magazine*, 16 (1746), 219–20.
2. Elcho, *Short Account*, p. 419.
3. Ray, *History*, pp. 312–13.
4. Ibid., pp. 313–14, National Army Museum 8711–48.
5. NA, SP54/30, fo. 143r.
6. Anon., 'Culloden Letter', *JSAHR*, 35 (1957), 183.
7. *Hardwicke*, ed. Yorke, vol. 1, p. 520.
8. NA, SP54/30, fo. 145r.
9. *Hardwicke*, ed. Yorke, vol. 1, p. 520.
10. NA, SP54/30, fo. 144v.
11. Elcho, *Short Account*, p. 420.
12. Maxwell, *Narrative*, p. 138.
13. NA, SP54/30, fo. 145r.
14. 'Culloden Letter' (1957), p. 184.
15. Elcho, *Short Account*, pp. 420–1.
16. A N C McLachlan, *A Sketch of Cumberland's Military Life* (1876), p. 287.
17. Elcho, *Short Account*, pp. 421–2.
18. J. Denistoun, *Memoirs of Sir Robert Strange* (1855), p. 55.
19. Findlay, *Wolfe in Scotland* (1928), pp. 103–4.
20. NA, SP54/30, fo. 146r.
21. Taylers, *1745*, p. 150.
22. Elcho, *Short Account*, p. 422.
23. Chambers, *Jacobite Memoirs*, p. 121.
24. Taylers, *1745*, p. 151.
25. Elcho, *Short Account*, p. 426.
26. Ibid., pp. 426–7.
27. Chambers, *Jacobite Memoirs*, p. 121.
28. Elcho, *Short Account*, p. 427.
29. Blaike, 'Origins', p. 210.
30. Johnstone, *Memoir*, p. 116.
31. Elcho, *Short Account*, pp. 427–8.
32. Henderson, *History*, p. 113.
33. Blaikie, 'Origins', p. 212.
34. Henderson, *History*, p. 113.
35. Home, *History* (1802), 221.
36. *Hardwicke*, ed. Yorke, vol. 1, p. 522.
37. Johnstone, *Memoir*, p. 118.
38. Elcho, *Short Account*, pp. 428–9.

39. Ray, *History*, pp. 349–51.
40. Blaikie, 'Origins', p. 212.
41. Tayler, *Miscellany*, p. 162.
42. 'Culloden Letter' (1957), p. 184.
43. McLachlan, *Sketch*, p. 287; *The Whitefoord Papers*, ed. W. Hewins (1898), p. 76.
44. Earl of Ilchester, *Letters to Henry Fox* (1895), p. 10.
45. McLachlan, *Sketch*, p. 288.
46. Ray, *History*, 345; BL, Stowe MSS 158, fo. 126r; RA, CP14/7.
47. Elcho, *Short Account*, pp. 429–31.
48. Blaikie, 'Origins', pp. lxix–lxx.
49. NAS, GD1/53/86/2.
50. Henderson, *Cumberland*, p. 251.
51. *Hardwicke*, ed. Yorke, vol. 1, p. 522.
52. 'Culloden Letter' (1957), p.184.
53. W H Anderson, 'The Battle of Culloden', *JSAHR* 1 (1921), 22.
54. Blaikie, 'Origins', p. 418.
55. Ray, *History*, pp. 333–4; *Whitefoord*, ed. Hewins, p. 77.
56. BL, Stowe, MSS, 158, fo. 214r.
57. Elcho, *Short Account*, pp. 423–4, 430.
58. Ray, *History*, p. 333.
59. *The Gentleman's Magazine*, 16 (1746), 210.
60. Taylers, *1745*, pp. 161–3.
61. Blaikie, *Itinerary*, p. 79.
62. Johnstone, *Memoir*, p. 119.
63. Blaikie, *Itinerary*, pp. 120–1.
64. Henderson, *Cumberland*, p. 253.
65. Hughes, *A Plain Narrative*, p. 40.
66. Home, *History*, p.167; Historical Manuscripts Commission, vol. 10, p. 443.
67. Blaikie, 'Origins', p. 212.
68. Ibid., p. 213.
69. Ibid., p. 214.
70. Maxwell, *Narrative*, p. 150.
71. Home, *History*, p. 166.
72. Ray, *History*, p. 334.
73. Anderson, 'Battle' (1921), p. 24.
74. Ray, *History*, p. 334.
75. Henderson, *History*, p. 115.
76. Home, *History*, p. 166n.
77. HMC Var., vol. 8, p. 167.
78. Home, *History*, p. 166.
79. *The Gentleman's Magazine*, 16 (1746), 209.
80. *Hardwicke*, ed. Yorke, vol. 1, p. 523; Reid, *Culloden*, p. 76.
81. Blaikie, 'Origins', p. 214.
82. 'Lyon', ed. Paton, vol. 1, pp. 67, 86, 87.

83. BL, Stowe MSS, 158, fo. 212r.
84. Johnstone, *Memoir*, p. 123; Henderson, *History*, p. 115.
85. BL, Stowe MSS, 158, fo. 213v.
86. 'Culloden Letter' (1957), p. 184.
87. Anon., *A Particular Account of the Battle of Culloden* (c.1746), p. 16.
88. *The Newcastle Courant*, 2731 (19–26 April 1746).
89. Henderson, *History*, p. 115.
90. Johnstone, *Memoir*, p. 123.
91. Hughes, *Plain Narrative*, p. 41.
92. Henderson, *History*, p. 115.
93. Anderson, 'Battle', 22.
94. Ibid.
95. Blaikie, *Itinerary*, p. 79.
96. 'Lyon', ed. Paton, vol. 1, p. 87.
97. Home, *History*, p. 172.
98. Elcho, *Short Account*, p. 433.
99. HMC Hastings, vol. 3, p. 55.
100. *The Gentleman's Magazine*, 16 (1746), 220.
101. *The Newcastle Courant*, 2731 (19–26 April 1746); *The Oxford Gazette or Reading Mercury*, 24 (28 April 1746).
102. Ray, *History*, p. 346.
103. HMC Hastings, p. 55.
104. *The Oxford Gazette or Reading Mercury*, 25 (5 May 1746).
105. HMC Hastings, pp. 55–6.
106. London Metropolitan Archives, WJ/SP/1746/06/15.
107. Elcho, *Short Account*, pp. 433–4.
108. Ray, *History*, p. 346.
109. BL, Stowe MSS, 158, fo. 213v.
110. Johnstone, *Memoir*, p. 123.
111. Home, *History*, pp. 168–9.
112. BL, Stowe MSS, 158, fo. 212v; J. Fergusson, *Argyll in the Forty Five* (n.d.), p. 172.
113. Home, *History*, pp. 169n–170n; Ray, *History*, p. 346.
114. Findlay, *Wolfe*, p. 108.
115. Anderson, 'Battle', p. 22.
116. HMC Laing, vol. 2, p. 367.
117. Home, *History*, p. 169.
118. *The Oxford Gazette or Reading Mercury*, 25 (5 May 1746).
119. LMA, WJ/SP/1746/06/15.
120. NA, MPF1/1; NAS, GD1/53/95/3; 109; Elcho, *Short Account*, p. 433.
121. Ibid., p. 434.
122. Henderson, *History*, p. 116.
123. Home, *History*, p. 170.
124. Henderson, *History*, p. 116; Home, *History*, p. 170.

125. S Boyse, *An Impartial History of the Late Rebellion in 1746* (1748), p. 149n.
126. *Walpole*, ed. Lewis, vol. 37, pp. 238–40.
127. *Hardwicke*, ed. Yorke, vol. 1, p. 524.
128. 'Lyon', ed. Paton, vol. 1, p. 380.
129. Whitefoord, ed. Hewins, p. 79.
130. Charles, *History*, p. 329; NAM, 8711–48.
131. *The Newcastle Courant*, 2731 (19–26 April 1746); *Whitefoord*, ed. Hewins, p. 78.
132. Anderson, 'Battle', p. 24.
133. Historical Manuscripts Commission, vol. 10, p. 443.
134. HMC Laing, vol. 2, p. 367.
135. *The Gentleman's Magazine*, 16 (1746), 219.
136. HMC Laing, vol. 2, p. 367.
137. LMA, WJ/SP/1746/06/15.
138. Historical Manuscripts Commission, vol. 10, p. 445.
139. *The Gentleman's Magazine*, 16 (1746), 209.
140. *The London Magazine* (1746), 199, 201.
141. Marchant, *History*, p. 385.
142. Ray, *History*, p. 346.
143. Anderson, 'Battle', p. 23; Royle, *Civil War*, p. 332.
144. Douglas, *History*, p. 189.
145. Ray, *History*, p. 339.
146. HMC Laing, vol. 2, p. 367.
147. Elcho, *Short Account*, p. 434.
148. Johnstone, *Memoir*, p. 126.
149. NAS, GD1/53/86/4.
150. Ibid., 931/15.
151. Ibid.
152. *Hardwicke*, ed. Yorke, vol. 1, pp. 552–3.
153. Ibid, p. 553.
154. T Pollard and N Oliver, *Two Men in a Trench* (2002), pp. 263, 285.
155. J Boswell, *The Journal of a Tour to the Hebrides with Samuel Johnson* (1958), pp. 128–9.
156. 'Lyon', ed. Paton, vol. 3, p. 56.
157. *Anti-Jacobin Review*, 13 (1793), 125.
158. 'Lyon', ed. Paton, vol. 1, p. 252.
159. Henderson, *History*, p. 116.
160. Ibid., p. 117.
161. *The Newcastle Courant*, 2731 (19–26 April 1746).
162. Hughes, *Plain Narrative*, p. 44.
163. Findlater, *Wolfe*, p. 108.
164. *The London Magazine* (1746), 235.
165. Pollard and Oliver, *Two Men*, p. 263; Barratt, *Cavaliers*, p. 193; Royle, *Civil War*, p. 531.

166. *The Westminster Journal*, 231 (5 May 1746).
167. Hughes, *Plain Narrative*, p. 44.
168. Anderson, 'Battle', p. 24.
169. LMA, WJ/SP/1746/06/15..
170. Boyse, *History*, p. 150n.
171. Ray, *History*, pp. 343–4; Elch, *Short Account*; pp. 461–2.
172. Starkey, *War*, p. 166.
173. LMA, WJ/SP/1746/06/15.
174. 'Lyon', ed. Parton, vol. I, pp. 32–3.
175. Boyse, *History*, p. 150.
176. HMC Hastings, p. 56.
177. 'Lyon', ed. Paton, vol. 1, pp. 32–3.
178. *Walpole*, ed. Lewis, vol. 19, p. 299.
179. *The Lockhart Papers*, vol. 2 (1817), p. 508.
180. Starkey, *War*, p. 166.
181. Elcho, *Short Account*, pp. 461–2.
182. 'Lyon', ed. Paton, vol. 3, p. 71.
183. *The Gentleman's Magazine*, 16 (1746), 272.
184. Johnstone, *Memoir*, p. 94.
185. NAS, GD1/931/15.
186. 'Lyon', ed. Paton, vol. 2, p. 4.
187. Hughes, *Plain Narrative*, pp. 46, 50.
188. Anderson, 'Battle', p. 23.
189. McLachlan, *Sketch*, p. 290.
190. Ibid., p. 300.
191. Ibid., p. 308.
192. Barratt, *Cavaliers*, p. 197.
193. Marchant, *History*, p. 395.
194. Historical Manuscripts Commission, vol. 10, p. 442.
195. 'Culloden Letter' (1957), pp. 184–5.
196. 'Lyon', ed. Paton, vol. 1, pp. 380–1.
197. *Hardwicke*, ed. Yorke, vol. 1, p. 528.
198. NRO, ZRI/27/4/66.

Chapter 6

1.   NA, SP36/83, fo. 222r.
2.   Anderson, 'Battle', p. 24.
3.   HMC Var., vol. 8, p. 168.
4.   BL, Add. MSS 32707, fo. 88v.
5.   D. Warrand, *More Culloden Papers* (1930), p. 71.
6.   RA, CP14/414.
7.   Tayler, *Miscellany*, p. 161.

8. *Hardwicke*, ed. Yorke, vol. 1, p. 528.
9. Johnstone, *Memoir*, p. 127.
10. Ibid.
11. Elcho, *Short Account*, p. 436.
12. Taylers, *1745*, p. 167.
13. Johnstone, *Memoir*, p. 127.
14. Ibid., p. 129.
15. Ibid.
16. Blaikie, 'Origins', p. 216.
17. Elcho, *Short Account*, pp. 436–8.
18. Ibid.
19. Taylers, *1745, p. 173.*
20. *The Gentleman's Magazine*, 16 (1746), 274.
21. M F Hamilton, 'The Locharkaig Treasure', *Miscellany VII, SHS*, 3rd series, 35 (1941), 132–68.
22. *Hardwicke*, ed. Yorke, vol. 1, p. 540.
23. NAS, GD248/48/4/9.
24. NLS, MS 3735, fo. 634r.
25. *Hardwicke*, ed. Yorke, vol. 1, p. 539.
26. NA, SP/54, 31/25.
27. Ray, *History*, p. 347.
28. Home, *History* (1802), pp. 384–6.
29. Ibid., pp. 387–8.
30. RA, CP14/405.
31. NA, SP54/31/27.
32. NA, SP36/83, fos. 222r–225r.
33. 'Lyon', ed. Paton, vol. 3, p. 74.
34. Warrand, *More Culloden Papers*, vol. 5, p. 71.
35. G. Menary, *Duncan Forbes of Culloden* (1936), p. 283.
36. D. Forbes, *Culloden Papers* (1815), p. 281.
37. Ibid., pp. 283–4.
38. *The Gentleman's Magazine*, 16 (1746), 236.
39. NA, SPS30/246r.
40. *The Gentleman's Magazine*, 16 (1746), 274.
41. Fergusson, *Argyll*, p.196.
42. *The General Advertiser*, 3620 (3 June 1746).
43. Anon., *A Journey through part of England and Scotland* (1746), p. 90.
44. Fergusson, *Argyll*, p. 204.
45. NAS, GD248/48/31.
46. Henderson, *History*, p. 122.
47. 'Lyon', ed. Paton, vol. 3, pp. 6–7.
48. NAS, GD248/48/40.
49. Wilson, *Wolfe*, p. 68.

50. NRO, ZRI/27/4/66.
51. Ray, *History*, pp. 348, 374–5.
52. NA, SPS, 54, 31/2.
53. McLachlan, *Sketch*, p. 294.
54. NA, SPS, 54, 31/9a, 17, 22.
55. Ibid., 17.
56. 'Lyon', ed. Paton, vol. 2, pp. 298–9.
57. Ibid., vol. 3, pp. 156–7.
58. *The Gentleman's Magazine*, 16 (1746), 263.
59. Ray, *History*, p. 341.
60. Ibid., p. 365.
61. Wilson, *Wolfe*, p. 68.
62. *Hardwicke*, ed. Yorke, vol. 1, p. 528.
63. *The Gentleman's Magazine*, 16 (1746), 210.
64. Ray, *History*, p. 366.
65. Fergusson, *Argyll*, p. 179; *The Gentleman's Magazine*, 16 (1746), 274.
66. Boyse, *Impartial History*, p. 154; Ilchester, *Letters*, p. 10.
67. LMA, WJ/SP/1746/06/15.
68. 'Lyon', ed. Paton, vol. 1, p. 381.
69. Ray, *History*, p. 376.
70. Johnstone, *Memoir*, pp. 133–4.
71. RA, CP15/78.
72. NA, SPS, 54, 30/253r.
73. *The Gentleman's Magazine*, 16 (1746), 272.
74. RA, CP14/354.
75. 'Lyon', ed. Paton, vol. 3, p. 164.
76. RA, CP14/92.
77. NA, SPS, 54, 30/221r.
78. RA, CP14/292.
79. NA, SPS54, 31/24A.
80. *Hardwicke*, ed. Yorke, vol. 1, p. 529.
81. Forbes, *Culloden Papers*, p. 285.
82. *The Gentleman's Magazine*, 16 (1746), 261.
83. *Private Correspondence*, ed. Lodge, p. 73.
84. *The Westminster Journal*, 234 (24 May 1746).
85. NA, SPS/54, 31/9a.
86. NA, SPS/54, 31/27.
87. NA, SPS/54, 32/4A.
88. Anderson, 'Battle', pp. 23–4.
89. Hughes, *Plain Narrative*, p. 47; P Rae, *The History of the Rebellion* (1746), p. 326.
90. J S Arnot and B Seton, 'Prisoners of the Forty Five', *Scottish Historical Society*, 3rd series, 13–15 (1928–9).
91. Henderson, *Cumberland*, p. 264.

92. McLachlan, *Sketch*, p. 301.
93. Ibid., p. 300.
94. Ibid., pp. 300–1.
95. RA, CP5/104.
96. Ibid., pp. 301–5.
97. NA, SPS/54, 30/285r.
98. NA, SPS/54, 31/24a.
99. Henderson, *History*, p. 123.
100. RA, CP14/392.
101. RA, CP15/101.

Chapter 7

1. *The Gentleman's Magazine*, 16 (1746), 374.
2. Ibid., p. 314.
3. *The Oxford Gazette or Reading Mercury*, 30 (9 June 1746).
4. *Hardwicke*, ed. Yorke, vol. 1, p. 542; NLS, MS 3735, fo. 701r.
5. Home, *History* (1802), pp. 389–91.
6. *The Gentleman's Magazine*, 16 (1746), 315.
7. *Hardwicke*, ed. Yorke, vol. 1, p. 542.
8. *The London Evening Post*, 2893, 2898, 2903, 2912 (20–22 May, 31 May–2 June, 12–14 June, 3–5 July 1746).
9. *The London Evening Post*, 2919 (19–22 July 1746).
10. *The London Evening Post*, 2913, 2918 (5–8 July, 15–17 July 1746).
11. *The Gentleman's Magazine*, 16 (1746), 315.
12. *The Gentleman's Magazine*, 16 (1746), 375.
13. Tayler, *1745*, pp. 194–5; NLS, MS 3734, fo. 771r.
14. *The London Evening Post*, 2920 (22–24 July 1746).
15. NLS, MS 3735, fo. 749r.
16. NLS, MS 3736, fo. 818r.
17. Ibid., fos. 811r–814r.
18. Home, *History*, pp. 181–2.
19. NA, SPS/54, 32/4a.
20. *The Gentleman's Magazine*, 16 (1746), 324.
21. Ibid.
22. NA, SPS54, 32/4a.
23. *Hardwicke*, ed. Yorke, vol. 1, p. 542.
24. Ibid., p. 547.
25. Ibid., pp. 542–3.
26. Ilchester, *Letters*, p. 13.
27. *The Newcastle Gazette*, 104 (11 June 1746).
28. *Hardwicke*, ed. Yorke, vol. 1, pp. 543–4.
29. Ilchester, *Letters*, p. 13.

30. *The General Advertiser*, 3628 (12 July 1746).
31. Hughes, *Plain Narrative*, p. 56.
32. Ibid., p. 57.
33. Boyse, *Impartial History*, p. 159.
34. WSRO, Goodwood MSS 111, 203.
35. *The Newcastle Gazette*, 103 (4 June 1746).
36. NLS, MS 3735, fo. 718v.
37. Douglas, *History*, pp. 232–3.
38. NA, SPS54, 32/11a.
39. NA, SPS54, 32/15.
40. NA, SPS54, 32/32.
41. NA, SPS54, 32/49a.
42. Whitworth, *William Augustus*, p. 93.
43. NAS, GD220/5/1961/4.
44. RA, CP17/300.
45. Ibid.
46. NAS, GD220/5/1632/2.
47. Henderson, *Cumberland*, p. 264.
48. Douglas, *History*, p. 234.
49. RA, CP16/74.
50. NAS, GD220/5/1632/2.
51. 'Lyon', ed. Paton, vol. 1, p. 91.
52. Ibid., vol. 3, p. 72.
53. Ibid., pp. 18, 58.
54. Ibid., vol. 1, pp. 93–4.
55. Ibid., p. 95.
56. Ibid., vol. 2, pp. 306–7.
57. Ibid., pp. 91–4.
58. Ibid., vol. 2, pp. 306–7.
59. NAS, GD 170/1055.
60. RA, CP16/8.
61. RA, CP16/59.
62. RA, CP17/466.
63. 'Lyon', ed. Paton, vol. 3, pp. 85–7, 29.
64. Ibid., vol. 1, p. 123.
65. Ibid., pp. 312–13, 303.
66. Ibid., vol. 2, p. 253.
67. 'Lyon', ed. Paton, vol. 2, pp. 79–80.
68. WSRO, Goodwood MSS 111, 204.
69. *The Oxford Gazette or Reading Mercury*, 30 (9 June 1746); 35 (14 July 1746).
70. NAS, GD220/5/1962/6.
71. Boyse, *Impartial History*, p. 158n.
72. Ilchester, *Letters*, p. 13.

73. Ibid.
74. *Hardwicke*, ed. Yorke, vol.1, p. 550.
75. WSRO, Goodwood MSS 111, 203.
76. W. McLeod (ed.), 'Persons Concerned in the Rebellion', *Scottish Historical Society*, 8 (1890), 385–6.
77. Whitworth, *William Augustus*, pp. 99–100.
78. RA, CP16/112.
79. *The Gentleman's Magazine*, 16 (1746), 315.
80. *Hardwicke*, ed. Yorke, vol. 1, p. 545.
81. *The Westminster Journal*, 235 (31 May 1746).
82. *The Gentleman's Magazine*, 16 (1746), 375.
83. NA, SPS, 54, 31/34.
84. RA, CP/15/433.
85. NA, SPS, 54, 31/35a.
86. RA, CP/16, 98, 144, 226.
87. NA, SP36/83, fos. 270r–271r, 293r–294v, 36/84, fo. 63r.
88. NA, SP36/83, fo. 302.
89. NA, SP36/83, fo. 381r.
90. NA, SP36/91, fo. 244r.
91. NA, SP36/83, fo. 389r, 36/91, fos. 242r–243r; RA, CP16/83–90.
92. NA, SP36/84, fo. 1r.
93. RA, CP15/315.
94. NA, SPS/54, 31/33A; RA, CP15/302.
95. RA, CP15/373.
96. RA, CP16/98.
97. Warrand, *Culloden Papers*, vol. 5, p. 104.
98. RA, CP15/302.
99. NA, SPS/54, 32/2b.
100. NA, SPS/54, 32/4a.
101. *Hardwicke*, ed. Yorke, vol. 1, p. 545.
102. NA, SPS/54, 32/13.
103. NA, SPS/54, 32/24b, 24c.
104. Douglas, *History*, p. 234.
105. Ray, *History*, pp. 371–2.
106. Ibid., pp. 372–3.
107. McLachlan, *Sketch*, p. 323.
108. RA, CP18/20.
109. Ray, *History*, p. 373.
110. McLachlan, *Sketch*, pp. 322, 325.
111. Ibid., pp. 324–5.
112. Ray, *History*, p. 388.
113. Boyse, *Impartial History*, p. 159.
114. *Walpole*, ed. Lewis, vol. 19, p. 273.

115. NA, SPS/54, 32/38.
116. NA, SP36/85, fos. 232r–233v.
117. Warrand, *More Culloden Papers*, vol. 5, p. 79.
118. HMC Laing, vol. 2, pp. 381–2.
119. Tayler, *Epilogue*, p. 136.
120. *Hardwicke*, ed. Yorke, vol. 1, pp. 556–7.
121. *The Gentleman's Magazine*, 16 (1746), 270, 329, 382.
122. Arnot and Seton, 'Prisoners', vol. 1, p. 156.
123. W A Speck, *Stability and Strife, England, 1714–1760* (1977), p. 251.
124. *Hardwicke*, ed. Yorke, vol. 1, pp. 607, 609.
125. N T Phillipson and R Mitchison, *Scotland in the Age of Improvement* (1996), pp. 8–9.
126. NAS, GD44/14/15/33.

Chapter 8

1.   BL, Add. MSS, 35598, fo. 208r.
2.   WYAS, Leeds, NP1514/21.
3.   Bodl. Don.c.108, fo. 41v.
4.   Clegg, 'Diary', ed. Voe, p. 570.
5.   'The Diary of Dr Richard Kay, 1716–1751', ed. W Brockbank and F Kenworthy, *Chetham Society* (1968), 109.
6.   Saville, 'Diaries', p. 270.
7.   Ibid., p. 271.
8.   Whiting, 'Yorkshire Diaries', p. 131.
9.   Saville, 'Diaries', p. 271.
10. Henderson, *History*, p. 121.
11. *The General Advertiser*, 3593 (2 May 1746).
12. NA, SPS/54, 30, 205r.
13. NAS, GD248/48/28.
14. *The Edinburgh Evening Courant*, 7783 (25 April 1746), 7784 (26 April 1746), 7786 (29 April 1746).
15. Saville, 'Diaries', pp. 272, 273–4.
16. A H Cooper, *Annals of Cambridge*, vol. 4 (1860), 225–55.
17. T Maddox, *Sermon* (1746), p. 17.
18. W Wood, *Sermon* (1746), pp. 6, 7.
19. BL, Add. MSS, 35598, fo. 208r.
20. Saville, 'Diaries', pp. 272, 274.
21. *The Gentleman's Magazine*, 16 (1746), 257.
22. *The London Magazine* (1746), 236.
23. Clegg, 'Diary', ed. Voe, p. 582.
24. Kay, 'Diary', p. 114.
25. Lancashire Record Office, PR2067; WYAS: Wakefield, D53/8/6.

26. York City Archives, HB43, pp. 199, 198, 214.
27. NA, SP36/83, fo. 387r; Tyne and Wear Archives, GU/TH/6/2; *The London Evening Post*, 2926 (5–7 Aug. 1746).
28. HMC Laing, vol. 2, p. 368.
29. Saville, 'Diary', pp. 273–4.
30. *Walpole*, ed. Lewis, vol. 19, p 273.
31. Ibid., p. 52.
32. *Letters*, ed. McCann, p. 214.
33. Ibid., p. 224.
34. Ibid., p. 235.
35. WSRO, Goodwood MSS 111, 261.
36. BL, Add. MSS, 35598, fos. 119r, 122r–123v.
37. *The Gentleman's Magazine*, 16 (1746), 366–7.
38. Oates, 'Hertfordshire and the Jacobite Rebellions of 1715 and 1745', *Herts Past and Present*, 3/3 (2004), 12.
39. NA, PL26/35/1; East Riding Record Office, QSF 153/B4.
40. *The York Journal* (14 Oct. 1746).
41. *Walpole*, ed. Lewis, vol. 19, p. 288.
42. HMC Var., vol. 8, p. 169.
43. Lewis, *Walpole*, vol. 9, p. 34.
44. Johnstone, *Memoir*, p. 134.
45. BL. Add. MSS, 33954, fo. 82r.
46. *Calendar of Political and Personal Satires III*, part 1(2), *1734–1750*, pp. 627, 633.
47. HMC Var., vol. 8, p. 173.
48. H Walpole, *Memoirs of the Reign of King George II*, vol. 1 (1847), p. 9.
49. Ibid., p. 38, vol. 2, p. 101.
50. Ibid., vol. 2, p. 157.
51. *Memoirs of the Reign of King George III*, vol. 2 (1894), pp. 158–9.
52. J Woodforde, *The Diary of a Country Parson, 1758–1802* (1987), p. 8.
53. *The Diary of a Village Shopkeeper: Thomas Turner*, ed. D. Vaisey (1998), p. 44.
54. *An Eighteenth Century Correspondence*, ed. L. Dickins and M. Stanton (1910), pp. 229, 324, 368.
55. Anon., *An Elegy on the death of William Duke of Cumberland* (1765).
56. *A Selection of the Papers of the Earls of Marchmont*, ed. G Rose, vol. 1 (1831), pp. 194–5.
57. J Boswell, *The Life of Samuel Johnson* (1992), p. 560, 560n.

Conclusion

1. Earl of Waldegrave, *Memoirs, 1754–1758* (1821), pp. 22–3.

Bibliography

Primary Sources

Manuscript

ROYAL ARCHIVES
Cumberland Papers (Microfilm), 7–18

NATIONAL ARCHIVES
State Papers: Scotland, 54/27–32
State Papers Domestic 36 (Microfilm)
Map of Culloden, MPF1/1

NATIONAL ARMY MUSEUM
8711–48, Alexander Tough's narrative

NATIONAL ARCHIVES OF SCOTLAND
GD1/53/86, 109
GD1/90
GD1/931
GD16/34
GD24/5/162
GD44/14
GD103/2
GD128/69/14
GD170/1055
GD220/5
GD248/48
GD1632

NATIONAL LIBRARY OF SCOTLAND
ADV.MS.23.2.28, 28.1.4
MS3734–6
MS16621

BRITISH LIBRARY
Newcastle MSS, 32705–32707
Hardwicke MSS, 35589, 35598
Stowe MSS, 158

BODLEIAN LIBRARY
Tucker Correspondence MS. Don.c. 107–108

EAST RIDING RECORD OFFICE
QSF 153/B4

LANCASHIRE RECORD OFFICE
PR2067

LONDON METROPOLITAN ARCHIVES
Culloden Letter, WJ/SP/1746/06/15

NORTHUMBERLAND RECORD OFFICE
Culloden Letter, ZRI/27/4/66

TYNE AND WEAR ARCHIVE SERVICE
GU/TH/6/2

WEST SUSSEX RECORD OFFICE
Goodwood MSS, 111

WEST YORKSHIRE ARCHIVE SERVICE: LEEDS
Newby Hall MSS 1514

WEST YORKSHIRE ARCHIVE SERVICE: WAKEFIELD
D53/8/6

YORK CITY ARCHIVES
House Book, 43.

PRINTED

Anderson, W H (ed.), 'The Battle of Culloden', *JSAHR*, 1 (1921), 21–4.
Anon., 'Culloden Letter', *JSAHR*, 35 (1957), 183–5.
Anon., *A Journey through part of England and Scotland* (*c*.1746).

Annual Register, vol. 8 (1765).

Bate, J, *A Parochial Letter to the inhabitants of St. Paul's Deptford, Kent* (1745).

Blaikie, W B (ed.), 'Origins of the Forty Five', *Scottish Historical Society*, 2nd series, 2 (1916).

—— 'Itinerary of Prince Charles Edward Stuart', *Scottish Historical Society* 27 (1897).

Blundell, N, 'The Great Diurnall of Nicholas Blundell, 1711–1719', ed. F Tyrer, *Record Society of Lancashire and Cheshire* (1970).

Boswell, J (ed.), *Boswell's London Journal, 1762–3*, ed. F Pottle (1950).

—— *The Life of Samuel Johnson* (1992).

Boyse, S, *An Impartial History of the Late Rebellion in 1745* (1748).

Burt, E, *Letters from a Gentleman in the North of Scotland*, vol. 2 (1754).

Calendar of Political and Personal Satires III, part 1(2), 1734–1750. British Museum.

Defoe, Daniel, *A Tour through the Whole Island of Great Britain*, ed. P Rogers (1971).

Clegg, J., 'The Diary of James Clegg', ed. V S Doe, vol. 2, *Derbyshire Record Society*, 3 (1979).

The Correspondence of the Dukes of Richmond and Newcastle, 1724–1750, ed. T J McCann (1984).

Dennistoun, J, *Memoirs of Sir Robert Strange* (1855).

Douglas, F, *History of the Rebellion in 1745* (1755).

The Diary of a Village Shopkeeper: Thomas Turner, ed. D Vaisey (1998).

The Edinburgh Evening Courant (1746).

An Eighteenth Century Correspondence, ed. L Dickins and M Stanton (1910).

Elcho, Lord, *A Short Account of the Affairs of Scotland, 1744–1746*, ed. E. Charteris (1907).

Forbes, D, *Culloden Papers* (1815).

Forbes, J M (ed.), *Jacobite Memoirs* (1834).

Forbes, R (ed.), 'Lyon in Mourning', *Scottish Historical Society*, vols. 1–3 (repr. 1975).

The General Advertiser (1746).

The Gentleman's Magazine, 9, 10, 15 and 16 (1740, 1741, 1745 and 1746).

Hardwicke, Earl of, *The Life and Correspondence of Philip Yorke, Earl of Hardwicke*, ed. P. Yorke, vol. 1 (1913).

Henderson, A, *The History of the Rebellion, 1745 and 1746* (1748).

—— *The Life of William Augustus, Duke of Cumberland* (1766).

Hill, J S, *False Zeal and Christian zeal distinguish'd or the essentials of popery described: A Sermon* (1745).

HMC Egmont = *Report on the Manuscripts of the Earl of Egmont*, vol. 1, ed. S C Lomax, vol. 2, ed. W Page (Historical Manuscripts Commission, 1905).

HMC Hastings = *Report on the Manuscripts of the Late Reginald Rawdon Hastings, Esq., of the Manor House, Ashby de la Zouche*, ed. R R Hastings (Historical Manuscripts Commission, vol. 78; 1928).

HMC Laing = *Report of the Laing Manuscripts Preserved in the University of Edinburgh*, ed. H Paton (Historical Manuscripts Commission, vol. 72; 1914).

HMC Var. = *The Manuscripts of the Hon. Frederick Lindley Wood Preserved at Temple Newsam, Leeds*, ed. F L Bickley (Historical Manuscripts Commission, vol. 8; 1913).

Home, J, *The History of the Rebellion* (1802).

—— *The History of the Rebellion in Scotland* (1822).

Hughes, M, *A Plain Narrative* (1746).

Ilchester, Earl of, *Letters to Henry Fox, Lord Holland* (1895).

Johnstone, Chevalier de, *The Chevalier de Johnstone: A Memoir of the Forty Five*, ed. B Rawson (1958).

Kay, R, 'The Diary of Richard Kay, 1716–1751', ed. W. Brocksbank and F. Kenworthy, *Chetham Society*, 3rd series, 16 (1968).

The Letters of Private Wheeler, 1809–1828, ed. B H Liddell Hart (2000), *The Lockhart Papers*, vol. 2 (1817).

The London Evening Post (1746).

The London Gazette (1746).

The London Magazine (1746).

Lord Hervey's Memoirs, ed. R. Sedgwick (1963).

'The Lyon in Mourning', ed. H Paton, *Scottish Historical Society*, 1 (1975).

McLachlan, A N C, *A Sketch of Cumberland's Military Life* (1876).

Maddox, T, *Sermon* (1746).

Marchant, J, *History of the Present Rebellion* (1746).

Maxwell, J, *Narrative of Charles Prince of Wales' Expedition to Scotland in the Year 1745* (1841).

'Memorials of John Murray of Broughton, 1740–1747', ed. R. Bell, *Scottish Historical Society* (1898).

Menary, G, *Duncan Forbes of Culloden* (1936).

The Newcastle Courant (1746).

The Newcastle Gazette (1746).

The Oxford Gazette or Reading Mercury (1746).

Patten, R, *The History of the Rebellion* (1717).

'Peter Clarke's Journal', ed. H. Paton, *Scottish Historical Society Miscellany* (1893), 513–22.

Private Correspondence of Chesterfields and Newcastle, 1744–46, ed. R Lodge (1930).

Rae, R, *The History of the Rebellion* (1746).

Ray, J, *A Compleat History of the Rebellion* (1753).

Ryder, D, *The Diary of Dudley Ryder, 1715–6*, ed. W. Mathews (1939).

Saville, A (ed.), 'Secret Comment: The Diaries of Gertrude Saville, 1722–1757', *Thoroton Society*, 41 (1997).

A Selection of the Papers of the Earls of Marchmont, ed. G Rose, vol. 1 (1831).

Tayler, A and H (eds), *The '45 and After* (1938).

Tayler, H, *A Jacobite Miscellany* (1948).

Waldegrave, Earl of, *Memoirs, 1754–1758* (1821).

Walpole, H, *Memoirs of the Reign of King George II* (1847).

——— *Memoirs of the Reign of King George III* (1894).

——— *The Correspondence of Horace Walpole*, ed. W S Lewis, vols 9, 18, 19 and 30 (1955).

The Westminster Journal (1746).

Warrand, D (ed.), *More Culloden Papers*, vol. 5 (1930).

The Whitefoord Papers, ed. W. Hewins (1898).

Whiting, C E (ed.), 'Two Yorkshire Diaries', *Yorkshire Archaeological Society Record Series*, 107 (1952), 3–135..

Wolfe, J (ed.), *Life and Letters of James Wolfe*, ed. B. Wilson (1909).

Wood, W, *Sermon* (1746).

The York Journal (1746).

Secondary Sources

BOOKS AND ARTICLES

Arnot, J G, and B S Seton, 'The Prisoners of the '45', *Scottish History Society*, 3rd series, 13–15 (1928–9).

Bailey, G, *Falkirk or Paradise! Falkirk Muir, 17 January 1746* (1996).

Barrett, J, *Cavaliers* (2000).

Barthorp, M, *The Jacobite Rebellions, 1689–1745* (1982).

Black, J, *Culloden and the '45* (1990).

——— *European Warfare, 1660–1815* (1994).

Charteris, E, *William Augustus, Duke of Cumberland*, vol. 1 (1913).

Clifton, R, *The Last Popular Rebellion: The Western Rising of 1685* (1984).

Cooper, A H, *Annals of Cambridge*, vol. 4 (1860).

Duffy, C, *The Military Experience in the Age of Reason* (1987).

—— *The '45* (2003).

Ewald, A C, *The Life and Times of Prince Charles Stuart* (1883).

Falkner, J, *Great and Glorious days, Marlborough's Battles, 1704–1709* (2002).

Fergusson, J, *Argyll in the Forty Five* (n.d.).

Findlay, J, *Wolfe in Scotland* (1928).

Fortescue, J, *The History of the British Army*, vol. 2 (1935).

Frey, L and M, *Societies in Upheaval* (1987).

Garde, L. du, *Bonnie Prince Charlie* (1974).

Hamilton, M F, 'The Locharkaig Treasure', *Scottish Historical Society Miscellany VII*, 3rd series (1941), 133–68.

Harris, T, *Revolution: The Great Crisis of the British Monarchy, 1685–1720* (2006).

Hartley, J, *The Go-Between* (1958).

Houston, R, 'The Ten Worst Britons', *BBC History Magazine*, 7 (2006), 1.

Langford, P, *A Polite and Commercial People: England, 1727–1783* (1997).

Lenman, B P, *The Jacobite Risings in Britain, 1689–1746* (1980).

McLeod, W, 'Persons concerned in the Rebellion', *Scottish Historical Society*, 8 (1890).

McLynn, F J, *Bonnie Prince Charlie* (1988).

Oates, J D, 'The Last Siege on English Soil, Carlisle, December 1745', *Transactions of the Cumberland and Westmorland Antiquarian and Archaeological Society*, 3 (2003), 169–84.

—— 'The Crisis of the Hanoverian State?', *JSAHR*, 81 (2003), 308–29.

—— 'Hertfordshire and the Jacobite Rebellions of 1715 and 1745', *Herts. Past and Present*, 3 (2004), 3–14.

—— 'Hessian Forces Employed in Scotland in 1746', *JSAHR*, 83 (2005), 205–14.

—— *The Jacobite Invasion of 1745 in North West England* (2006).

Oxford Dictionary of National Biography (2004).

Petrie, C, *The Jacobite Movement* (1932).

Phillipson, N T, and R. Mitchison, *Scotland in the Age of Improvement* (1996).

Plumb, J, *England in the Eighteenth Century* (1950).

—— *The First Four Georges* (1956).

Pollard, T, and N Oliver, *Two Men in a Trench* (2002).

Prebble, J, *Culloden* (1961).

—— *Glencoe* (1967).

Preston, D, *The Road to Culloden Moor* (1995).

Reid, S, *1745: A Military History of the Last Jacobite Rising* (1996).
—— *Wolfe* (2000).
—— *Culloden Moor* (2005).
Roberts, J, *The Highland Wars* (2002).
Royle, T, *The Civil War* (2006).
Sadler, T, *Culloden: The Last Charge of the Highland Clans* (2006).
Simpson, A, *Culloden and the Four Unjust Men* (2000).
Speck, W A, *Stability and Strife: England, 1714–1760* (1977).
—— *The Butcher: The Duke of Cumberland and the Suppression of the '45* (1981)
Starkey, A, *War in the Age of the Enlightenment, 1700–1789* (2003).
Szechi, D, *1715: The Great Jacobite Rebellion* (2006).
Tey, J, *The Daughter of Time* (1951).
Whitworth, R, *William Augustus, Duke of Cumberland* (1993).
Williams, E N, *Dictionary of British and European History, 1485–1789* (1979).
Woosnam-Savage, R C, *1745: Charles Edward Stuart and the Jacobites* (1995).
Youngson, A J, *The Prince or Pretender: A Study in the Writing of History* (1985).

Index

191